ENGLISH EPISCOPAL ACTA

28

CANTERBURY 1070–1136

ENGLISH EPISCOPAL ACTA

ENGLISH
EPISCOPAL ACTA
28

CANTERBURY 1070–1136

EDITED BY

MARTIN BRETT

AND

JOSEPH A. GRIBBIN

Published for THE BRITISH ACADEMY
by OXFORD UNIVERSITY PRESS

Oxford University Press, Great Clarendon Street, Oxford OX2 6DP

Oxford New York
Auckland Bangkok Bogotá Buenos Aires Cape Town Chennai
Dar es Salaam Delhi Hong Kong Istanbul Karachi Kolkata
Kuala Lumpur Madrid Melbourne Mexico City Mumbai Nairobi
São Paulo Shanghai Singapore Taipei Tokyo Toronto

Oxford is a registered trade mark of Oxford University Press
in the UK and certain other countries

Published in the United States
by Oxford University Press Inc., New York

© The British Academy, 2004

Database right The British Academy (maker)

British Library Cataloguing in Publication Data
Data available

ISBN 0–19–726301–1

Typeset by J&L Composition
Printed in Great Britain
on acid-free paper by
Antony Rowe Limited
Chippenham, Wiltshire

CONTENTS

LIST OF PLATES

(between page lxxx and page lxxxi)

PREFACE

This collection, modest though its scale, has been very long in the making, and is the work of many hands. Christopher Cheney's name must stand first. His contribution is apparent at every stage, from the conception of the volume to its completion. Shortly before he died he was able to read an early draft, on which he commented with all his characteristic generosity, penetration and wit. The charters of Lanfranc were mostly listed and discussed by the late Dr Margaret Gibson; some of the charters of Anselm were collected by Dom Schmitt for his edition of the letters, and later translated by Dr Walter Fröhlich. The charters of Ralph and William were originally collected by the late Denis Bethell in his unpublished study of archbishop William. It was first supposed that we would produce the volume together, and his drafts lie behind the editions of the acts of both archbishops, though they have been substantially revised. His tragically early death prevented him from completing his work. The division of labour between the editors has broadly been along the lines that MB is responsible for all the commentary, and some of the text, while JG has contributed much to the text and to the index; without JG's energetic commitment to the cause the enterprise would probably never have reached a conclusion.

Many others have contributed in other ways. The charters of archbishop Ralph were examined in more detail by Dr Amanda Clark in her 'Ralph d'Escures, Anglo-Norman abbot and archbishop' Ph.D. Dissertation, University of California, Santa Barbara, 1975, and we have turned to her work on many occasions; we are grateful for her permission to exploit it throughout the section on Ralph. Professor Nicholas Vincent was, as ever, an unfailing source of new and unexpected information. Michael Gullick has been equally generous with information and judgement, and detected a grave omission at the last moment. Kathleen Thompson and Daniel Power provided essential help with the archives of Sées. The regular meetings of the editors of other volumes in the series have been a constant source of information, encouragement and guidance. The contribution of Professor Christopher Brooke and the General Editors is less visible yet even more pervasive. We owe a particular debt to Dr Teresa Webber, whose analysis of the hands and generous advice have provided a rigour of palaeographical analysis, and a breadth of comparative material, far beyond our reach.

Our work would also have been impossible without the unfailing kindness of the authorities and staff of the British Library, the National Library of Wales, the Bibliothèque nationale at Paris, the Cambridge University Library, the Bodleian Library, Lambeth Palace, the Public Record Office, St George's Chapel at Windsor, the librarians and archivists of Corpus Christi and Trinity College in Cambridge, Corpus Christi and New College, Oxford, the keepers of the cathedral muniments at Canterbury and Durham, and the Record Office archivists and their staff at Chelmsford, Dover, Maidstone, Norwich and Strood. Though all these have been unstinting in their help, none bears any responsibility for the result. Such merit as the outcome may have is attributable to others. Its failings are ours alone.

MANUSCRIPT SOURCES CITED

ORIGINAL AND PURPORTED ORIGINAL CHARTERS OF THE ARCHBISHOPS

Canterbury, Dean and Chapter
  C.A. (Chartae Antiquae): A 2: p. 91; C
  1193: *15*; L 70: *66*; S 350: *38*; Y 57: *14*
Chelmsford, Essex Record Office
  D/DPr 150 (Colne Priory estate
  archives): +*43*
Durham UL, Archives & Special Collections,
  Durham Cathedral Muniments
  1.1. Archiep. 3: +*3*
London, Lambeth Palace
  Carte Misc.: V. 110: +*76*
London, British Library
  Add. charter 7214: *63*
  Campbell charter vii.1 : *5*; vii. 5: *16*

Cotton charter viii. 19: +*8*
Harley charter 43 G 18: +*33*
London, Public Record Office
  DL 25/105: *64;* DL 25/106: *65*
  DL 27/ 46: *36*
  E 40/4985: *80;* E 40/5005: *35;* E 40/6689:
  47; E 40/7915: *62;* E 40/15415: *49;*
  E 40/15416: *46*; E 40/15739: *81*
  E 41/464: *48*
Oxford, New College Archive
  no. 13152: +*32*
Strood, Medway Archives and Local Studies
  Centre
  DRc/T 48: +*29*; T 49: +*27*; T 50: *24*

COPIES, MENTIONS AND OTHER MANUSCRIPTS CITED

Aberystwyth, National Library of Wales
  ms 7851: *93, 94*
  ms 17110E: *50, 79*
Alençon, Archives de l'Orne
  ms H 938: *92*
Alençon, Bibliothéque Municipale
  ms 190: *92*
Cambridge, University Library
  Add. ms 3020: *96, 97*
  ms Ee 5.31: *23, 74,* +*76*
  ms Ll. 2.15: +*1, 20, 68*
  ms Mm 4.19 : *13*
Cambridge, Corpus Christi College
  ms 111: **11, 56n*
  ms 189: *16*
  ms 298: **67*
  ms 369: *56n*
Cambridge, Trinity College
  ms R. 5. 33: **+4, *45, 56n*
Canterbury, Cathedral Library
  ms Lit. B 2: p. 107n

Canterbury, Dean and Chapter
  C.A. (Chartae Antiquae): A 2: *app.*; C 156:
  *67; C 157: **67*; C 158: **67*; C 204 : *18*;
  N 26: *23*; S 317: *16*;
  Register A: *16, 18, 38, 39, *67*
  Register B: *16, 66*
  Register E: *18, 38, 39*
  Register I: *16, 18, 38, 39*
  Register P: *16*
Chatsworth House
  ms 73A: **10*
Chelmsford, Essex Record Office
  D/DPr 149 (Colne Priory estate
  archives): +*43, 70*
Dover, East Kent Archives Centre
  Sa/LC1–5; Sa/ ZB 4/16; Sa/ ZT2:
  p. 107n
Durham UL, Archives & Special Collections,
  Durham Cathedral Muniments
  Cartuarium I: +*3*
  Cartuarium III: +*3*

Eaton Hall, Chester
  ms 1: *21*
Glasgow, University Library
  ms Hunterian U. 2. 6: *82*
Lincoln, Lincolnshire Archives
  Bishop's register I: *31*
London, Guildhall Library
  ms 9531/4: *56*
London, Lambeth Palace
  Carte Misc.: V/111: *74*
  Reg. Warham: *57, 58, 74, 75, +76, 80, 81, 84, 85*
  ms 59: *16, 17*
  ms 303: **67*
  ms 1131 (part 2): *19, 40*
  ms 1212: *16*
London, British Library
  Add. ms 6159: *18*; 40734: **10*; 57946: p. 92
  Arundel 68: p. liin
  Cotton charter ii. 21: *23*
  Cotton charter Vitellius B 3 (destroyed): *+7, +28*
  ms Cotton Claudius A vi: *37*; Claudius B vi: *44*; Claudius C ix: *44*; Claudius D x: *68*; Claudius E iv: *10*; Domitian v: *14*; Domitian x: *5, 6n, 24, 25, 26, 53, 55, +88*; Faustina A viii p. 102; Faustina B v: *+7, +8n, +27, +28, +29, +54, +89*; Galba E ii: *72*; Galba E iii: *67*; Julius B iv-v: p. 107n; Nero C vii: *95n*; Nero D i : **10*; Otho D iii: **10*; Tiberius E ix: *+43*; Vespasian A xxii: *+7, +29n*; Vespasian B xi: **69*; Vespasian B xv: *+43n*; Vespasian E iv : *59*; Vespasian E xxv: *77, 78, 86*; Vitellius E xv: *61*
  ms Egerton 3031: *77, 86*
  ms Harley 1708: *86*;
  1965: *21*; 3601: **60*; 6203: *71*
  ms Lansdowne 448: *81*
London, Public Record Office
  C 53/55: *5*; C 53/63: *5*;
  C 53/122: *5*; C 53/123:*5*;
  C53/ 134: *22, 51, 52*
  C 56/32: *5;* C 66/413: *5*; C 66/530: *5*
  E36/137: *18n*
  E 36/138: *18n, 39n*
  E 40/6689: *47*

E 40/7915: *62*
E 40/14176: *48n*
E 40/14810: **95*
E 40/15427: *48n*
E 41/437: *80–1*
PRO Trans 31/8/140b/3: *92*
SC 13/F 154: p. lxi
London, Society of Antiquaries
  ms 194: *74n*
Maidstone, Centre for Kentish Studies
  DRb/ Ar1/1: *74*; Ar 1/13: *24, 74* ; Ar 1/17: *+90*
  DRb/ Ar 2: *5, 6, +7, 24, +27*
  U 120/Q 13: *74, 75, +76*
Norwich, Norfolk Record Office
  DCN 40/ 1: *23*; 40/ 2 : *23*; 40/ 8: *73*
Oxford, Bodleian Library
  ms Dodsworth 39: *61*
  ms Gough Essex 1: *56n*
  ms Rawlinson B 329: *71*
  ms Smith 90: *+7*
  Top. Salop d 2: *93*
Oxford, Corpus Christi College
  ms 256: **67*
Paris, Bibliothèque nationale
  ms Cinq cents de Colbert 190: *12*
  ms Coll. du Vexin IV: *42*; VIII: *42*; XIII: *42*
  ms fr. 18953 : *92*
  ms lat. 12884: *12*; 13905: *12*
Sées, Archives épiscopales
  Liber Albus of Sées : *92*
Strood, Medway Archives and Local Studies Centre
  DRc/L 5/1: *+30*; 16/3: *+90*
  DRc/R 1: *5, 7n 10, 24, 25, 26, 53, 87, +88*
  DRc/T 48: *+29*; T 57: *26, 52, +88*; T 58: *5*; T 60: *5*; T 65: *5*; T 66: *5*; T 373: *+30*; T 380: *74*
Truro, Cornwall Record Office
  ART 6/7: p. 92
Vatican, Archivio Segreto
  Vat. Register 18: *18*
Windsor, St George's Chapel Archives
  XI E 5: *21*
  XI G 29: *34*

PRINTED BOOKS AND ARTICLES CITED, WITH ABBREVIATED REFERENCES

Acta Lanfranci	ed. Plummer in *ASC* i 287–92; also ed. J.M. Bately *The Anglo-Saxon Chronicle, a collaborative edition, 3. MS A* (Cambridge 1986) 84–9.
Acta of. . .Chichester	*The acta of the bishops of Chichester 1075–1207* ed. H. Mayr-Harting (CYS lvi) 1964
Acta S. Langton	*Acta Stephani Langton Cantuariensis archiepiscopi (A.D. 1207–1228)* ed. K. Major (CYS l) 1950
Ancient charters royal and private prior to AD 1200	ed. J.H. Round (PRS x,1888)
Anglia sacra	ed. H. Wharton 2 vols (London 1691)
Anglo-Norman Durham	*Anglo-Norman Durham 1093–1193* ed. D. Rollason, M. Harvey, M. Prestwich (Woodbridge 1994)
Annales monastici	ed. H.R. Luard 5 vols (RS 1864–9)
Annals of St Neots with Vita prima sancti Neoti	eds D. Dumville and M. Lapidge (The Anglo-Saxon Chronicle 17, Cambridge 1985)
ANS	*Anglo-Norman Studies* (Proceedings of the Battle Conference)
Anselmi opera	*Sancti Anselmi Cantuariensis archiepiscopi opera omnia* ed. F.S. Schmitt 6 vols (Edinburgh 1946–61). See also *Anselmo d'Aosta*, Fröhlich, *Letters*
Anselmo d'Aosta	*Anselmo d'Aosta, arcivescovo di Canterbury, Lettere.* 3 vols (Biblioteca di cultura medievale, 1988–93) ed. and trans. I. Biffi, A. Granata and C. Marabelli
Arch. Cant.	*Archaeologia Cantiana* (1858–)
Archer, T.A.	'The children of Ranulf Flambard', *EHR* ii (1887) 103–12
Armitage Robinson, J.	*Gilbert Crispin, abbot of Westminster* (Notes and documents relating to Westminster Abbey 3 1911)
ASC	*Two of the Saxon Chronicles parallel,* ed. C. Plummer and J. Earle 2 vols (Oxford 1892–99)
Bannister, 'Cartulary'	A.T. Bannister, 'A lost cartulary of Hereford cathedral', *Trans. of the Woolhope Naturalists' Field Club* (1914–17) 268–77
Barlow, F.	*William Rufus* (London 1983, corr. repr. 2000)
Basset charters	*Basset charters c. 1120 to 1250* ed. W.T. Reedy (PRS ns l 1995 for 1989–91)
Bates, *Acta*	D. Bates, *Regesta regum Anglo-Normannorum. The acta of William I (1066–1087)* (Oxford 1998)
Bateson, M.	'The Huntingdon song school and the school of St Gregory's, Canterbury', *EHR* xviii (1903) 712–3
Bethell, 'Richard'	D. Bethell, 'Richard of Belmeis and the foundation of St Osyth's', *Trans. of the Essex Archaeol. Soc.* 3s ii (1970) 299–328
Bethell, 'St Osyth'	D. Bethell, 'The lives of St. Osyth of Essex and St. Osyth of Aylesbury', *Analecta Bollandiana* lxxxviii (1970) 75–127
Bethell, 'William'	D. Bethell, 'William of Corbeil and the Canterbury York dispute', *Journal of ecclesiastical history* xix (1968) 145–59

Bethell, 'Black monks' D. Bethell, 'English black monks and episcopal elections in the 1120s', *EHR* lxxxiv (1969) 673–98

Birch, *Catalogue* Walter de Gray Birch, *Catalogue of seals in the Department of manuscripts in the British Museum* 6 vols (London 1887–1900)

Bishop, *Scriptores* T.A.M. Bishop, *Scriptores regis* (Oxford 1961)

Blair, J. 'The Surrey endowments of Lewes priory before 1200', *Surrey Archaeological Collections* lxxii (1980) 97–126

Bloom, J.H. *English seals* (London 1906)

Boehmer, H. *Die Fälschungen Erzbischof Lanfranks von Canterbury* (Leipzig 1902)

Book of Llan Dâv *The text of the Book of Llan Dâv* ed. J.G. Evans (Oxford, 1893)

Bouvris, J-M. 'Le "livre rouge" de l'abbaye de St-Martin', *Annales de Normandie* xliii (1993) 255–7

Box, E.G. 'Donations of manors to Christ Church, Canterbury, and appropriation of churches', *Arch. Cant.* xliv (1932) 103–119

Brett, *English church* M. Brett, *The English church under Henry I* (Oxford 1975)

Brett, 'Forgery' 'Forgery at Rochester', *Fälschungen im Mittelalter* iv 397–412 (6 vols, Schriften der MGH xxxiii 1988–90)

Brett, M. 'A supplementary note on the charters attributed to archbishop Lanfranc', *Lanfranco di Pavia*, ed. G. D'Onofrio 521–7

Brooke, 'English *acta*' C.N.L. Brooke, 'English episcopal *acta* of the twelfth and thirteenth centuries', *Medieval ecclesiastical studies in honour of Dorothy M. Owen* ed. M.J. Franklin and C. Harper-Bill (Studies in the history of medieval religion vii, Woodbridge 1995) 41–56

Brooke, C.N.L. 'Episcopal charters for Wix priory', *Medieval miscellany* 45–63

Brooke, C.N.L. 'London and Lambeth in the eleventh and twelfth centuries', *Report of the Friends of Lambeth Palace Library for 1972* (1973) 11–23

Brooks, N. *The early history of the church of Canterbury* (Leicester 1984)

Brunel, C. 'Les actes faux de l'abbaye de Saint-Valery', *Le moyen âge* 2s xiii (1909) 94–116, 179–96

Cal. Ch. Rolls *Calendar of the Charter Rolls* (1216–1516) 6 vols (HMSO 1903–27)

Cal. Pat. Rolls *Calendar of the Patent Rolls preserved in the Public Record Office* (HMSO 1891–)

Calendar of Chancery Warrants (HMSO 1927)

Calendar of entries in the papal registers relating to Great Britain and Ireland *Papal Letters* i 1198–1304 (HMSO 1893)

Canterbury and the Norman Conquest ed. R. Eales and R. Sharpe (London/Rio Grande 1995)

Canterbury cathedral nave K. Blockley, Margaret Sparks and Tim Tatton-Brown, *Canterbury cathedral nave: Archaeology, history and architecture* (Canterbury 1997)

Canterbury professions *Canterbury professions*, ed. M. Richter (CYS lxvii 1973)

Cart. Aldgate *Cartulary of Holy Trinity, Aldgate* ed. G.A.J. Hodgett (London Record Society vii 1971)

Cart. Colchester *Cartularium monasterii sancti Johannis Baptiste de Colecestria* ed S.A. Moore 2 vols (Roxburgh Club 1897)

Cart. Colne *Cartularium prioratus de Colne* ed. J.L. Fisher (Essex Arch. Soc. Occasional publications i 1946)

Cart. Lewes *The chartulary of St Pancras of Lewes* cal. L.F. Salzman (Sussex Record Soc. xxxviii 1932, xl 1934)

Cart. Oseney	*Cartulary of Oseney abbey* ed. H.E. Salter 6 vols (Oxford Hist. Soc. lxxxix-xci, xcvii-viii, ci 1929–36)
Cart. Shrewsbury	*Cartulary of Shrewsbury abbey* ed. U. Rees 2 vols (Aberystwyth 1975)
Cartae Glam.	*Cartae et alia munimenta quae ad dominium de Glamorgancia pertinent* ed. G.T. Clark (rev. ed. by G.L. Clark) 6 vols (Cardiff 1910)
Cartularium Saxonicum	ed. Walter de Gray Birch 3 vols (London 1885–93)
Cartulary of Worcester cathedral priory (Register I)	ed. R.R. Darlington (PRS ns xxxviii 1968)
Chaplais, 'Seals'	P. Chaplais, 'The seals and original charters of Henry I', *EHR* lxxv (1960) 260–75, reprinted in *Essays in medieval diplomacy and administration* (London 1981)
Chaplais, 'Original charters'	P. Chaplais, 'The original charters of Herbert and Gervase, abbots of Westminster (1121–1157)', in *Medieval miscellany* 89–110 repr, in *Essays* (as above)
Chart. Boxgrove	*Chartulary of the priory of Boxgrove* ed. L. Fleming (Sussex Record Soc. lix 1960)
Chart. Chester	*Chartulary or register.of the abbey of St Werburgh, Chester* ed. J. Tait 2 vols (Chetham Soc. ns lxxix 1920, lxxxii 1923)
Charters of King David I	*The charters of King David I* ed. G.W.S. Barrow (Woodbridge 1999)
Charters of St Augustine's abbey, Canterbury and Minster-in Thanet	ed. S. Kelly (Anglo-Saxon charters v 1995)
Cheney, C.R.	*Notaries public in England in the thirteenth and fourteenth centuries* (Oxford 1972)
Cheney, *EBC*	C.R. Cheney, *English bishops' chanceries, 1100–1250* (Manchester 1950)
Cheney, C.R. and M.G. (eds)	*The letters of pope Innocent III (1198–1216) concerning England and Wales* (Oxford 1967)
Cheney, C.R.	'The deaths of popes and the expiry of legations in twelfth-century England', *Revue de droit canonique* xxviii (1978) 84–96
Cheney, C.R.	'On the acta of Theobald and Thomas, archbishops of Canterbury', *Journal of the Society of Archivists* vi (1981) 467–81
Cheney, M.G.	'The compromise of Avranches of 1172 and the spread of canon law in England', *EHR* lvi (1941) 177–97
Chester charters	*The charters of the Anglo-Norman earls of Chester, c. 1071–1237* ed. G. Barraclough (Record Soc. of Lancashire and Cheshire cxxvi 1988)
Chibnall, M.	'History of the priory of St Neots', *Proc. Cambridge Antiquarian Soc.* lix (1966) 67–74
Chibnall, M.	'The relations of Saint Anselm with the English dependencies of the abbey of Bec', repr. from *Spicilegium Beccense* (1959) 521–30 in *Piety, power and history in medieval England and Normandy* (Aldershot 2000)
Chron. Battle	*Chronicle of Battle Abbey* ed. and trans. Eleanor Searle (OMT 1980)
Chronicles of the reigns of Stephen, Henry II. and Richard I . . .	ed. R. Howlett 4 vols (RS 1884–9)
Chronicon abbatiae de Evesham	ed. W.D. Macray (RS 1863)

Chronique de Saint-Pierre- ed. R.-H. Bautier and M. Gilles (Sources d'histoire médiévale 1979)
le-Vif de Sens

Chronique du Bec ed. A. Porée (Société de l'histoire de Normandie 1883)

Churchill, I.J. 'Table of Canterbury archbishopric charters', *Camden Miscellany xv* (Camden 3s xli 1929)

Colker. M.L. 'The life of Guy of Merton by Rainald of Merton', *Mediaeval Studies* xxxi (1969) 250–61

Colker, 'Latin texts' M.L. Colker. 'Latin texts concerning Gilbert, founder of Merton priory', *Studia monastica* xii (1969) 241–71

Colker, 'Polemic' M.L. Colker, 'A hagiographic polemic', *Mediaeval Studies* xxxix (1977) 60–108

Colvin, 'List' H.M. Colvin, 'A list of the archbishop of Canterbury's tenants by knight-service in the reign of Henry II', *Kent Records* (Kent Archaeological Society, Records Publication Committee xviii, 1964) 1–40

Consuetudines Burienses *The customary of the Benedictine Abbey of Bury St Edmunds in Suffolk* ed. A. Gransden (Henry Bradshaw Society xcix 1973 for 1966)

Conway, A.E. 'The owners of Allington castle, Maidstone (1086–1279)', *Arch. Cant.* xxix (1911) 1–39

Conway Davies, J. Conway Davies, *Episcopal acts . . . relating to Welsh*
Episcopal acts *dioceses* 2 vols (all published) (Historical Soc. of the Church in Wales i 1946, iii-iv 1948)

Councils *Councils and Synods with other documents relating to the English Church 1. A.D.871–1204* ed. D. Whitelock, M. Brett and C.N.L. Brooke 2 vols (Oxford 1981)

Cowdrey, *Lanfranc* H.E.J. Cowdrey, *Lanfranc, scholar, monk and archbishop* (Oxford 2003)

Crick, 'Antiquity' J. Crick, 'The marshalling of antiquity: Glastonbury's historical dossier' in *The archaeology and history of Glastonbury abbey* ed. L. Abrams and J. P. Carley (Woodbridge 1991) 217–43

Crosby, *Bishop and chapter* E.U. Crosby, *Bishop and chapter in twelfth-century England* (Cambridge 1994)

Crouch, D. *The Beaumont twins* (Cambridge 1986)

CRR *Curia regis rolls* (HMSO 1922–)

Culture of Christendom *The culture of Christendom. Essays in medieval history in memory of Denis L.T. Bethell* ed. M.A. Meyer (London/Rio Grande 1993)

Cust. Roff. *Custumale Roffense* ed. J. Thorpe (London 1788)

CYS Canterbury and York Society

Dart, *Canterbury* J. Dart, *The history and antiquities of the cathedral church of Canterbury* (London 1726)

DB *Domesday Book, sive Liber censualis Willelmi primi regis Angliae* ed. A. Farley et al. 4 vols (Record Commission 1783–1816)

De iniusta vexatione *De iniusta vexacione Willelmi episcopi* ed. H.S. Offler in *Camden Miscellany xxxiv* (Camden 5s 10, 1997) 49–104; also Simeon i 170–95.

Delisle, L. 'Recueil de 109 chartes originales de Henri II', *Bibliothèque de l'École des chartes* lxix (1908) 541–80

Diceto *The historical works of Master Ralph de Diceto* ed. W. Stubbs 2 vols (RS 1876)

Dickinson, J.C. *The origins of the Austin canons and their introduction into England* (London 1950)

Domesday monachorum   *The Domesday monachorum of Christ Church Canterbury* ed. D.C. Douglas (Royal Historical Society 1944)

Douglas, D.C.   *Feudal documents from the abbey of Bury St Edmunds* (British Academy Records of the Social and Economic History of England and Wales viii 1932)

Du Boulay, 'Bexley'   F.R.H. Du Boulay, 'Bexley church: some early documents', *Arch. Cant.* lxxii (1958) 41–53

Du Boulay, *Lordship*   F.R.H. Du Boulay, *The Lordship of Canterbury* (London 1966)

Ducarel, A.C.   *Anglo-Norman antiquities considered, in a tour through England and Normandy* (London 1767)

Duchesne, A.   *Histoire genealogique des maisons de Guines, d'Ardres, de Gand et de Coucy* (Paris 1631)

Duncombe, *History*   J. Duncombe and N. Battely, *History and antiquities of the three archiepiscopal hospitals, and other charitable foundations, at and near Canterbury* (1785) in J. Nichols, *Bibliotheca topographica Britannica* i no. xxx.

Durham episcopal charters   *Durham episcopal charters 1071–1152* ed. H.S. Offler (Surtees Soc. clxxix 1968 for 1964)

EA   *Epistolae Anselmi* in *Anselmi opera* ed. F.S. Schmitt, vols iii–v cited by number

Eadmer, *Historia*   *Eadmeri Historia novorum in Anglia* ed. M. Rule (RS 1884)

Eadmer, *Vita Ans.*   *The life of St Anselm, archbishop of Canterbury* ed. R.W. Southern (NMT 1962, corrected repr. in OMT 1972).

Eales, R.   'Local loyalties in Norman England: Kent in Stephen's reign', *ANS* viii (1986) 88–108

Early Yorkshire charters   13 vols, i–iii ed. W. Farrer (Edinburgh 1914–6); index to i–iii ed. C.T. Clay and E.M. Clay, and iv–xii ed C.T. Clay as Yorkshire Archæological Society Record Series, Extra series i–x, 1935–65

EEA   *English episcopal acta*

EHR   *English historical review*

Eyton, *Antiquities*   R.W. Eyton, *Antiquities of Shropshire* 12 vols (London 1854–60)

Facsimiles of English royal writs to 1100   ed. T.A.M. Bishop and P. Chaplais (Oxford 1957)

Facsimiles of national manuscripts   4 vols (Ordnance Survey 1865–8)

Faith and fabric   *Faith and fabric: a history of Rochester cathedral* ed. N. Yates and P. Welsby (Woodbridge 1996)

Fasti   D.E. Greenway (and, for viii, J.S. Barrow), *Fasti Ecclesiae Anglicanae 1066–1300* (London 1968–)

Feodarium prioratus Dunelmensis   ed. W. Greenwell (Surtees Soc. lviii 1872)

First Register of Norwich cathedral priory   ed. H.W. Saunders (Norfolk Rec. Soc. xi 1939)

Fleming, R.   'Christ Church Canterbury's Anglo-Norman cartulary' in *Anglo-Norman political culture and the twelfth-century renaissance* ed. C.W. Hollister (Woodbridge 1997) 83–155

Fleming, 'Lists'   R. Fleming, 'Christchurch's sisters and brothers: an edition and discussion of Canterbury obituary lists' in *Culture of Christendom* 115–53.

Flight, *Bishops and monks*   C. Flight, *The bishops and monks of Rochester 1076–1214* (Kent Archaeological Soc. Monographs ser. 6 1997)

Foliot, *Letters* *The letters and charters of Gilbert Foliot* ed. A. Morey and C.N.L. Brooke (Cambridge 1967)

Fröhlich, *Letters* W. Fröhlich (trans.), *The letters of Saint Anselm of Canterbury* 3 vols (Cistercian Studies publications xcvi–xcvii, cxlii 1990–4)

Galbraith, V.H. 'Press-marks on the deeds of Lewes priory' *Sussex Archaeological Coll.* lxv (1924) 196–205

Gameson, R. *The manuscripts of early Norman England* (Oxford 1999)

Gervase *The historical works of Gervase of Canterbury* ed. W. Stubbs 2 vols (RS 1879–80)

Gesta abbatum monasterii sancti Albani ed. H.T.Riley 3 vols (RS 1867–9)

Gesta Normannorum ducum of William of Jumièges, Orderic Vitalis, and Robert of Torigni ed. and trans. E. M.C. van Houts 2 vols (OMT 1992–5)

Gesta Stephani ed. and trans. K. Potter, rev. R.H.C. Davis (OMT 1976)

Gibson, *Lanfranc* M. Gibson, *Lanfranc of Bec* (Oxford 1978)

Gorham, G.C. *The history and antiquities of Eynesbury and St Neots* 2 vols (London 1820–4)

Greatrex, J. *Biographical register of the English cathedral priories of the province of Canterbury* (Oxford 1997)

Green, *Government* J. Green, *The Government of England under Henry I* (Oxford 1986)

Green, *Sheriffs* J. Green, *English sheriffs to 1154* (PRO Handbooks no. 24 1990)

Gullick, 'Eadmer' M. Gullick, 'The scribal work of Eadmer of Canterbury to 1109', *Arch. Cant.* cxviii (1998) 173–89

Gullick and Pfaff, 'Pontifical' M. Gullick and R.W. Pfaff, 'The Dublin pontifical (TCD 98 [B.3.6]): St Anselm's?', *Scriptorium* lv (2001) 284–94

Haines, C.R. *Dover priory* (Cambridge 1930)

Haines, R.M. 'Bishops and politics in the reign of Edward II', *Journal of ecclesiastical history* xliv (1993) 586–609

Hart, C. *The early charters of Essex. The Norman period* (University of Leicester. Dept. of English Local History, Ocasional papers 11 1957)

Harvey, P.D.A. and A. McGuiness *A guide to British medieval seals* (London 1996)

Hasted, E. *The history and topographical survey of the county of Kent* (2 ed. Canterbury 1797–1801, repr. 1972)

Heads *Heads of religious houses: England and Wales* i. *940–1216* ed. D. Knowles, C.N.L. Brooke and V.C.M. London (2 ed. Cambridge 2001); ii *1216–1377* ed. D.M. Smith and V.C.M. London (Cambridge 2001)

Heads Scot. *Heads of religious houses in Scotland from twelfth to sixteenth centuries* ed. D.E.R. Watt and N.F. Shead, (Scottish Record Society ns xxiv 2001).

Heslop, 'English seals' T.A. Heslop, 'English seals from the mid-ninth century to 1100', *Journal of the British Archaeological Association* cxxxiii (1980) 1–16

Heslop, 'Forgeries' T.A. Heslop, 'Twelfth century forgeries as evidence for earlier seals: the case of St Dunstan' in *St Dunstan: his life, times and cult* ed. N. Ramsay, M. Sparks and T. Tatton Brown (Woodbridge 1992) 299–310

Hist. Abingdon *Historia ecclesiae Abbendonensis* ii ed. and trans. J. Hudson OMT (2002), also J. Stevenson as *Chronicon monasterii de Abingdon* 2 vols (RS 1858)

Historiae Dunelmensis scriptores tres	(Surtees Soc. ix 1839)
Historians York	*Historians of the church of York and its archbishops* ed. J. Raine 3 vols (RS 1879–94)
HMC	Reports of the Royal Commission on Historical Manuscripts
Hollister, C.W.	*Henry I* (New Haven/London 2001)
Hoyt, R.S.	'A pre-Domesday Kentish assessment list', *Medieval miscellany* 189–202
Hugh the Chanter	*Hugh the Chanter. History of the archbishops of York* ed. C. Johnson, rev. by M. Brett, C.N.L. Brooke and M. Winterbottom (OMT 1990)
Hunn, J.R.	'A medieval cartulary of St Albans abbey', *Medieval Archaeology* xxvii (1983) 151–2
Huntingdon	Henry of Huntingdon, *Historia Anglorum* ed. D. Greenway (OMT 1996)
Huws, 'The making'	D. Huws, 'The making of *Liber Landavensis*', *National Library of Wales Journal* xxv (1987) 138–41
Italia Pontificia	ed. P. Kehr, W. Holtzmann and D. Girgensohn 10 vols (Berlin 1906–62)
Jeayes, I.H.	*Descriptive catalogue of Derbyshire charters* (London 1906)
JL	P. Jaffé, rev. W. Wattenbach, S. Loewenfeld, F. Kaltenbrunner and P. Ewald, *Regesta pontificum Romanorum* 2 vols (Berlin 1885–8)
Johanek, P.	*Die Frühzeit der Siegelurkunde im Bistum Würzburg* (Quellen und Forschungen zur Geschichte des Bistums und Hochstifts Würzburg xx 1969)
Johannis . . . Glastoniensis chronica siue historia de rebus Glastoniensibus	ed. T. Hearne 2 vols (Oxford 1726)
John of Salisbury, *Historia pontificalis*	ed. M. Chibnall (NMT 1956, corr. repr. OMT 1986)
John of Worcs.	*The chronicle of John of Worcester* ii–iii ed. R. R. Darlington and P. McGurk (OMT 1995, 1998)
Johnson, C. and Jenkinson, H.	*English court hand AD 1066 to 1500* 2 vols (Oxford 1915)
Ker, N.R.	*Catalogue of manuscripts containing Anglo-Saxon* (Oxford 1957)
Ker, N.R.	*English manuscripts in the century after the Norman Conquest* (Oxford 1960)
Keynes, S. (ed.)	*Facsimiles of Anglo-Saxon charters* (Anglo-Saxon charters. Supplementary series i, 1991)
Kissan, B.W.	'An early list of London properties', *Transactions of the London and Middlesex Archaeological Society* ns viii (1938) 57–69
Knowles, D. and Hadcock, R.N.	*Medieval Religious houses: England and Wales* (2 ed. Harlow 1971, reissued 1994)
Lanfranc, *Letters*	*The letters of Lanfranc, archbishop of Canterbury* ed. H. Clover and M. Gibson (OMT 1979)
Lanfranci opera	*Beati Lanfranci . . . opera omnia quæ reperiri potuerunt* ed. L. D'Achery (Paris 1648), partially repr. in PL cl 9–764
Lanfranco di Pavia e l'Europa del secolo XI	ed. G. D'Onofrio (Italia sacra 51, 1993)
Leclercq, 'Écrits spirituels'	Leclercq, J., 'Écrits spirituels d'Elmer de Cantorbéry' in 'Analecta monastica ii', *Studia Anselmiana* xxxi (1953) 45–123

Legg, J. Wickham and W.H. St John Hope — *Inventories of Christ Church, Canterbury* (Westminster 1902)

Leland, *Collectanea* — *Joannis Lelandi antiquarii de rebus Britannicis collectanea* ed. T. Hearne 6 vols (2 ed. 1770)

Leland, *Itinerary* — J. Leland, *Itinerary of John Leland in or about the years 1535–43* ed. L. Toulmin Smith 5 vols (London 1906–10)

Letters of John of Salisbury — ed. W.J. Millor, H.E. Butler and C.N.L. Brooke 2 vols (NMT 1955, corr. repr. 1986, OMT 1979)

Letters of Osbert of Clare — ed. E.W. Williamson (Oxford 1929)

Levison, W. — *England and the continent in the eighth century* (Oxford 1946)

Liber Eliensis — ed. E. O. Blake (Camden 3s xcii 1962)

Liber memorandorum ecclesie de Bernewelle — ed. J.W. Clark (Cambridge 1907)

Life of Christina — *The Life of Christina of Markyate* ed. and trans. C.H. Talbot (rev. ed. OMT 1987)

Life of Gundulf, bishop of Rochester — ed. Rodney Thomson (Toronto medieval Latin texts vii, 1977)

Literae Cantuarienses — ed. J.B. Sheppard 3 vols (RS 1887–9)

Lohrmann, D. — 'Formen der *Enumeratio bonorum* in Bischofs-, Papst- und Herrscherurkunden (9.–12. Jahrhundert)', *Archiv für Diplomatik* xxvi (1980) 281–311

Loyd. L.C. and D.M. Stenton (eds) — *Sir Christopher Hatton's book of seals* (Oxford 1950)

MacMichael, N.H. — 'The descent of the manor of Evegate in Smeeth with some account of its lords', *Arch. Cant.* lxxiv (1960) 1–47

Malmesbury, *GP* — *Willelmi Malmesbiriensis monachi de gestis pontificum Anglorum libri quinque* ed. N. E. S. A. Hamilton (RS 1870)

Malmesbury, *GR* — *Gesta regum Anglorum* ed. and trans. R.A.B. Mynors, R.M. Thomson and M. Winterbottom 2 vols (OMT 1998–9)

Malmesbury, *HN* — *Historia novella* ed. E. King, trans. K.R. Potter (OMT 1998)

Medieval miscellany — *Medieval miscellany for Doris Mary Stenton* ed. P. M. Barnes and C.F. Slade (PRS ns xxxvi 1962 for 1960)

Memorials Anselm — *Memorials of St Anselm* ed. R.W. Southern and F.S. Schmitt (Auctores Britannici medii aevi i 1969)

Memorials of St Dunstan — ed. W. Stubbs (RS 1874)

Memorials of St Edmund's abbey — ed. T. Arnold 3 vols (RS 1890–6)

MGH — *Monumenta Germaniae historica*

Miller, E. — *The Abbey and bishopric of Ely* (Cambridge 1951)

Mon. Angl. — *Monasticon Anglicanum* ed. R. Dodsworth and W. Dugdale, rev. ed. by J. Caley, H. Ellis and B. Bandinel 6 vols in 8 (London 1817–30, repr. 1846). First ed. *Monasticon Anglicanum* ed. R. Dodsworth and W. Dugdale 3 vols (London 1655–73)

Morgan, M. — *The English lands of the abbey of Bec* (Oxford 1946)

Musset, L. — *Les actes de Guillaume le Conquérant et de la reine Mathilde pour les abbayes caennaises* (Mémoires de la Société des Antiquaires de Normandie xxxvii 1967)

Nicholl, D. — *Thurstan, archbishop of York (1114–1140)* (York 1964)

Nichols, J. — *Bibliotheca topographica Britannica* 10 vols (London 1780–1800)

Niemeyer, G., — 'Die *Miracula S. Mariae Laudunensis* des Abtes Hermann von Tournai', *Deutsches Archiv* xxvii (1971) 135–74

NMT — Nelson's Medieval Texts (Edinburgh/London)

Norwich charters	*The charters of Norwich cathedral priory* ed. B. Dodwell 2 vols (PRS ns xl 1974, xlvi 1985)
Oakley, A.	'The cathedral priory of St Andrew, Rochester' *Arch. Cant.* xci (1975) 47–60
Offler, H.S.	'The early archdeacons in the diocese of Durham', *Trans. of the Architectural and Archaeological Society of Durham and Northumberland* xi (1962) 189–207
Oliver, G.	*Monasticon dioecesis Exoniensis* (Exeter 1846–54)
OMT	Oxford Medieval Texts
Orderic	*The Ecclesiastical History of Orderic Vitalis* ed. M.Chibnall 6 vols (OMT 1968–80)
Parisse, *Actes*	*A propos des actes d'évêques. Hommage à Lucie Fossier* ed. M. Parisse (Nancy 1991)
Pipe Roll	*Magnum rotulum scaccarii . . . de anno tricesimo-primo regni Henrici primi* ed. J. Hunter (1833, repr. with corrs for the PRS in 1929)
PL	J-P. Migne, *Patrologia Latina* 221 vols (Paris 1844–64)
Porée, *Histoire du Bec*	A. Porée, *Histoire de l'abbaye du Bec* 2 vols (Evreux 1901)
PRS	Pipe Roll Society
PUE	W. Holtzmann, *Papsturkunden in England* 3 vols (Abhandlungen der Gesellschaft der Wissenschaften zu Göttingen. Phil.-hist. Klasse. Neue Folge 25, no. 1. Dritte Folge nos 14, 33. Berlin 1930–52)
Rady, J., T. Tatton-Brown and J.A. Bowen	'The archbishop's palace, Canterbury', *Journal of the British Archaeological Association* cxliv (1991) 1–60
Reading cart.	*Reading abbey cartularies* ed. B. Kemp 2 vols (Camden 4s xxxi 1986, xxxiii 1987)
Recueil de chartes et documents de Saint-Martin-des-Champs	ed. J. Depoin 5 vols (Archives de la France monastique xiii, xvi, xviii, xx, xxi, 1912–21)
Reedy, W.T.	'The first two Bassets of Weldon—*novi barones* of the early and mid-twelfth century', *Northamptonshire Past and Present* iv (1969–72) 241–5, 295–8
Reg. ant.	*The Registrum antiquissimum of the cathedral church of Lincoln* ed. C.W. Foster and K. Major 12 vols (Lincoln Record Soc. xxvii-ix, xxxii, xxxiv, xli-ii, xlvi, li, lxii, lxvii-viii 1931–73)
Reg. Hethe	*Registrum Hamonis de Hethe* ed. C. Johnson 2 vols (CYS xlviii-ix, 1914–48)
Reg. regum	*Regesta regum anglo-normannorum, 1066–1154* ed. H.W.C. Davis, C. Johnson, H.A. Cronne, R.H.C. Davis 4 vols (Oxford 1913–69)
Reg. Roff.	*Registrum Roffense* ed. J. Thorpe (London 1769)
Registres de Grégoire IX	ed. L. Auvray 4 vols (Bibliothèque des Écoles françaises d'Athènes et de Rome 2s ix 1890–1955)
Rollason, D.	*The Mildrith legend* (Leicester 1982)
Rolls and register of Bishop Oliver Sutton	ed. R. Hill (Lincoln Record Soc. xxxix, xliii, xlviii, lii, lx, lxiv, lxix, lxxvi 1948–76)
Rot. chart.	*Rotuli chartarum in turri Londinensi asservati* ed. T.D. Hardy (Record Commissioners 1837)
Round, *CDF*	J.H. Round, *Calendar of documents preserved in France, illustrative of the history of Great Britain and Ireland* (HMSO 1899)
Round, J.H.,	*Geoffrey de Mandeville* (London 1892, repr. New York 1972)
RS	Rolls Series (London 1858–1911)
Salter, H.E.,	*Facsimiles of early charters in Oxford muniment rooms* (Oxford 1929)

Saltman, *Theobald*   A. Saltman, *Theobald, archbishop of Canterbury* (London 1956)

Sawyer   P.H. Sawyer, *Anglo-Saxon charters: an annotated list and bibliography* (Royal Hist. Soc. 1968)

Saxl, F.   *English sculptures of the twelfth century* (London 1954)

Scammell, G.V.   *Hugh du Puiset, bishop of Durham* (Cambridge 1956)

Scholz, B.W.   'Eadmer's life of Bregwine, archbishop of Canterbury, 761–764', *Traditio* xxii (1966) 127–48

Sherwood, 'Leeds'   L. Sherwood, 'The cartulary of Leeds priory', *Arch. Cant.* lxiv (1951) 24–34

Simeon   *Symeonis monachi opera omnia* ed. T. Arnold 2 vols (RS 1882–85)

Somner, *Antiquities*   W. Somner, *Antiquities of Canterbury* 2 ed. by N. Battely (London 1703) repr. with introduction by W. Urry (Wakefield 1977)

Southern, R.W.   'St Anselm and Gilbert Crispin, abbot of Westminster', *Mediaeval and Renaissance Studies* iii (1954) 78–113

Southern, *St Anselm* (1990)   R.W. Southern, *Saint Anselm: a portrait in a landscape* (Cambridge 1990)

Southern, *St Anselm* (1963)   R.W. Southern, *Saint Anselm and his biographer* (Cambridge 1963)

Southern, R.W.   *Medieval humanism and other studies* (Oxford 1970)

St Benet of Holme   *St Benet of Holme 1020–1210* ed. J.R. West 2 vols (Norfolk Record Soc. ii-iii 1932)

St Gregory's cartulary   *Cartulary of the priory of St Gregory, Canterbury* ed. A.M. Woodcock (Camden 3s lxxxviii 1956)

Stapleton, T.   'Observations upon the succession to the barony of William of Arques. . .', *Archaeologia* xxxi (1846) 216–37

Stenton, D.M.,   *English justice between the Norman conquest and the Great Charter, 1066–1215* (Philadelphia 1964)

Stoke by Clare cartulary   ed. C. Harper-Bill and R. Mortimer 3 vols (Suffolk charters iv-vi 1982–4)

Suger, *Vie de Louis VI le gros*   ed. H. Waquet (Paris 1964)

Tatton-Brown, 'Beginnings'   T. Tatton-Brown, 'The beginnings of St Gregory's priory and St John's hospital', in *Canterbury and the Norman Conquest* 41–52

Tatton-Brown, T.   'The beginnings of Lambeth Palace', *ANS* xxiv (2001) 203–14

Taxatio   *Taxatio ecclesiastica Angliæ et Walliæ auctoritate P. Nicholai IV. circa A.D. 1291* (Record Commission 1802)

Text. Roff.   *Textus Roffensis. Rochester Cathedral Library manuscript A. 3. 5* ed. P. Sawyer (Early English Manuscripts in Facsimile vii 1957, xi 1962); earlier (incomplete) ed. T. Hearne (Oxford 1720)

Thompson, *Women religious*   S. Thompson, *Women religious; the founding of English nunneries after the Norman conquest* (Oxford 1991)

Torigni   *Chronique de Robert de Torigni, abbé du Mont-Saint-Michel* ed. L. Delisle 2 vols (Société de l'histoire de Normandie 1872–3)

TRHS   *Transactions of the Royal Historical Society*

Two chartularies of the priory of St Peter at Bath   ed. W. Hunt (Somerset Record Soc. vii 1893)

Twysden, *Scriptores*   R. Twysden, *Historiae Anglicanae scriptores decem* 2 vols (London 1652)

UGQ   *Ungedruckte Anglo-Normannische Geschichtsquellen* ed. F. Liebermann (Strassburg 1879)

Urry, *Canterbury*   W. Urry, *Canterbury under the Angevin kings* (London 1967)

Urry, 'Normans'   W. Urry, 'The Normans in Canterbury', *Annales de Normandie* viii (1958) 119–38

Valor   *Valor ecclesiasticus temp. Henr. VIII. auctoritate regia institutus* 6 vols (Record Commission 1810–34)

van Caenegem, *Lawsuits*   R.C. van Caenegem, *English lawsuits from William I to Richard I* 2 vols (Selden Soc. cvi-vii for 1990–1)

Vaughn, S.   *Anselm of Bec and Robert of Meulan* (Berkeley/LA 1987)

Vincent, N.   'Some pardoners' tales: the earliest English indulgences', *TRHS* 6s xii (2002) 23–58

Vita Herluini   ed. J. Armitage Robinson, *Gilbert Crispin* 87–110; also ed. Evans in *The works of Gilbert Crispin, abbot of Westminster* eds A. S. Abulafia and G.R. Evans (Auctores Britannici medii aevi vii 1986) 183–212

Vita Lanfranci   ed. M. Gibson in *Lanfranco di Pavia* 659–715; also *PL* cl 29–58 (incomplete) from *Lanfranci opera omnia*

Wallace, W.   *The Life of St. Edmund of Canterbury* (London 1893)

Wallenberg, J. K.   *The place-names of Kent* (Uppsala 1934)

Ward, J.C.   'The lowy of Tonbridge and the lands of the Clare family in Kent, 1066–1217', *Arch. Cant.* xcvi (1980) 119–31

Webber, 'Scribes'   T. Webber, 'The scribes and handwriting of the original charters' in *The earldom of Chester and its charters: a tribute to Geoffrey Barraclough* ed. A.T. Thacker (Journal of the Chester Archaeological Society lxxi 1991) 137–51.

Webber, 'Script and manuscript'   T. Webber, 'Script and manuscript production at Christ Church, Canterbury, after the Norman Conquest' in *Canterbury and the Norman Conquest* 145–58

Whitelock, D.   *Anglo-Saxon wills* (Cambridge 1930)

Wilmart, A.   'La tradition des lettres de S.Anselme; lettres inédites de S.Anselme et de ses correspondants', *Revue Bénédictine* xliii (1931) 38–54

'Winchcombe annals 1049–1181'   ed. R.R. Darlington in *Medieval miscellany* 111–137

Woodman, F.   *The architectural history of Canterbury Cathedral* (London 1981)

Zarnecki, G., Holt, J. and Holland, T.   eds. *English Romanesque Art 1066–1200* (London 1984)

OTHER ABBREVIATIONS

add.	add, addition
appx	appendix
archbp	archbishop
archdn	archdeacon
BL	British Library
BN	Bibliothèque nationale, Paris
Bodl.	Bodleian Library, Oxford
bp	bishop
c.	*circa*
Cal.	Calendared
cf	compare
corr.	corrected
d.	died
D. & C.	Dean and Chapter
ed., eds	editor, editors
esp.	especially
ex.	exeunte
HMSO	Her (His) Majesty's Stationery Office
in.	ineunte
kg	king
lhs	left-hand side
Mr	Master
mun.	muniments
m.	membrane
NLW	National Library of Wales
om.	omit, omission
Pd	Printed
PRO	Public Record Office, London
rhs	right-hand side
UL	University Library

INTRODUCTION

THE COLLECTION AS A WHOLE

The charters published here differ from those in most earlier volumes of the series in a number of ways, with important consequences. There are firstly fewer. Eighty-four acts and thirteen mentions of lost acts is a modest haul in absolute terms. Under another aspect, however, the total is more impressive, for the period they cover ends earlier than any other volume, and the approximate number of episcopal *acta* which can be placed before 1136 so far assembled for every diocese in England amounts to no more than some 400; only York with some eighty for the same period, many also suspicious, has even half as many.[1] This calculation is certainly approximate and probably significantly overstated. Few authentic episcopal *acta* were dated, and many provide few internal clues to their date. Correspondingly the inclusion of all texts for long-lived bishops such as Henry of Blois at Winchester or Nigel of Ely which cannot be proved to be later than 1136 undoubtedly inflates the figure substantially. It is remarkable how many of the dateable charters of bishops who took office before 1135 and died well into the reign of Stephen or later fall into the later years of their pontificates. Given the incompleteness or inaccessibility of the studies of French episcopal *acta*, in spite of the energy with which they are now being pursued, it is difficult to make cogent comparisons across the Channel. What we do have is a detailed survey of surviving original acts from French dioceses from 1050 to 1121—a period more or less coincident with the rule of Lanfranc, Anselm and Ralph. The collection below includes ten credible originals in the name of Anselm and Ralph, as well as five which are manifestly or probably spurious. Though Bourges and Reims are far better represented, and Canterbury was a very large province by any standard, the seven surviving originals for Sens, six for Tours and four for Rouen cast Canterbury in a rather more favourable light.[2] It is

---

[1] These figures are drawn from the earlier volumes of *EEA, Acts of Chichester, Durham episcopal charters* ed. H.S. Offler, and the forthcoming volumes for Rochester, Worcester and Ely. I am very grateful to Mrs Cheney and Nicholas Karn for supplying the figures for their volumes in preparation.
[2] M. Courtois in Parisse, *Actes* 71–77; B-M. Toch et al., *La diplomatique française du haut moyen âge* (Turnhout, 2001) i 349, 355, 337.

in general true to say that there is a sharp break between the episcopal acts attributed to Anglo-Saxon bishops and those from after the Conquest.[3] Given the very small number of surviving charters, authentic or not, attributed to the bishops of the first two generations after 1066, it seems reasonable to assume that most acts of episcopal authority in those years were not recorded by formal grant, and that the period covered here represents the dawn of a new sort of document, with all the interest and difficulty that such a period offers. By that criterion the sample looks rather more impressive.

Secondly, an alarming proportion of the texts are at best dubious, at worst manifest forgeries. This does not render them devoid of interest, but they are evidence for periods later than that of their purported issue. It is only rarely possible, however, to date the composition of these forgeries at all precisely. Again, the early texts in other volumes often excite suspicion, but not on the scale found here. In part the explanation lies in the large number of charters relating to the cathedral priory of Rochester, a notorious centre of forgery from the mid-twelfth century through to at least the end of the thirteenth— of the eighteen charters here treated as certainly inauthentic, ten concern Rochester and are only known from its archives. The position is rather more troubling than this might suggest. It may be that Rochester was wholly exceptional in its enthusiasm for 'modernising' its archives, but it may equally well be observed that it is now also exceptional for the survival of its early cartulary in the Textus Roffensis. This provides a relatively secure standard against which to compare those texts found only in later compilations.[4] For most houses we have no such test. It is more or less impossible to determine how many charters surviving only in later copies would prove suspect or manifestly false if we had either single-sheet originals or much earlier copies against which to judge them. Two examples below illustrate the point with worrying clarity. Only the script of +33, archbishop Ralph's Battle charter, reveals its status, for its diplomatic and content would arouse little suspicion in a copy. Similarly, +32, Anselm's supposed confirmation to St Valery,

[3] Brooke, 'English *acta*' 44–5. The 166 surviving charters attributed to pre-conquest bishops are listed in P. Sawyer, *Anglo-Saxon charters* nos 1244–1409. Many are post-conquest forgeries, and a high proportion of the surviving authentic texts are leases for Worcester or Winchester, which seem to have only two parallels at Canterbury (Sawyer nos 1389–90 of 1020–1028). The only more conventional Canterbury texts in Sawyer's list which command any confidence are a small group from 798–before 870 (Sawyer nos 1258, 1264–9), a letter of Dunstan of 980 × 988 (Sawyer no. 1296), and two grants by archbp Eadsige (Sawyer nos 1400–1). S. Kelly, editing no. 1401 in her *Charters of St Augustine's abbey Canterbury and Minster-in Thanet* (Anglo-Saxon charters v, 1995) as no. 37 suggests that it began as a St Augustine endorsement to the royal grant Sawyer no. 1050.
[4] But see +88 and the cautionary note to 25.

would be troubling in a transcript, but the content allowed Salter to make a good case for its authenticity; its seal however is more or less decisive. A high proportion of the texts below exist in this world of shadows. The charters of Malling, Minster-in-Sheppey and Leeds, in particular, inspire anxiety, but the case against most of them remains unproven. The criteria for assessing the authority of texts are also peculiar to this early stage in the evolution of English episcopal acts. While marked eccentricities of form may excite suspicion in a late-twelfth-century act, for this earlier period the reverse is true. The texts which command most confidence are those which follow no fixed pattern of formulation, physical appearance or sealing. Many of the manifest later forgeries, and more of those that are suspicious, arouse distrust precisely because they conform too closely to the conventions of a later age.

A third distinction concerns the origin of these texts. Neither form nor script nor physical appearance suggests that these early archiepiscopal charters form any coherent body of diplomatic practice. There is little evidence of a scribe working in the archbishop's household and writing acts for more than one beneficiary. William's charter for the small house of canons at Calke may be an example of an archbishop's scribe at work, for the hand has some features characteristic of Canterbury practice, though it has not been identified elsewhere. Four original acts, one of Ralph and three of William, concerning Bexley, an archiepiscopal church, and its grant to Holy Trinity, Aldgate, are written in one hand, but this is found also in an act for Christ Church priory, and in cathedral priory books, and the scribe was presumably a member of the community.[5] It is more or less axiomatic that forgeries are constructed by or for the beneficiaries.[6] However, many even of the credible texts below are written in scripts which suggest that they also were written by the beneficiary, or use formulae which may be familiar elsewhere in their archive, few though there are which preserve many private acts before 1136. In many respects the acts collected here are more instructive when read grouped under beneficiaries than under the name of each archbishop. Correspondingly, the commentary on their diplomatic usage is to be read rather as an account of a small sample of acts of the period than as the analysis of a chancery.

---

[5] below, pp. lxiv–vi.

[6] There is no clear sign in this collection of the 'professional' forger working for a number of clients, such as the notorious Guerno of St Medard (W. Levison, *England and the continent in the eighth century,* Oxford 1946, 207–23), or Osbert of Clare (P. Chaplais, 'Original charters'), or the skilled but anonymous craftsman unmasked by Christopher Brooke in 'Episcopal charters for Wix priory', *Medieval miscellany* 45–63, though one may lurk in the shadows behind +33 below.

It can never be known how many early acts have been lost. Nevertheless, the three distinctive features of the collection set out above combine to suggest that the number was always low. It is difficult to believe that Christ Church lost any acts of Lanfranc it may once have had, especially since it seems possible to reconstruct a cartulary of the house produced very soon after his death.[7] Further, the absolute number of grants relating to places and people outside the archbishop's immediate jurisdiction is small, but the proportion remains significant. Even if one excludes the authentic acts for Rochester, with its exceptionally close relationship to the archbishopric,[8] thirty-one credible acts and five improbable ones deal with churches or men neither in Kent nor on the archbishop's estates outside the county. In principle one may look across all England for evidence of the archbishop's action. Yet outside Canterbury and Rochester, even archives and inventories as rich as Abingdon, Lincoln or Ramsey produce little or nothing. The existence of forgeries in part reflects the high value which would later be attached to early archiepiscopal authority, and encourages one to suppose that at least some form of earlier acts would have been preserved with care. The incoherence of the forms in the acts, and the apparent importance of beneficial drafting, do nothing to encourage the view that even archbishop William's clerks were accustomed to their systematic production. On a longer perspective, what is most striking is the gap between this meagre haul and the astonishing explosion of acts for archbishop Theobald. From the perspective of 1136 a new, and largely unheralded, era was about to begin.

Lastly, we are much better informed about the careers of the archbishops than we are about most of their suffragans. Even if one sets aside the modest letter collection which survives for Lanfranc, and the much larger one for Anselm, or the remarkably detailed account of Anselm (and to a degree his successor) given by Eadmer's *Historia novorum,* the abundant chronicles of the reign of Henry I provide much more material on the archbishops' careers than may be extracted from their charters. A comparison of the itineraries at the end of this volume with those in earlier editions in the series makes the point at a simple level. More generally, we can know no medieval archbishop of Canterbury more intimately than Anselm in his letters, his prayers and reflections, and his theological works. Yet, even if none had survived, we would still know more of how contemporaries perceived him and his successors than we would of almost any other bishop of the realm under king Henry. While the charters of most of the archbishops' contemporaries are a

[7] See the notes to 16 below.
[8] Brett in *Faith and fabric* 20–22, summarising the earlier literature.

prime source for their careers and purposes, those printed here supplement what is known elsewhere rather than replace it.

THE ARCHBISHOPS AND THEIR HOUSEHOLDS

The period covered in this collection begins with the arrival of the first archbishop of Canterbury appointed by king William I, after the deposition of Stigand by papal legates at the Easter council of 1070, and ends only months after the death of the Conqueror's youngest son Henry I, and before the political crises that followed had reached any intensity.

Lanfranc's career has been studied with masterly care, and needs only a brief summary here.[9] He was born in Pavia c. 1010 to Heribald and Rosa, later commemorated at Canterbury,[10] and later tradition made his father one of those who declared the rights and laws of the city. The extent of his own legal education is a matter of continuing dispute, but certainly his own works give only the slightest indication of a familiarity with such legal learning as was available in Pavia in his youth.[11] Around 1030, for reasons which are nowhere adequately explained, he left Italy with some of the pupils he had attracted, and travelled along the Loire valley, eventually settling in the remote centre of Avranches shortly after Normandy had descended into tumult at the death of duke Robert in 1035, where he is said to have taught for some three years. In 1042 he abandoned the world and took the monastic habit at the struggling community which Herluin had founded at Le Bec eight

[9] Gibson, *Lanfranc* has lost none of its value, and remains fundamental both as a study and as a guide to the earlier literature; her chapter in *A history of Canterbury cathedral* ed. P. Collinson, N. Ramsay and M. Sparks (Oxford 1995) 38–68 carries the story of the community further. See too now Cowdrey, *Lanfranc*, which offers a valuable alternative perspective.

[10] Fleming, 'Lists', 146, 137n.

[11] The difficulty in describing Lanfranc's early life stems in part from the steady enhancement of the story after his death, particularly in the *Vita Lanfranci* written at Bec c. 1140. The fullest, and most sceptical, account of this is by Margaret Gibson, in her 'The image of Lanfranc' and edition of the *Vita: Lanfranco di Pavia e l'Europa del secolo XI* ed. G. D'Onofrio (Italia sacra 51, 1993), 21–8, 659–715. Her account of the sources in *Lanfranc* 195–205 remains essential. For a recent analysis of legal education in Northern Italy, which downplays the resources available very considerably see A. Winroth, *The making of Gratian's 'Decretum'* (Cambridge 2000) 157–70. For the earliest and least highly coloured account, in Gilbert Crispin's *Vita Herluini* of 1109 × 1117, I have used the edition of J. Armitage Robinson in his *Gilbert Crispin* 87–110; he used the *editio princeps*, apparently based on a good and early lost Bec copy as well as a twelfth-century manuscript from Rochester and a fifteenth-century one from Bec. Gillian Evans in *The works of Gilbert Crispin, abbot of Westminster*. edited by A. S. Abulafia and G.R. Evans (Auctores Britannici medii aevi vii, 1986) 183–212 used the late and eccentric ms Cambridge UL ms Add. 3096, unknown to Robinson, but not the earlier edition.

years earlier. His arrival, and the flood of pupils attracted by his teaching, transformed the fortunes of the house.[12] Three years later he became prior, and abbot Herluin's chief support. In 1049 he was among those brought to the papal curia to debate the doctrines of Berengar of Tours, and was at Leo IX's synod at Rome in April 1050, in part at least to vindicate his own orthodoxy. By the end of the 1050s he stood high in the regard of the duke, and of pope Nicholas II, and in 1063 he became first abbot of duke William's magnificent new foundation at St Etienne of Caen. After the death of archbishop Maurilius in 1067 he was said to be sought as his successor at Rouen, but to have refused.[13] However, after the deposition of archbishop Stigand by papal legates at the Council of Winchester at Easter 1070, king William set about securing Lanfranc as his successor. At a meeting of the Norman clergy attended by the legate Ermenfrid Lanfranc was persuaded to agreement, not least by the urging of abbot Herluin. He crossed the Channel, and on 15 August, according to the Worcester chronicle, the king 'made him archbishop of the church of Canterbury', though Eadmer's *Life* of Dunstan claims that this was the date at which he was first received at Canterbury 'more electi antistitis'.[14] A fortnight later he was consecrated by eight or nine bishops in the cathedral church, which was largely ruinous after the catastrophic fire of 1067. Over the next nineteen years the English church was to undergo profound change. Although it is usually difficult to pin down precisely Lanfranc's involvement in these changes beyond his own diocese, there is something like unanimity among the early sources that he stood in an exceptionally close relationship with the king. In secular and ecclesiastical business he was a leading figure under the Conqueror, and did much to secure the succession of William Rufus. Certainly he presided over a sequence of councils of the English Church of unparalleled regularity and importance, which legislated among other issues for the movement of sees, the abolition of simony, a qualified imposition of celibacy upon the clergy in higher orders, the relation of secular and ecclesiastical justice, and the assertion of ecclesiastical control over appointments to parish churches. This was reform, indeed, but more in the spirit of Leo IX than Gregory VII. Lanfranc resisted every effort by Gregory to persuade him to visit Rome, and after 1080 he seems to have maintained a cool neutrality between Gregory and the anti-pope Clement III.

---

[12] Such at least is the account of Gilbert Crispin in *Vita Herluini* 95–6; Lanfranc's name, however, stands thirty-fifth on the profession-list of Bec, which suggests a considerable, if not necessarily a wealthy, community—Porée, *Histoire du Bec* i 629.

[13] *Vita Lanfranci* c. 5 (ed Gibson 682).

[14] John of Worcs. iii 14; *Materials Dunstan* 232.

It is certainly striking that two of the three letters written by Clement to Lanfranc were copied into the archbishop's own copy of Pseudo-Isidore by Eadmer, apparently very soon after their arrival.[15] Similarly, when Odo of Bayeux fell foul of the Conqueror in 1083 or William of Durham under Rufus in 1088, Lanfranc was ruthless in rejecting the claims of the aggrieved bishops to the protection of their order—claims abundantly supported by the Pseudo-Isidore collection Lanfranc did so much to disseminate in England.[16] His wider influence is part of the history of the whole English Church. From the narrower perspective of the archbishopric Lanfranc's achievement was clear and largely enduring.

His extended obit conveniently catalogues his works as they were viewed from Christ Church.[17] Reconstruction of the cathedral advanced rapidly after his arrival. The new cathedral bore a marked resemblance to Lanfranc's former church at Caen, though the crypt is most closely matched by the contemporary cathedral which his turbulent neighbour, bishop Odo, was to consecrate at Bayeux in 1077—the same year in which the church was sufficiently near completion to be dedicated.[18] The church was further splendidly enriched with treasures, some of gold, some inlaid with gems and all of wonderful workmanship. In the inventory of the vestments of the cathedral in 1316 there were still three chasubles, four copes, a tunic and a dalmatic remembered as the gift of Lanfranc; they were all in black, but magnificently ornamented with gems and richly embroidered in gold with circles, leaves and beasts.[19] At the same time he rebuilt the monastic offices on a vast scale, to house a community which rapidly rose from around twenty to sixty and more, and was conceived for a hundred and fifty, if we may believe Gervase

---

[15] Gullick, 'Eadmer' 180–1.

[16] For the dispute with bp William see most recently M. Philpott, 'The *De iniusta vexacione Willelmi episcopi primi* and canon law in Anglo-Norman Durham', *Anglo-Norman Durham* 125–37; M. Gullick, 'The English-owned manuscripts of the *Collectio Lanfranci* (s.xi/xii)' in *The legacy of M.R.. James* ed. L. Dennison (Donington 2001) 99–117 marks a significant advance in the study of Lanfranc's canon-law collection.

[17] Gibson, *Lanfranc* 227–9.

[18] For Lanfranc's cathedral see three important studies published since Gibson's work: F. Woodman, *The architectural history of Canterbury Cathedral* (London 1981); *Medieval art and archaeology at Canterbury before 1220* (British Archaeological Association Conference Transactions v 1982), particularly the studies by Richard Gem and H.J.A. Strik; Kevin Blockley, Margaret Sparks and Tim Tatton-Brown, *Canterbury Cathedral nave: Archaeology, history and architecture* (Canterbury 1997), esp 23–30, 111–23.

[19] J. Wickham Legg and W.H. St John Hope, *Inventories of Christ Church, Canterbury* (Westminster 1902) 51, 53, 57.

of Canterbury.[20] The library was stocked with fine books, many corrected in his own hand.[21] Concern for the fabric went hand in hand with a determined campaign to recover estates lost to his church, and to Rochester, in the years of confusion under Stigand. At Pennenden Heath he recovered a great string of these, and the king's favour enabled him to add more. Outside the city wall he founded the church of St Gregory for a small community of canons, apparently in part at least to serve his new hospital the other side of Northgate street for the poor and infirm, and a leper house at Harbledown, a mile or two up the London road.[22] At the north-western corner of the nave he also built an archiepiscopal residence; significantly the excavators interpreted a large chamber-block attached to it as a residence for his household.[23] The obituarist praised him too for the construction of many and handsome churches and houses on the archiepiscopal estates, for the comfort and honour of his successors and the relief of poverty for his men. The work of restoration at Rochester, which was near ruin when Lanfranc came to Canterbury, was equally striking. Under Gundulf, the second monk of Caen to succeed the last Anglo-Saxon bishop, a substantial monastic community replaced the tiny group of canons, and a new cathedral was built; Lanfranc encouraged the conversion of the community, contributed generously to the new church, recovered estates for it with the same zeal he had showed for Christ Church and added more. The price Rochester paid was to be subjected to a more formal subordination than any other bishopric; the election of the bishop was in the hands of Canterbury, the knights of the church answered to the archbishop, not directly to the king, and the bishop took over many of the functions of a deputy to the archbishop which had formerly been performed, as it seems, by a *chorepiscopus* based in the ancient church of St Martin in Canterbury.[24] For the community at Christ Church not the least of Lanfranc's achievements was to secure the formal submission of the archbishop of York to Lanfranc's own highly idiosyncratic vision of the primacy of Canterbury, involving a personal act of submission. The subordination of Rochester was scarcely less extraordinary in the common practice of the

---

[20] Eadmer speaks of some sixty after the deposition of abbot Aethelnoth of Glastonbury in 1077/8 in *Memorials Dunstan* 420; Gervase of Canterbury ii 368.

[21] But see Webber, 'Script and manuscript' 148.

[22] Tatton-Brown, 'Beginnings'.

[23] J. Rady, T. Tatton-Brown and J.A. Bowen, 'The archbishop's palace, Canterbury', *Journal of the British Archaeological Association* cxliv (1991) 1–60, esp. 5, 30–32; T. Tatton-Brown, *Lambeth Palace* (London 2000).

[24] Brett, 'Gundulf and the cathedral communities of Canterbury and Rochester', *Canterbury and the Norman Conquest* 16–19, and above xxvi n.

Latin Church, but it was only to be diluted slowly over the next century and a half. The primacy, on the other hand, was to prove a fearful burden after Lanfranc's death; once the issue was carried beyond England to the papal court there were almost overwhelming forces of law and custom against it.[25] The ultimately unavailing struggle of Lanfranc's successors to maintain it overshadowed the last years of Anselm and much of the career of Ralph and William. In this, as in many other respects, Lanfranc's masterful rule became the standard against which the monks of Christ Church judged his successors, and largely found them wanting.

Lanfranc had never doubted that the fortunes of the Church in England were wholly dependent on the stability of the new Norman regime, and he played an active part in maintaining king William's throne. He played a key role in suppressing the revolt of 1075, he acted as a justice, he sided resolutely with the king against those bishops who fell foul of him, he took some part in the knighting of prince Henry, the king's youngest son, in 1086,[26] and the following year had a decisive influence in ensuring the succession of William Rufus. Two years later he died at Canterbury on 28 May, and was buried before the cross at the west end of the monks' choir. At his anniversary two hundred years later the monks of Christ Church still dressed the church as they did for the feast of St Augustine himself.[27]

In assessing the nature of the household which sustained Lanfranc and his successors, one has to bear in mind the elastic sense which the *familia* had then, and continues to bear in the modern literature. At its narrowest, it may mean no more than the small group who attended to the archbishop's domestic needs. Du Boulay called attention to a thirteenth-century custumal which listed the expected complement of these servants in terms which may well have held good from the time of Lanfranc himself—an almoner, the 'summus clericus de familia', an usher, a single knight, some messengers, a cross-bearer, a monk, a washerwoman, an 'emptor', a door-keeper, a baker and the chief steward.[28] Their closeness to their master could give these servants an importance well beyond the apparent modesty of their offices, but we can only occasionally distinguish who exercised them. Beyond this circle there is a rather larger one, and often better attested, which involved those clerks and laymen in whom the archbishop reposed a special confidence, and who were,

[25] There is a brief summary of the issues in Hugh the Chanter xxx–xlv; a fuller bibliography would need a chapter to itself; for later developments see below.

[26] Orderic iv 120–1 and n.

[27] *Fasti* ii 1; *Life of Gundulf* 52; Fleming, 'Lists' 128; Dart, *Antiquities*, appx p. xxxi.

[28] Du Boulay, *Lordship* 253.

it seems, largely dependent on him for their material support. Beyond that again is the larger group of those who held lands or churches from him, and looked to him as their patron and lord, though not regularly fed at his table. Finally there is the largest and most diffuse group of neighbours, connections and friends, often landholders or clerks of substance, who appear occasionally in the narrative sources. One may suspect that they form a significant part of the witness-lists of the archbishops after Lanfranc, but one can rarely be confident. Other witnesses may as probably appear for other reasons, as potential objectors to the transaction, by virtue of some local office or even by mere chance.

For Lanfranc the only act to illuminate this world is the exasperating **9**, recording the presence at one of his judgements of two royal judges at work in the area, his old friend Gilbert the abbot of Westminster, his nephew abbot Paul of St Albans, the sheriff 'et maxima parte de familia ipsius domini archiepiscopi'. One can however supply the lack to some extent from other material. The laymen closely tied to his service are to be found scattered through the pages of the *Domesday monachorum*: Godfrey the steward, Ralph the chamberlain, Richard the constable, William the bursar (*dispensator*), Roger and Osbern the butlers, though only Godfrey the steward and the two butlers are clearly listed among the knights of the archbishop.[29] Some leading clerics also appear in other sources. Not surprisingly Lanfranc sought to gather about him trusted colleagues from Normandy. Of these the one whose functions are most fully described is Gundulf, the monk of Bec, possibly prior of Caen, and later bishop of Rochester. According to his *Life* Lanfranc brought him to England with him, and appointed him 'rei familiaris suae procuratorem'; the biographer speaks of his omnicompetence, his special concern with the poor, his expedition to London on their behalf and the likelihood that he would slip out at night to ensure the horses were being well-treated. In another anecdote the *Life* illustrates the complexities of the household of a monastic archbishop with a monastic chapter, showing Gundulf as also a leading member of the community at Christ Church.[30] After he became bishop of Rochester, and Lanfranc abandoned the services of a *chorepiscopus* at Canterbury, Gundulf became the archbishop's constant deputy; at least according to the *Life*, the archbishop delegated to him virtually the entire burden of dedicating churches, ordaining clergy and confir-

---

[29] *Domesday monachorum* 81, 83, 95 (and cf p. lxxxi n below); 82; 85, 93, 95; 87; 105.
[30] *Life of Gundulf* 32–4; cf *Materials Dunstan* 413–4.

mation throughout his diocese.[31] Three further monks of Caen and Bec, all destined to high office, are also known to have joined Lanfranc. Ralph and William had been monks at Caen. Ralph, the future prior of Rochester and abbot of Battle, accompanied Lanfranc to England; Walter, abbot of Evesham from 1077, was described by the abbey chronicle as Lanfranc's former chaplain; a little later, much to his abbot's distress, Gilbert Crispin of Bec was summoned to the archbishop's side, where he seems to have remained until promotion to Westminster around 1085. The high offices all were to hold suggest that none would have been confined to the monastic community, any more than Gundulf had been.[32] Nevertheless, the significance and scale of Lanfranc's achievements remain much clearer than the means and resources with which they were achieved.

Like Lanfranc, Anselm had enjoyed a great reputation at Bec, came to England relatively late in his life, and together with Lanfranc was remembered by the monks of Christ Church with their saints and martyrs.[33] Like him too, he has been studied with outstanding sympathy and care.[34] In almost all other respects the contrast is much more remarkable. His career as archbishop was marked by long periods of conflict with the king, he spent much of his pontificate in exile, he left far less obvious a mark upon the Church in England, at least in the short term. The remarkable detail in which we can follow his career owes much to the labours of Eadmer, his constant companion and confessor, yet at least part of Eadmer's motive for writing was to justify his friend and master against the charge that he had abandoned, if not actually betrayed, the Church in England. and even more his church at Canterbury.

Anselm was born in 1033 at Aosta, in Savoy, the son of Ermenburga, and Gundulf, both of whom were duly commemorated at Canterbury.[35] At the

---

[31] *Life of Gundulf* 52. It is possibly significant that the form of profession to Canterbury produced in the 1090s is made 'Dorobernensi ecclesiae eiusque vicari[o]', Gullick and Pfaff, 'Pontifical' 288.

[32] *Chron. Battle* 116; Malmesbury, GP 137 (placing him at Caen at least for a time), *Chronicon abbatiae de Evesham* ed. W.D. Macray (RS 1863) 96, calling him a m. of Cerisy; *EA* 103, below 9. See too the group of monks of Bec and Caen who followed Lanfranc, discussed in Cowdrey, *Lanfranc* 150–1.

[33] Dart, *Canterbury* Appx p. xxvi.

[34] What follows is based almost wholly on Southern, *St Anselm* (1963) and (1990), which are not usually further cited. *Councils and synods* i(2) 639–52, 655–705 provide some further references. A much more 'political' account is offered by S. Vaughn, *Anselm of Bec and Robert of Meulan* (Berkeley/LA, 1987); see too, again from another perspective, Hollister, *Henry I* 117–30. 149–203, partly developing his 'William II, Henry I and the Church', in *Culture of Christendom* 183–205.

[35] Fleming, 'Lists' 144, 141.

age of twenty-three he left home and travelled for some three years in
Burgundy and France, before going to Bec to study with Lanfranc, whose
reputation was now established. A little later, and not without hesitation, he
became a monk. In the list of monks professed at Bec his name stands sixty-
eighth, directly after Gundulf, the later bishop of Rochester.[36] When
Lanfranc was sent to be abbot of the duke's new foundation at Caen, Anselm
succeeded him as prior; when abbot Herluin died at a ripe age in 1079,
Anselm succeeded him, apparently without debate, and ruled Bec for fourteen years of considerable prosperity and growing influence. After Lanfranc's
death he was an obvious candidate to succeed him at Canterbury, where he
was well-known from earlier visits, not least because of his remarkable hold
on the regard of many of the leading Norman magnates. King William, however, was even less willing to forgo the revenues of the archbishopric than he
was of the growing number of other churches kept vacant over the years, as
he was straining every sinew to seize Normandy from his brother, and the
archbishopric remained unfilled for four years.[37] Anselm was in England on
abbey business in the autumn of 1092, and at the Christmas court the king
was urged to make an appointment at Canterbury. He is said to have replied
that there would be no archbishop but him; shortly afterwards he fell seri-
ously ill at Gloucester. His counsellors all urged him to provide for his soul,
and most of all to remove the scandal of the vacancy at Canterbury. Anselm
was hurriedly summoned to the king's side, and on 6 March, in the teeth of
his protests, the bishops and king more or less forced the office on him. After
securing the consent of duke Robert, the archbishop of Rouen and the
monks at Bec, further negotiations followed, in which Anselm sought the
king's consent to the restitution of all the lands of Canterbury as Lanfranc
had held them, free of the tenures the king had created during the vacancy,
to judgement on other lost lands Lanfranc had not recovered, to an acknowl-
edgement that Anselm was already bound to obedience to pope Urban II—
whom Normandy but not England had already recognised—and to the
maintenance of the relationship which the Conqueror had maintained with
Lanfranc. Though the king's responses were at best qualified, at Winchester
Anselm was formally invested with the archbishopric, and on 25 September
he was enthroned at Canterbury; six weeks later he was consecrated at
Canterbury on 4 December in the presence of archbishop Thomas of York
and all the bishops of England but the elderly and infirm bishops of
Worcester and Exeter.

---

[36] Porée, *Histoire du Bec* i 629.
[37] For the election see too F. Barlow, *William Rufus* 299–308.

In the next three years all the difficulties foreseen by Anselm, at least in Eadmer's account, proved occasions of deepening conflict. The king resisted acknowledging pope Urban and allowing Anselm to secure his pallium as long as possible, and only did so in 1095 in return, it was believed, for securing a wide liberty in his management of church affairs. The legate Walter of Albano came to Canterbury with the pallium, which Anselm took up from the high altar of Christ Church on 27 May 1095.[38] The king would not allow Anselm to celebrate the councils the archbishop thought necessary for the well-being of the Church, demanded heavy contributions from Canterbury for his Welsh campaign, and resisted all Anselm's urgings to take thought for vacant churches or to allow him to visit Rome to consult the pope. By the autumn of 1097 Anselm felt his position to be untenable; he had received virtually no support from his fellow-bishops, and the king was proving ever more intransigent. On 15 October he took what was to be his final leave of the king, and prepared to cross the sea for Rome, with or without the king's consent. On 8 November he sailed from Dover to Wissant, on a journey which took him on to Bari and to Rome for the memorable councils of 1099. The king seized the archbishopric into his hands, but pope Urban offered little practical support, and Anselm left for a prolonged stay at Lyon.

The sudden death of Rufus in 1100 led to the the new king's almost instant invitation for Anselm to return. On 23 September Anselm landed at Dover. King Henry was a great deal more cautious than his brother, and the threat of an invasion from Normandy would have made an open breach very dangerous. Even so, relations between king and archbishop were strained from their first meeting, when Anselm refused to accept re-investiture with the archbishopric on the basis of the papal condemnation of 1099, though that did no more than rehearse earlier condemnations since at least 1078. Though Anselm would not consecrate any bishops who had received investiture, yet he was allowed to celebrate a council at Michaelmas 1102 which ruled on many of the issues which had pre-occupied Anselm under Rufus, and to enjoy the fruits of the archbishopric. By 1103, however, the deadlock over investitures had become complete, and Anselm set off again for Rome to consult pope Paschal II in April. Again the pope offered honour and welcome, but little readiness to act with resolution on his behalf, and Anselm retired once more to Lyon. As he made his way there William Warelwast on the king's behalf forbade him to return to England without accepting the king's rights; the king then took the Canterbury estates into his own hand. Over the

---

[38] Eadmer, *Historia* 72–3; below p. xlii n.

next two years negotiations continued between king and pope, and to a lesser degree between king and archbishop. By March 1106 Henry and Paschal had agreed a formula whereby the king would yield his right to invest, but would retain, at least in the interim, his right to receive homage. On this basis Anselm returned to England in the late summer, though his health was poor; at a royal council at the beginning of August 1107 the settlement was confirmed, and on 11 August the end of the dispute was signalled by Anselm's consecration of five bishops at Canterbury. The following year Anselm and Thomas, the archbishop-elect of York, celebrated a council at London at Whitsun on the mechanism for enforcing clerical celibacy, an issue which had raised innumerable difficulties after its first English promulgation in strict form in 1102. A couple of months earlier, Anselm had buried his most constant supporter, bishop Gundulf, at Rochester. Immediately after the council he appointed Ralph, abbot of Sées, as his successor. From the moment of his consecration Anselm had been aware that York was in no way reconciled to the subjection imposed on archbishop Thomas I in 1072. There had been a confused debate over the primatial title in 1093; archbishop Gerard, who was already consecrated as bishop of Hereford, was at last brought to a qualified undertaking to observe the same obedience at York as he had promised at Hereford before his death in May 1108; his designated successor, Thomas II, and even more the canons of his cathedral, showed much greater determination to resist. Almost Anselm's last act was to threaten Thomas with excommunication and suspension from priestly office unless he either submitted or resigned (**14**). On 21 April 1109 Anselm died, and was buried beside Lanfranc the next day.[39]

 Compared to his predecessor, Anselm showed little inclination for the minutiae of ecclesiastical business, even when he was any position to conduct it. Nevertheless, a good deal can be discovered about the circle of companions, servants and friends that surrounded him. Apart from the clear *spuria*, and the exceptional and suspicious **23**, three of his charters have witness lists which are instructive in their contrasts. In **15**, a grant of nine holdings outside the walls of Canterbury to the portreeve, the witnesses are almost all drawn from the circle of leading Englishmen of the city, with whom Anselm seems to have enjoyed closer relations than his correspondence might readily suggest. It is noteworthy that, with the possible exception of Godfrey of Thanington, elsewhere described as a steward, none is known to have been in his direct service, and that there is no overlap with the witnesses of the com-

---

[39] *Councils* i(2) 655–707; Eadmer, *Historia* 206; Margaret Sparks in *Canterbury Cathedral nave* 121.

panion grant by prior Ernulf and the monks, who were all apparently local Norman knights. In **16**, the restoration of an estate in Essex to Christ Church, the witnesses are headed by the archdeacon, followed by the sheriff (who was commemorated at Christ Church, and whose wife is described as Anselm's spiritual daughter[40]), three local knights and bishop Gundulf's nephew. Only **26**, the slightly suspect grant to Rochester, has a predominantly clerical witness list, the prior of Christ Church, the archdeacons of Canterbury and Rochester, Baldwin of Tournai, Joseph and Eadmer, monks of Canterbury with exceptionally close links with the archbishop, and two knights.

His clerical circle is much more prominent in the narrative sources and in his letters, and has been analysed in some detail by Sir Richard Southern. The most visible of its members is bishop Gundulf, who escorted the archbishop-elect around the Canterbury estates between his election and consecration, did his best to mediate between Anselm and both Rufus and Henry I, and carried the chief burden in watching over his interests when he was in exile. Yet, for all his services, and the warm friendship which linked them, Gundulf can scarcely be described as a member of his household. Others were plainly closer to him, at least physically. When Anselm came to England in 1092 he was accompanied by two monks of Bec, Baldwin, the former advocate of the bishop of Tournai, and Eustace. Baldwin quickly took a leading part in the new archbishop's entourage, 'a man energetic in monastic and secular affairs whom the archbishop placed in charge of his affairs', elsewhere called his 'provisor et ordinator' (or 'dispensator'). At the height of Rufus' indignation with Anselm in 1095 he could think of no more effective means of putting pressure on the archbishop than by exiling Baldwin as his principal counsellor, with two other unnamed clerks. Though soon restored, he accompanied Anselm into exile in both 1097 and 1103, and acted as his intermediary with the pope in 1102 and again in 1104 and 1106–7. He was at his deathbed in 1109, and then drops out of sight.[41] Eustace clearly remained a confidant, and accompanied Anselm on his second journey to Rome in 1103, though at least in Eadmer's account he is a much shadowier figure.[42] The other two monks who shared Anselm's second exile were both from Christ Church,

---

[40] Fleming, 'Lists' 143, *EA* 356.

[41] *Memorials Anselm* 238; Eadmer, *Historia* 67, 132, 171, 386, 417; Eadmer, *Vita Ans.* 81, 99, 134, 143; *EA* 338, 349; Malmesbury, *GP* 123. Compare however 39 below. which could just possibly be a further attestation, though it is most natural to see this unspecified witness as a layman. It is tempting to identify him with Dom Baldwin, a kinsman of an abbot Andrew, who carried Elmer of Canterbury's ep. ii, Leclercq, 'Écrits spirituels' 64–5.

[42] *Memorials Anselm* 227, 238.

Alexander and Eadmer. Southern suggests that Alexander came to take a leading place in Anselm's circle from 1100, and certainly he was his emissary to Rome in early in 1102; his *Dicta* and *Miracula* are a precious further insight into Anselm's conversation and thought, if overshadowed by the scale of Eadmer's vivid accounts.[43] Though Eadmer was as constantly with Anselm as Baldwin, and may have acted occasionally as his secretary and even spiritual director, his character, and his own account of their journeys, suggest that he was better suited for the role of confidant than agent. So far as we can know, and Eadmer tells us much about himself, he was never entrusted with independent action. For some time Boso, the future abbot of Bec, was another of Anselm's circle. He was summoned to Canterbury very shortly after the archbishop's consecration, and sent by him to the Council of Clermont in 1095, and returned to report on its outcome—though the events of 1099–1100 make one wonder how fully he understood what was said there. He returned from Bec with Anselm to England in 1106, and remained with him until his death.[44] Other monks too, Gilbert of Bec, Anselm's 'familiaris' and messenger in 1105, Robert who 'is accustomed to look after our business' in 1104, or Joseph, entrusted with the management of some archiepiscopal lands, appear briefly in Anselm's letters.[45] His nephew, another Anselm, the later legate and abbot of Bury, joined his uncle around 1098, and returned to England with him in 1100; he was apparently with his uncle in his second exile, at least for a while; his temperament, and his youth, seem not to have given him a significant role in the household as we now know it.[46]

The context of Eadmer's portrait of Anselm is overwhelmingly monastic, but to some extent this may be misleading. The two anonymous but influential clerks whom Rufus exiled in 1095 remind one of other actors who probably mattered more to Anselm than to Eadmer. Scattered references suggest some of the names of these clerks in the background of Eadmer's account. During his first exile he was accompanied by Adam the clerk, and in his second exile by Robert the clerk; earlier Rainer, a client of countess Ida of Boulogne, had spent an extended period in his household.[47] An otherwise

---

[43] Ibid. 20; *EA* 223, 311, 325.

[44] *Vita Bosonis* in *Lanfranci opera* appx. 47. Even the distracted transmission of the canons of Clermont makes it clear that Urban there condemned both investiture and homage, though Anselm appeared unaware of this until 1099.

[45] *EA* 378, 289, 330–1. Charles Homer Haskins, 'A Canterbury monk at Constantinople, *c.* 1090,' repr. from *EHR* xxv (1910) 293–5 in his *Studies in mediaeval culture* (Oxford 1929) 160–3.

[46] The younger Anselm joined his uncle in Rome in 1098; cf Eadmer, *Vita* 104n, 169, *EA* 211 and was with him in Lyon in *c.* 1103 (*EA* 268); Southern, *St Anselm* (1963) 10–11.

[47] Eadmer, *Vita Ans.* 124; *EA* 331, 235.

unidentified William, chaplain to the archbishop, is known only from two acts connected with countess Adela of Blois, the king's sister, of 1102 × 1104.[48] There is lastly the case of Norman: according to Eadmer he was Anselm's clerk and chaplain, a Norman by name and birth; nevertheless it is very tempting to identify him with the Norman, born in Thanet and a former student of Anselm's in France, who was sent to the archbishop by the canons of Colchester for direction to a suitable house where he could study the life of the regular canons, and was recommended by him to the abbot of Mont-St-Eloi. After stays in Chartres and Beauvais he returned to become first prior of the influential house of canons at Holy Trinity Aldgate in 1107 × 8.[49] If so, he was to have a more substantial career beyond the household than most of Anselm's circle. While many of Lanfranc's familiars went on to high office, Anselm's did not. Apart from the priors of Christ Church whom he appointed, Ernulf in 1096, later abbot of Peterborough and bishop of Rochester, or Conrad in 1108 × 9, briefly abbot of St Benet at Hulme, or Eadmer in his brief and disastrous career as bishop-elect of St Andrews in 1120 × 1, none is known to have received significant preferment. There may be some force in Hugh the Chanter's suggestion that king Henry never wholly forgave Anselm for their prolonged dispute.[50] This may also account in part for the five-year vacancy that followed. While the king took the archiepiscopal lands into his hands, the monks retained control of their own estates, and bishop Ralph performed all the diocesan offices of the archbishop.[51]

It was not until the spring of 1114 that the king summoned the bishops and magnates to a great council at Windsor to take thought for a new appointment. Although it was widely believed that he favoured his physician, abbot Faricius of Abingdon, he gave way with unexpected ease before the objections, particularly of the bishops, that they would accept no monk. Since the Canterbury party was equally insistent in their demand for one, bishop Ralph of Rochester was put forward as a compromise candidate; his well-known affability brought him ready acceptance, and he was postulated on 26 April.[52] On Saturday 16 May he was enthroned at Canterbury.

---

[48] *Recueil de chartes et documents de Saint-Martin-des-Champs* ed. J. Depoin (Archives de la France monastique xiii 1912) i nos 96–7.

[49] *Memorials Dunstan* 246; *EA* 234; *Cart. Aldgate* 225–7; *Heads* i 173.

[50] Hugh the Chanter 22.

[51] Eadmer, *Historia* 221–2. It was probably as deputy for the archbp that Ralph consecrated the crypt chapel at Bury St Edmunds, which jealously guarded its exemption from its own diocesan, and promoted Baldwin to the priorate, perhaps in 1112, *Consuetudines Burienses* 114.

[52] Eadmer, *Historia* 221–3; Malmesbury, *GP* 125–8; *Hist. Abingdon* (ed. Stevenson) ii 287; D. Bethell, 'Black monks', 675–6; Brett, *English Church* 73.

Archbishop Ralph was born around 1068, the son of Seffrid d'Escures and his first wife Rascendis.[53] Seffrid, whose name suggests kinship with the lords of Bellême, held extensive lands in the neighbourhood of Alençon, and made substantial grants from them to the foundation of Roger, vicomte of the Hiémois and Mabel his wife, the heiress of Bellême, at St Martin of Sées, first established with monks from St Evroul. Among his other children were a daughter, Hugh canon of Sées and Seffrid, the son of his second wife, who entered St Martin as a monk and later became abbot of Glastonbury and bishop of Chichester.[54] Ralph entered the house in youth, rose to be prior in 1088 and the next year abbot, in the eleventh year after his profession. He was to hold office under increasingly difficult circumstances for sixteen years. For some time the house prospered. Roger of Bellême had already taken monks from St Martin's to establish a substantial monastery at Shrewsbury around 1083, and in Ralph's time the family made extensive further grants to Sées, notably in Pembrokeshire and Lancashire. A curious sidelight on the abbot's concerns is thrown by some questions he put to archbishop Anselm, already apparently long familiar to him, around 1095. One of his monks had accepted orders from bishop Herewald of Llandaff when the bishop was under Anselm's interdict, and another had helped a wife with poisonous herbs to kill her husband. Anselm's reply ended with what was to prove a grim presage of future events, a declaration that his life as archbishop had provided not a moment's satisfaction.[55]

The death of William Rufus was disastrous for St Martin and the abbot. In 1102 abbot Ralph was in England when Robert of Bellême and his brothers rose against king Henry, for after the fall of Bridgnorth the men of Shrewsbury sent Ralph to the king with the keys to the fortress.[56] Count Robert, who had become an increasingly exacting neighbour, now made intolerable demands on Sées after his expulsion from England, including apparently a demand for homage; by 1104 both bishop Serlo and abbot Ralph had fled to the protection of king Henry. England was then full of such exiles, but Ralph is said to have been unusually unwilling to burden his

---

[53] The following account is largely an abbreviated version of the forthcoming entry in the new *DNB*. The principal sources for Ralph's earlier career are Orderic iv 168–70; Malmesbury, *GP* 127–8; Round, *CDF* 232–9. Paris, BN fr. 18953 contains a xvii c. history of Sées, citing, inter alia, the lost 'Livre rouge' (for which see also BN lat. 13818, fos 198–201).

[54] For a possible sister 'Azeliz', for whom the archbp purchased land near Canterbury, see 52 below.

[55] *EA* 175.

[56] Malmesbury, *GR* i 718.

hosts with too long or exacting a stay.[57] He first appears at Durham that September, to attend the translation of St Cuthbert to the new cathedral; it was a remarkable gathering, including another future archbishop, William of Corbeil, as well as three other abbots and Alexander, shortly to succeed his brother as king of the Scots.[58] In 1106 Ralph was at least for a while back in Normandy, where he visited Anselm at Bec during his protracted illness in mid-summer.[59] Since Orderic says that he was only abbot for sixteen years he is unlikely to have exercised continuing authority at Sées, although all the sources continue to refer to him as abbot until 1108 and his successor may not have been elected until 1110.[60]

The new archbishop's first act was to remove the custodians of the estates of the archbishopric and replace them with his own men; to wider approval he arranged his own replacement at Rochester by abbot Ernulf of Peterborough, the former prior of Christ Church, whom he invested with the bishopric in the chapter-house of Canterbury on 28 September 1114. On 10 October he took him to Rochester and installed him in his see. Emissaries set off for Rome late in the year to seek papal confirmation of Ralph's translation and a pallium. According to the letters of support for his election which they carried the new archbishop was too infirm to make the journey himself, the first sign of the chronic ill-health which was to dog his later years. The ambassadors received at first an icy reception, since pope Paschal was already indignant at the reluctance of the English church to refer serious matters to his judgement and to render Peter's Pence; an episcopal translation without the previous consent of Rome was conceived as a particular affront. Only the intercession of abbot Anselm of St Saba, nephew to the late archbishop, at length secured pope Paschal's agreement, conveyed in letters of the most grudging assent of 30 March 1115. Abbot Anselm was charged with raising all these matters with the king, as well as with the pallium for Ralph. On 27 June the legate was received in procession at Canterbury by the archbishop, eight of his bishops and the communities of Christ Church and St Augustine. The legate laid the pallium in its silver casket on the high altar of the cathedral, the archbishop swore his oath of fidelity to the pope and assumed the pallium. After enthronement on the seat of St Augustine he proceeded immediately to consecrate Theulf as bishop of Worcester. Very shortly afterwards

[57] Hollister, *Henry I* 154–63.
[58] Simeon, i 256–61
[59] Eadmer, *Vita* 136.
[60] *Gallia Christiana* xi (1759) 720 cites unspecified charter evidence for the election of abbot Hugh in 1110; Dr Clark, in her unpublished study cited in the preface, found no evidence of Ralph's presence at Sées after 1104 in the abbey archives.

he appointed John, his sister's son and one of the recent embassy to Rome, as his archdeacon.[61]

The legate also bore a less welcome gift, a detailed requisitory of the pope's grievances against the English church, which he delivered to the king at his court at Westminster in September 1115; Canterbury had long resisted any legation except for their own archbishop. Yet more pressingly for Ralph, the archbishop-elect of York, Thurstan, was refusing to make a profession to Canterbury. On the advice of the legate Cono, who was then threatening the entire Norman episcopate with suspension for failing to attend his councils, he was also considering a direct appeal for consecration by the pope, while Ralph refused in terms to consecrate him unless he professed, even if confronted by a papal command.[62] It was agreed to send the blind but infinitely experienced ambassador bishop William of Exeter to Rome to seek a resolution to these difficulties. Another rose almost at once, over the place of consecration of Bernard, the queen's chancellor, as bishop of St Davids. Although it is far from clear that any claim to independence was involved Ralph categorically refused to meet the demand of Robert, count of Meulan and the king's most trusted adviser, that he be blessed in the royal court or anywhere but Canterbury. It was eventually settled that Bernard should make his profession and receive his blessing at Westminster, the favourite residence of the queen he had served for many years.

Late in the year Alexander king of the Scots wrote to seek the archbishop's advice on finding a new bishop of St Andrews; in the context of the time the king's proposal that a new bishop should be consecrated at Canterbury rather than by the archbishop of York must have seemed extremely timely, though nothing seems to have come of the proposal immediately. In March 1116 the archbishop was among those who swore allegiance to William the young king at Salisbury, an occasion which also saw the king compel Thurstan of York to renounce his see rather than profess to Canterbury, in spite of letters of powerful support secured on Thurstan's behalf from pope Paschal. Shortly afterwards Thurstan crossed to Normandy to join the king, where he was allowed to resume his status as elect and continued to press his case. In August abbot Anselm returned to Normandy with a new legatine commission for England, a clear indication of the failure of the mission of the bishop of

---

[61] Gullick and Pfaff, 'Pontifical' 286, 293, notice the special form for the reception of a pallium entered in the Canterbury pontifical at about this time. Eadmer's accounts of the delivery of Anselm's pallium in 1095 and Ralph's in 1115 are remarkably close, but the references to the oath and enthronement in the rubric are closer to 1115: Eadmer, *Historia* 72–3, 229–37.

[62] For what follows the chief authorities are Eadmer and Hugh the Chanter. The notes to the intinerary below supply more detailed references. See too *Councils and synods* i(2) 709–25.

Exeter. A council of English magnates in the presence of the queen therefore urged Ralph himself to undertake a journey to Rome to present his case. In September the archbishop arrived in Rouen to confer with the king, and soon afterwards set out for Rome with a substantial company. The journey was a desperate one.

At La Ferté Ralph fell ill with an ulcer of the face, and for a month his life was despaired of. Further delayed by bad weather, the archbishop and his companions spent Christmas at Lyon. After crossing the Alps the bishop of Norwich was struck down by yet graver sickness at Piacenza and had to return to Normandy. The rest eventually reached Rome in March only to find that it was under assault from the emperor Henry V, and that the pope had fled to Benevento. The archbishop nevertheless celebrated mass in St Peter's on 12 March, but could communicate with the pope only through messengers, and they secured no more than empty courtesy. On the other hand, Thurstan's representatives, who arrived with the pope a few days later, received unequivocal support. Apparently with pope Paschal's consent Ralph spent eight days with the emperor during a period of anxious shuttling between Rome and Sutri, but it became increasingly clear that the rumours of the pope's imminent return were baseless. By the end of the year Ralph was back at Rouen after much suffering and no gain.

On hearing of the death of Paschal in January 1118 Thurstan left York and made his way secretly to the king in Normandy, armed with papal letters commanding Ralph to consecrate him without a profession, and hoping for equally determined advocacy from Paschal's successor. Ralph remained with the king, partly no doubt to strengthen the king's resolve to require a profession, partly because the legate Anselm still awaited the king's leave to cross to England to exercise his legation, partly perhaps in the hope that a new pope would be more sympathetic. In June he was present at the deathbed of the king's most trusted counsellor, Robert of Meulan (42), and in September he attended an important royal council at Rouen where the legate Cono denounced the imperial anti-pope and the king took counsel on the war raging along the Norman frontier. The new pope, Gelasius II, proved as staunch a friend to Thurstan as his predecessor had been and wrote to Ralph in uncompromising terms, commanding him to consecrate Thurstan without a profession, but Gelasius died suddenly at Cluny in January 1119. His successor, Calixtus II, proved no less insistent on Thurstan's rights; the state of war with France and Anjou and the uncertainty over the pope's movements yet again frustrated Ralph's attempts to go to plead his case in person; a messenger did succeed in delivering a letter of impassioned complaint but received predictably short shrift from Calixtus.[63] In July (probably in 1119, rather than 1118), as the archbishop was taking off his vestments after the mass for the translation of St Benedict, he suffered a severe stroke. After a few days he made a partial recovery but his speech was permanently impaired and his movement restricted; for some time at least he could only travel in a litter.

In May pope Calixtus had announced his intention of hearing the dispute between Canterbury and York at a council to be held at Reims in October, to which Ralph and Thurstan were both summoned. A large delegation of English bishops set out, as did Thurstan, but Ralph was too ill, and Canterbury's case was chiefly represented by his half-brother Seffrid, shortly to become abbot of Glastonbury, and his nephew, John the archdeacon. In spite of their protests the pope consecrated Thurstan on 19 October, the Sunday before the council, leaving the issue of the profession to be disputed elsewhere. The king, enraged by what he chose to represent as a breach of faith, forbade Thurstan to enter England and disseised him of his estates, swearing that he should never enter England so long as the king lived. On 4 January 1120 Ralph was received with ceremony at Canterbury after an absence of three and a half years; on 4 April he was well enough to conse-crate David bishop of Bangor at Westminster. At this point king Alexander renewed his application for a new bishop of St Andrews, this time specifying Eadmer of Canterbury as his candidate. As a thorn in the flesh of Thurstan, if not in the event as chief of the Scottish bishops, this was a choice which the archbishop could scarcely oppose, and Eadmer was sent off on his ill-starred adventure with the archbishop's blessing and king Henry's leave. Meanwhile, however, the pope's support for Thurstan was unwavering, and faced by a threat of interdict Henry submitted; at Christmas 1120 Ralph and the other bishops met the king at London and accepted defeat, if only for the moment. Thurstan returned to England and his church a few weeks later.

On 25 November the king's only legitimate son had drowned in the White Ship, two years after his mother's death, and a second marriage was settled with remarkable haste at the London court. The new queen was Adelisa of Louvain, whom Henry married at Windsor on 29 January 1121. Though Ralph had consecrated bishop Richard of Hereford at Lambeth on 16 January he was too unwell to perform the wedding, but insisted on taking part in the coronation the following day. His celebrated ease of manner had broken down entirely under the pressure of illness and failure, and he broke

---

[63] *Historians York* ii 228–51.

off the ceremony on seeing the king wearing the crown which it was the archbishop's cherished right to place upon his head. With unexpected restraint
the king agreed to untie the thong below his chin and Ralph was ultimately
persuaded to replace the crown and allow the mass to proceed. After the wedding he accompanied the king the short way to Abingdon, where he consecrated the royal clerk Robert as bishop of Chester on 13 March. He was back
in Canterbury in the summer to entertain yet another papal legate, Cardinal
Peter Pierleone, the later anti-pope Anacletus II, at Canterbury and seized
the opportunity to display the largely forged privileges of his see; in return
Peter is said to have offered large if vague promises of support at the curia.
Ralph was again ill at Michaelmas, and so could not attend the council where
the king pressed Thurstan once more to agree to make a profession, though
without success. His last recorded act was to consecrate Gregory of Dublin
at Lambeth on 2 October. By now he was failing fast; he does not certainly
attest any later royal charters, and Eadmer has nothing to report of him from
then until his death at Canterbury on 20 October 1122. He was buried,
according to Eadmer 'in medio aulae maioris ecclesiae', three days later.[64]

The theme of the primacy dispute, in which Ralph suffered a devastating
reverse, so dominates the surviving accounts of his pontificate that it is easy
to ignore a considerable body of testimony to his high qualities of mind and
character. In later years Gervase of Canterbury praised him for his wisdom
and eloquence, though he saw his breach with Calixtus as the origin of
Thurstan's triumph and the beginning of St Augustine's claim to independence. William of Malmesbury allowed that he was well-born, affable (even to
a fault, at least until his health broke down), learned and eloquent, though he
added that his reputation declined as his rank rose. Even a York supporter
could call him worthy of his high office, as it were a lesser pope, barely second to a king to whom he was right arm, heart and eye.[65] For all his pre-
occupations he was generous to the monks of Canterbury as well as
Rochester and a friend to the Cluniac monks of Lewes, the canons of St

---

[64] He was clearly still suffering severe after-effects from his stroke in 1121–2: Scholz, *Traditio* xxii
(1966) 146. The date of his death is variously given as Friday 20 Oct.—Eadmer, *Historia* 302,
ASC i 250, Simeon ii 267, Orderic vi 318, *GP* 132, *Cust. Roff.* 37, Fleming, 'Lists' 143, *Anglia
sacra* i 7, 56, or 19 Oct.—some mss of John of Worcs. iii 152, Paris, BN lat. 13905 fo. 77, *UGQ*
78. The most natural reading of Eadmer is that Ralph was buried in the nave, perhaps close to
Anselm and Lanfranc. However, according to Gervase, *Historia* i 10, at least after the completion of the new choir (consecrated in 1130) he lay before the altar of St Benedict in the north
transept.

[65] Gervase i 10–11; Malmesbury, *GP* 126–7, 132 and n; *Historians York* ii. 262; Simeon i 257: 'of
great courtesy and piety, and magnificently instructed in the holy scriptures'; *Life of Christina*
84: 'supremely learned in both sacred and divine law, and loved by all for his graceful piety'.

Osyth, the nuns of Malling and the resolute Christina of Markyate. At Abingdon, a house for which he also seems to have had some affection, he intervened to make peace when the monks fell out with their abbot. In Wales, Ireland and Scotland he sought to maintain the influence of Canterbury as vigorously as any of his predecessors.

Only one work of his certainly survives apart from his letters to Anselm and to the pope, a sermon on the feast of the Assumption of the Virgin. Originally delivered to the monks of Sées in French it was translated into Latin at the request of abbots William of Fécamp and Arnulf of Troarn; travelling under false colours as the work of Anselm it survives in some fifty manuscripts. There was even an Anglo-Saxon translation from the Latin text found in a single manuscript, probably from Canterbury or Rochester.[66]

The long vacancy after Anselm's death may explain the modest overlap between the known familiars of Ralph and those of his predecessor. Eadmer attests the mildly dubious **54**, with Joseph, another of Anselm's household, and plainly remained close to the new archbishop. He travelled to Rome with him in 1117, and stayed by his side in Normandy until the beginning of 1119. A further measure of continuity was provided by Ernulf's return from Peterborough to Rochester, and by the continuing importance of the Cauvel family in Canterbury (**36**). Otherwise the impression given by Ralph's eight charters with witness lists is of a sharp break. The only regularly recurrent witness is his nephew, John the archdeacon of Canterbury. While his prominence is not surprising, it is in marked contrast to the apparent distance between Anselm and his predecessor, archdeacon William.[67] John's close association with his archbishop is probably the grounds for the wholly exceptional description of him in **48** as his chancellor, an office one may well suppose invented by the Lewes scribe for the purpose of his document, rather than a defined function. The appearance of Roland 'medicus' in two acts is no cause for surprise either, given Ralph's health, and he may have been in regular attendance.[68] The appearances of Ansfrid the steward, both as a witness and as the addressee of acts concerning Canterbury estates, are rather more remarkable, for he had been Gundulf's steward at Rochester, does not appear in Canterbury documents under Anselm, and retained much closer and more enduring links with Rochester. He came to hold some Christ

---

[66] For the literature on the sermon, printed among works of Anselm as *PL* clviii 644–9, see N.R. Ker, *Catalogue of manuscripts containing Anglo-Saxon* (Oxford 1957) no. 209 art. 44.

[67] *EA* 230, 360, 374, 380. *EA* 360 suggests that a dispute between the archbp and his archdn had been sufficiently serious to require a formal agreement in writing after its resolution. John attests 35, 39, 52–3, 55.

[68] 39, 49.

Church land at Stisted, on a contentious tenure, and was later briefly to be sheriff of Kent. Hugh the monk of Rochester who attests **53** is almost certainly Hugh of Trottiscliffe, the future abbot of St Augustine's, for he was already a leading figure in the Rochester community, and he was one of those sent by Ralph to reclaim a Norfolk estate for Christ Church. One can be fairly sure that Ralph's translation strengthened the ties between Canterbury and Rochester yet further.[69] Although they only appear occasionally, there is another group of clerks who have a larger interest. Alan the clerk appears as a witness three times, Giffard and Lupellus the chaplains only once, and on that basis could scarcely be claimed as members of his household. However, all three appear regularly under archbishop William, Lupellus explicitly as one of his clerks, and so suggest for the first time the existence of a body of secular clergy who served successive archbishops.[70] Outside the charters one further member of Ralph's household can be identified, Hugh 'de Digniaco', a layman formerly attached to the community at Tewkesbury, who long

---

[69] Ansfrid attests 35, 49, 52–3 under Ralph, and 64, 74–5, 80–81 under William, and is also addressed in 35, 62. He was identified with Ansfrid the sheriff, lord of of Allington and holder of Stisted as a life tenure from Canterbury, by Agnes E. Conway, 'The owners of Allington castle' in *Arch. Cant.* xxix (1911) 9–10, a valuable study only partially compromised by the indiscriminate use of forged and genuine documents from Rochester. After his death and apparently 1136–9 his son John seized Stisted (Ex); see below 16 and note. Later Rochester held land in Stisted of the gift of Ansfrid—*Reg. Roff.* 118. Ansfrid first appears as sheriff in *Reg. regum* ii no. 1728 of 1131 × 1133 (if genuine, as no. 1867 almost certainly is not), and for the last time in 1136 (*Reg. regum* iii no. 142; Green, *Sheriffs* 51); *Pipe Roll* 66–7; for his daughter Adelicia see *EEA* viii no. 96. For his Rochester connections see *Text. Roff.* fos 188 no. 132 (the only probable document defining his stewardship as that of the bishop of Rochester), 198r-v no. 181 of 1107 × 8, 193v no. 170 of 1108–14, 197 no.178, 196v-7 no. 177 with William of St Albans, his knight and 198v–9v no.183 (the last three of 1115 × 1124); *EEA* Rochester no. 4 (the witness-list may be genuine, and to be dated *c.* 1108, though the act as we have it is a later forgery), 118–20; *Cust. Roff.* 37. He is to be distinguished from Ansfrid the clerk, with whom he attests *Text. Roff.* nos 132, 181, but see below p. lxxxi note. For Hugh see Saltman, *Theobald* 537, *Reg. Roff.* 119.

[70] It is uncertain whether a string of attestations by Alan the clerk (or chaplain) in 35–6, 39, 62, 80–1, Saltman, *Theobald* nos 55, 86, 147, 161, 310 all refer to the same man, and whether he is to be identified with Alan 'de Welles', another frequent witness under Theobald; as Alan 'de Wilna' is mentioned in *Letters of John of Salisbury* i no. 107 of 1159–61 the second possibility may seem unlikely. Giffard attests 52, 62, 80; it is tempting to identify him with the royal chaplain who accompanied archbp William to Rome for his pallium in 1123 (*ASC* i 252), with the chaplain who appears with a number of others close to the king as a witness to a deed of the chapter of St Pauls before 25 Nov. 1120 in *EEA* xv no. 17, and with the recipient of Leclercq, 'Écrits spirituels' 99–100 ep. x—a letter full of affection even though they now rarely met. A Giffard the chaplain of Lympne attests the Sandwich plea of 1127 (below p. 107) but the name is found elsewhere in the area; Giffard attests of William of Pagham attests nos 80–1 below. Lupellus attests 36, 80–1. As a former chaplain of archbp William he went to the papal court in 1139 to plead Stephen's case against the empress (John of Salisbury, *Historia pontificalis* ed. Chibnall 83).

served him, and entered the service of Seffrid his half-brother after his death.[71]

After archbishop Ralph's death the king moved with most unusual speed to replace him. Within four months he summoned a council to Gloucester, where the disputes of 1114 were played out again, though with greater intensity and to an unexpected conclusion. Even before the council the bishops, led by Roger of Salisbury and Robert of Lincoln (until his sudden death on 10 January 1123), were demanding a secular clerk; their position was the stronger since Ernulf of Rochester was then the only monk-bishop in office, and he was too ill to attend. Again the prior and monks of Canterbury demanded a monk. For two days they held out, but they were eventually compelled to accept a short-list of four candidates, from whom about 4 February they chose William of Corbeil, first prior of the house of regular canons of St Osyth.[72]

William's earlier career is much more difficult to reconstruct than that of his predecessors.[73] His name suggests that he came in some sense from Corbeil, on the right bank of the Seine, long a threat to the kings of France, which passed to the royal domain under Louis VI around 1112; the earlier counts had close connections with the counts of Blois/Chartres, and so indirectly with the dukes of Normandy.[74] Nothing is known of his parentage, though he had at least two brothers, Helgot and Rainulf.[75] His first clearly recorded occurrence is at the translation of St Cuthbert in 1104, in the company of the future archbishop Ralph, where he is described as a clerk of Ranulf Flambard. Since he was apparently already a man of some standing in 1104, he is unlikely to have been born much after 1080. He seems to have remained in Flambard's service for some time, if we may believe a charter of bishop Ranulf. This is of very dubious authenticity but its most recent editor

[71] *Letters of Osbert of Clare* ed. E.W. Williamson (Oxford 1929) 71, 203. Williamson suggests he came from Digny, some forty miles from Sées; Tewkesbury had been refounded by Robert fitz Hamo, brother of Haimo the sheriff of Kent who had close connections with Canterbury (above p. xxxvii, below, note to 74).

[72] The names of the other candidates are not recorded, but another canon and prior, Robert de Béthune of Lanthony, later bp of Hereford, may have been one of them. So at least William of Wycombe claimed in his *Life—Anglia sacra* ii 305—if this is not a reference to the Rouen election of 1130.

[73] Denis Bethell's 'The archiepiscopate of William of Corbeil 1123–36' is the only full-length study of his career. Elements in it were published in a series of important articles, listed in the bibliography, but much of value has never been published. See too D. Nicholl, *Thurstan, archbishop of York (1114–1140)* (York 1964); *Councils and synods* i(2) 725–61.

[74] Suger, *Vie de Louis VI le gros* ed. H. Waquet (Paris 1964) 88–90, 150–2.

[75] One of these, or possibly a third, became a canon of Aldgate: below nos 63, 65, 80–1 and n.; Sandwich plea of 1127 (below p. 107).

believes the witness list to be drawn from a respectable source after *c.* 1112; it is subscribed by William 'clerico meo de Curbuil'.[76] In 1123 Thurstan of York and prior Adelold of Nostell were able to give him a good character, perhaps on the basis of their acquaintance with him in the north. His early life is reported in a confused passage in the *Miracles of St Mary of Laon*, written, with much literary artifice, by Hermann of Tournai around 1142. This describes a fund-raising expedition of some canons of the cathedral to England, undertaken apparently between Lent and September 1113. On their travels they came to Canterbury, where they were well entertained by the monks of St Augustine and William the archbishop. William was well-known to them from his earlier stay in the house of the bishop of Laon. He had gone there to study under Anselm of Laon, as many other protégés of English clerics were to do. While staying in the bishop's house he had taught the sons of Radulf, sometime chancellor of the king of England. It has long been supposed that the Radulf involved may well be Ranulf Flambard, who was sufficiently important under Rufus to suggest to others outside the realm that he had been chancellor, who certainly had sons he sought to advance in the church, and had William in his service by 1104. If so, it is tempting to suppose that William's encounter with Flambard's sons was the opening which led to his joining the bishop's service.[77] However, Flambard's apparently oldest son is said to have been no more than twelve in 1102, and another Ranulf, who also had at least one child, was royal chancellor between 1107 and his death in January 1123.[78] There is firmer reason to believe that William had come into close and familiar contact with Anselm at some point, and he was known to Alexander, a figure very close to Anselm. In the second recension of his *De miraculis* Alexander reports the story of William's devotion to the

[76] Above p. xli and n.; H. S. Offler, 'The early archdeacons in the diocese of Durham', *Trans. of the Architectural and Archaeological Society of Durham and Northumberland* xi (1962) 189–207, esp. 197–8 nn and 207n, and *Durham episcopal charters* no. 10. Offler's lower date is based on the assumption that once William had a position in Kent he could not still be described as a clerk of Flambard; if true that would suggest a date for the list before the summer of 1113, since the *Miracula S. Mariae* place him at Canterbury by then. His upper date is based on the assumption that the witness list was always attached to a Finchale text; if it was not, then the earliest date possible is that of Michael's archdeaconry, which probably began after 1107—*Fasti* ii 37.

[77] *PL* clvi 961–1018, on which see now G. Niemeyer, 'Die *Miracula S. Mariae Laudunensis* des Abtes Hermann von Tournai', *Deutsches Archiv* xxvii (1971), 135–74, esp. 141, 186–7. T.A. Archer first proposed Flambard in his 'The children of Ranulf Flambard' *EHR* ii (1887) 103–12, though with prudent reserve; see Southern, 'Ranulf Flambard', *Medieval humanism and other studies* (Oxford 1970) 183–205, 184–8, a much revised version of his paper in *TRHS* 4s xvi (1933), for Flambard's special status, 201–2 for his family. Southern does not discuss the Laon text.

[78] Bethell, 'William' 146–7n, 'Richard' 306; Orderic v 322 and n.; Green, *Government* 160 accepts the identification with the chancellor in a valuable summary of English contacts with Laon.

cult of the archangels as he had heard it from his own lips.[79] Whatever one makes of the *Miracula* of Laon, William was certainly also established in Kent in the circle of archbishop Ralph by 1116, for as a canon 'Dorovernensis' that year he accompanied him on his ill-starred expedition to Italy. This probably indicates St Martin of Dover, a wealthy house in which both the archbishop and Flambard had an interest, rather than St Gregory of Canterbury; this is more consistent with Hugh the Chanter's usage, and Alexander's anecdote is set in a house at Dover where William fell gravely ill while already contemplating conversion to the religious life.[80] When he was forced on the monks of Christ Church in 1123 they could at least say that he was familiar to them as a man of modest life and sound learning.[81] Very soon after his return from the Italian expedition, if not earlier, he had also secured the patronage of bishop Richard of London. According to the lost life of St Osyth by William de Vere, the bishop called to him 'clericum insignem Gul. de Curbuil, totius literature communis peritum, quem ob probitatem morum et literature et secularis providentiae ad se vocaverat'. This suggests that he had not yet fulfilled his desire for the religious life, attested by Alexander, though it was not long before he took the habit at the house of canons of Aldgate, a house much in favour with the queen, other members of the court, and bishop Richard. Within a year or two he was appointed first prior of the bishop's new foundation of canons at St Osyth in Essex, from which he was elected to Canterbury.[82] William's career before his election, however imperfectly it can be recovered, shows him with strong connections both with bishops active in royal service and with Canterbury. If Hugh the Chanter may be believed, however, he had no substantial previous acquaintance with the king, who had to ask archbishop Thurstan what sort of man he might be; if true, this underlines yet further the exceptional character of an election where king Henry is represented in the numerous sources as doing little more than hold the ring among competing interests.[83]

---

[79] Simeon ii 269; *Memorials Anselm* 26, 266–8, an addition made sufficiently long after the second recension was otherwise complete to raise the possibility that it is by another hand. Stylistically there is nothing to suggest this, and the editors accepted it.

[80] Bethell, 'William' 147–54; Hugh the Chanter 82 n 2. Nevertheless, the canons of Laon had found him at Canterbury earlier, and in a position to offer effective hospitality.

[81] Simeon ii 269.

[82] Bethell, 'William' 154, 'Richard' 306; 'St Osyth' 120; Leland, *Itinerary* v 169 (where the text may need emendation); *Cart. Aldgate* 228. Though the cartulary's testimony is late, it seems inherently likely that William would have spent at least a short while in the habit somewhere before his promotion, and William was a benefactor of the house as archbp—below nos 80–1. For the date of the foundation of St Osyth see below, no. 56 and note, p. 108.

[83] Hugh the Chanter 184.

The scars of Thurstan's dispute with archbishop Ralph were at once re-opened by Thurstan's offer to consecrate the new archbishop, and its brisk rejection. Instead William was consecrated at Canterbury on either 18 or 25 February by Richard of London, William of Winchester and other suffragans.[84] On 13 March he set off for Rome for his pallium, accompanied by a large delegation from England; Thurstan of York travelled separately. At the *curia* William received a very hostile reception, and Hugh the Chanter claims he would have been compelled to resign Canterbury for a lesser see were it not for the intercession of Thurstan and the emperor Henry V, with whom the pope had recently come to agreement over investitures.[85] Further dispute over the primacy was then adjourned until the arrival of a legate in England to hear the issue. By July the archbishop was back at Canterbury with his pallium to consecrate Alexander of Lincoln and Godfrey of Bath. The promised legate, John of Crema, arrived in Normandy around midsummer 1124, where William had arrived too, possibly for a series of appointments to English churches from which the king had summoned delegations for the purpose. In Lent 1125 the legate arrived in England, and celebrated a legatine council at Westminster on 8 September—the first of its kind since the two councils of 1070. Accompanied by both archbishops the legate then returned to Normandy, where an agreement was reached that Thurstan would make a profession in return for the cession of three bishoprics, if the pope would agree. In Rome, however, the agreement was rejected, largely because William denied some of its terms; the effect of this was to leave York free of any obedience to William as primate, but a temporary and papal alternative was offered with the appointment of William as legate; this grant was renewed later by Innocent II, so that for most of the period 1126–36 William could style himself legate and, in principle at least, intervene throughout the English church. By 26 June he was back in England. William celebrated two councils which were clearly legatine, in 1127 and 1129. The acts of the council of 1127 survive, but those of 1129, although it was well-attended and lasted five days, do not. It commended the feast of the Immaculate

---

[84] John of Worcs. iii 152 claims he was consecrated by the bp of Winchester, Gervase of Canterbury ii 380 by Richard of London; John's testimony is the earlier, and Gervase may have supplied Richard's name on the basis of the precedence of his see (*Councils and synods* i(2) 612–3 and refs). Diceto i 244, otherwise following John, adds that Richard then suffered from paralysis, perhaps as an explanation of the unexpected event. Richard of London had suffered a stroke around 1118 (Bethell. 'St Osyth' 120), though he was involved with the discussions before William's consecration—Hugh the Chanter 184–6.

[85] Bethell, 'William' 155–6, K. Leyser, 'England and the empire in the early twelfth century' repr. from *TRHS* 5s x (1960) 61–83, esp. 79–83 in his *Medieval Germany and its neighbours 900–1250* (London 1982) 191–214.

Conception of the Virgin, but was dismissed contemptuously by the Peterborough chronicler: 'it turned out to be all about archdeacons' wives and priests' wives', though the king frustrated even that object, according to Henry of Huntingdon, in return for large payments from the married clergy.[86] On 4 May 1130 William dedicated the splendid new chancel of Christ Church, which had been begun under prior Ernulf and largely completed by prior Conrad;[87] three days later he consecrated the new church at Rochester.

In April 1132 he was at London, where he was joined by the archbishops of Rouen and York to hear one more stage in the claim of Urban of Llandaff against St Davids. Here he received formal confirmation of the grant of the church of Dover, which the king had promised at the consecration of the cathedral two years earlier; **63** below shows that other business was done there. The Llandaff claim was clearly not settled, for a second council early the next year met at London to consider it further, and to hear a dispute between the archbishop and Alexander of Lincoln, taken further at a second gathering at Winchester; both parties crossed to Normandy in 1134 to continue their contest, but its origins and outcome are alike unknown.[88] William's last substantial recorded action followed the death of king Henry on 1 December 1135 and Stephen's rush to England to seek the crown. With his fellow magnates the archbishop had sworn to accept Matilda in 1127, but he was persuaded to agree to consecrate Stephen on 22 December in return for an undertaking from Stephen to restore and maintain the liberties of the Church, an undertaking guaranteed by bishop Henry of Winchester. He accompanied the new king to Reading for the burial of king Henry, and attended the Oxford gathering at which Stephen fulfilled his promises before the coronation by the grant of his celebrated charter of liberties for the Church.[89] Six months later William died on 21 November, and was buried in the north transept at Canterbury beside archbishop Ralph. The irony of lay-

---

[86] *Councils and synods* i(2) 750–4; Huntingdon 482–4.

[87] Woodman, *Architectural history* 45–76; Gervase i 12–16; Malmesbury, *GP* 138; Eadmer, *Historia* 75; the obit of prior Conrad in Lambeth Palace ms 20 (also found in BL ms Arundel 68 fo. 16v)—pd in J. Wickham Legg and W.H. St John Hope, *Inventories of Christ Church, Canterbury* (Westminster 1902) 44—is detailed and instructive on its decoration.

[88] Huntingdon 488–90, the sole authority for the quarrel.

[89] Malmesbury, *HN* 6, 28, 32; *Gesta Stephani* 4–12; John of Worcs. iii 176–82, 214; Huntingdon 700; John of Hexham in Simeon ii 288; *Reg. regum* iii no. 271. For recent accounts of these familiar events see E. King (ed.), *The anarchy of Stephen's reign* (Oxford 1994) 6–11, Hollister, *Henry I* 474–82.

ing their first canon-archbishop before the tomb of St Benedict may not have escaped the monks.[90]

Contemporaries remembered William's qualities and achievements in very different ways. William of Malmesbury thought him pious, adequately sociable, and neither passive nor rash, though a grave disappointment to the secular bishops who hoped for a leader more sympathetic to the lordly pleasures of hunting, hospitality, fine clothing and a rowdy retinue. To some extent this acid view of the episcopate may be reflected in the criticism of the canon Henry of Huntingdon, who dismissed him as without a single praiseworthy quality, and believed his early death was a just punishment for his consecration of Stephen in defiance of his oath. Similarly, the author of the *Gesta Stephani* thought he had a fine presence, but was too mean to spend the treasure he accumulated on the poor. Generous hospitality to potential benefactors and personal austerity tended to represent opposing virtues in early-twelfth-century England. More surprisingly, Gervase of Canterbury reports his memory as that of a man of eminent piety and wisdom. If Hugh the Chanter was outraged by his resolute pursuit of the primacy, he yet has Thurstan of York describing him as a 'good clerk and a simple and devout man'.[91]

His achievements as archbishop were indeed not negligible. He clearly enjoyed the confidence of his king, for Henry was generous to him. In 1127 he gave him the castle and constableship of Rochester, where he built the splendid keep; in a damaged account of the knight-service of Canterbury William was remembered as having secured valuable concessions which were preserved until the days of Becket; more generally, the series of writs on behalf of the archbishop and monks between 1123 and 1135 is notably longer than that for Anselm and Ralph.[92] He may have conducted at least one visitation of another diocese (73), something which Ralph once proposed,

[90] The two versions of John of Worcs. iii 222 differ; one having him die at an unspecified manor away from Canterbury, the other in the city on 20 Nov. Gervase, i 96, ii 383 has him falling ill at Mortlake, and being carried to Canterbury to die. For 21 Nov. see Fleming, 'Lists' 145, *UGQ* 5, Gervase i 99, 'Winchcombe annals' 128; *Fasti* ii 4 and n. 3. Gervase i 10 describes his tomb; compare above p. xlv n.

[91] Malmesbury, *GP* 146–7 and note; Huntingdon, *Hist.* 608, 700 (where he is much warmer to the monks Lanfranc, Anselm, Ralph and Theobald); *Gesta Stephani* 10; Gervase ii 380; Hugh the Chanter, *Historia* 190; compare Southern, *St Anselm* (1963) 140–1 on Sampson of Worcester, and M.L. Colker 'The life of Guy of Merton', *Mediaeval Studies* xxxi (1969) 258 c. 10 on an austere prior of Taunton expelled for lack of hospitality.

[92] *Reg. regum* ii nos 1475, 1606; John of Worcs. iii 166–7; Colvin, 'List' 23. For less specific writs, patronage as defence against harm described by Southern in his 'Henry I' (*Medieval humanism* 222–5), and unaffected in this aspect by the important discussion in Green, *Government* 171–93, see *Reg. regum* ii nos 1388, 1417, 1511, 1522 (of which 1615 is a duplicate), 1703.

though we know only of his failure to do so; he appears as the custodian of the rights of the vacant diocese of Hereford (77–8); he confirmed rights of churches in dioceses with which he had no other known connection on a larger scale than any of his predecessors.[93] If his grants to Canterbury were modest, and his known generosity to Aldgate and St Osyth less ample than one might have expected, he attempted the conversion of three religious foundations.

The history of the nunnery of St Sexburga at Minster in Sheppey is remarkably obscure. There is a persistent tradition that the house had fallen on hard times, and that William effectively refounded it around 1130, though no early source for this is recorded. The surviving charters for the house seem to confirm the fact, if not the date, for several of the core endowments are attributed to William's purchase. On the evidence of documents now lost archbishop Courtenay claimed in 1395 that the house was originally founded for canonesses of the order of St Augustine, which would certainly be consistent with William's interests, though it seems to have been reckoned Benedictine from an early date. A number of the endowments listed in William's charters were subsequently lost, but the house survived at a level of modest prosperity to the dissolution.[94] He was also responsible for a major change to Lanfranc's foundation at St Gregory's. At some point he sought out canons of Merton to establish a community of regular canons to replace the earlier clerks there. The recent excavations have shown how profound a transformation this represented, with the complex of chapels of the first community replaced by a substantial conventual church with a large cloister surrounded by all the usual offices. William's sole surviving act on their behalf (68) does not inspire complete confidence, but the grant of a church from a fee held from the archbishop to increase the endowment offers something of a parallel to the grant of Gillingham church to Minster-in Sheppey. The Merton foundation history places the refoundation of St Gregory's after

---

[93] Brett, *English church* 67, 82–97, a discussion based on an uncritical approach to the charter evidence; below p. lvii.

[94] Leland, *Collectanea* i 89 attributes the restoration of Minster-in-Sheppey to William, without offering a date. Below nos 84–5, and the notes to 85; Thompson, *Women religious* 201–2, 226. E. Hasted, *The history and topographical survey of the county of Kent* (2 ed. Canterbury 1797–1801, repr. 1972) offers some unexplained dates in the history of St Sexburga. At iv 239 he attributes the gift of Gillingham to 22 Henry I, and at vi 218 he attributes a refoundation to archbp William in 1130; I have not been able to trace any early authority for either, though the 1130 date has often been repeated since.

the founding of Cirencester, conventionally dated 1131, and before the establishment of St Lô.[95]

William's most spectacular attempt to transform an earlier community was altogether more contentious. At the dedication of Christ Church in May 1130 king Henry honoured the event with the gift of the rich and ancient minster church at Dover. The charter recording the grant is said to have been decided at Northampton, but confirmed during the council held at Westminster in April 1132. It is clear from the text that the grant was intended to allow the archbishop to create a new community of regular canons, though the gift is made to both the archbishop and to Christ Church, and it was a surprising use for a benefaction made at the consecration of the cathedral. It is probably an indication of the archbishop's sense of anxiety that he sent messengers to Innocent II very soon to secure a bull confirming both the grant and the purpose. William pressed on with the new church with great energy, for by 1136 it was ready for the arrival of the canons he had chosen from Merton. Though the archbishop was already failing, and was too ill to leave his manor at Mortlake, he sent the bishops of St Davids and Rochester, prior Elmer of Christ Church and archdeacon Helewise to accompany the canons with their carts and possessions to their new church. As they prepared for their formal introduction, however, Jeremiah the sub-prior of Christ Church demanded that they abandon the ceremony as an assault on the rights of Christ Church, to which the king had given the house. When the bishops replied that they were acting on the instructions of the archbishop and with the consent of the prior, Jeremiah appealed against them and the prior to Rome. The bishops and canons then withdrew, intending to consult the archbishop. He was by now dying, and was carried to Canterbury; his grief at the frustration of his purpose is said to have hastened his end. Immediately afterwards the monks sent twelve of their number to establish a monastic community at Dover, which eventually remained a priory of Christ Church. The dispute was an unedifying one, casting a gloomy light on the relations between the

[95] Colker, 'Latin texts' 263, good evidence for the Merton origin of the canons, even though Leland, *Collectanea* iii 54 (citing an apparently lost life of St Mildrith, for which compare Huntingdon 691n) suggests they came from St Osyth, and cf ibid. i 89; Saltman, *Theobald* no. 59; Tatton-Brown, 'Beginnings' 41–50. Algar bp of Coutances received a letter from Innocent II congratulating him on his election, and approving his plan to convert St Lô to a community of canons regular, written on 2 March 1132 (JL 7547); it is much less clear when canons were actually sent.

archbishop and his monks, which would not otherwise have appeared particularly tense.[96]

Plainly the arrival of a regular canon at Canterbury involved a great deal of change, and unsurprisingly the priors of St Osyth's, Leeds and St Gregory's appear occasionally, with one or two other canons, among the witnesses to William's acts.[97] There is much more, however, to suggest continuity. On the death of Ernulf of Rochester William replaced him with archbishop Ralph's nephew, the archdeacon of Canterbury, and as bishop John continues to appear regularly in William's company, as does Ansfrid the steward. The three clerks of Ralph mentioned earlier continue to attest, as do Canterbury knights already familiar under Ralph, and a few monks.[98] It is possible that the Rochester link grew even stronger. Helewise the archdeacon was already in office at Rochester under Ernulf, and continued under John, the former archdeacon of Canterbury, who became bishop of Rochester in 1125. From then on an archdeacon Helewise, said by Gervase to be a regular canon, also appears regularly as archdeacon of Canterbury in William's acts, and no other archdeacon appears in either diocese until after archbishop William's death. It is easy to suppose, if impossible to prove, that he held both offices between 1125 and 1136.[99] In **61** Ralph Basset, son of the notable justice and king's servant, is described by the archbishop as 'clericus noster', but he does not appear in any witness list, and it cannot be determined to what extent, if at all, he was ever a working member of the household. Under Ralph and William there are just sufficient witness-lists to show the frequent

---

[96] *Reg. regum* ii no. 1736 and JL 7736, both printed from the Dover cartulary in *Mon.* iv 538 nos vii-viii; Gervase i 96–99, ii 383–4; there is a robust account of these events in C.R. Haines, *Dover priory* (Cambridge 1930) 60–69. Relations between prior Elmer and the archbp were apparently cordial, if Elmer's letter vii addressed to a William 'venerande pater' is indeed addressed to the archbp. If so, then letter viii is probably also to him, since they are clearly related: Leclercq, 'Écrits spirituels' 88–96.

[97] Fulk prior of St Osyth, 85, 87–8; Fulk prior of Leeds, 85, Alured the canon (later prior of St Gregory) 80–1, 87, and see Saltman, *Theobald* nos 55, 60–1, 161; Abel the canon, 87; Roger the canon 63; Simon the canon (probably also called Siward), 62, 80–1.

[98] Above pp. xlvi–vii and nn. For the knights see below p. lxxxii; a new figure in William's charters is Haimo son of Vitalis, a considerable figure in Kent, for whom see particularly Urry, *Canterbury* 51–3, 63–4, Du Boulay, *Lordship* 357, 388. Son of Vitalis, the tenant of bp Odo of Bayeux, he was a benefactor of Rochester—*Text. Roff.* fo. 185v no. 121, and cf *Reg. Roff.* 210, and also appears at the Sandwich plea of 1127 (below p. 107); his sister married William calvellus the portreeve of Canterbury. For monks, see Robert 64, Alan 80–1, Eadmer 88.

[99] Below, nos 53, 65, 80–1, 87, 96; *Text. Roff.* fos 179v (no. 94), 191v (no. 163), 194v (no. 175), 196v-7 (nos 177–8), 198v-9 (no. 183); Gervase i 97, 106; Colker, 'Latin texts' 265–6; commemorated at Canterbury as 'frater noster' on March 10 in Fleming, 'Lists' 135. He may also be concealed behind the archdn 'Henry' who appears with archbp William in the evidently untrustworthy charter of count Manasseh of Guines, noted below at pp. 92–3.

presence of a group of local families and a few clerks when the archbishops granted their charters, but not enough for us to discriminate between neighbours, visitors, tenants and intimates in any but the loosest way. Here too the brilliant circle which gathered around archbishop Theobald represents a new departure.

CONTENTS OF THE ACTA

The great majority of the acts, credible or not, are grants or confirmations of lands and churches. The interlocking interests of Canterbury and Rochester, the wide extent of the archiepiscopal lands beyond the diocese on its narrowest interpretation and the pre-existing connections of the archbishops with some churches outside Kent, make it difficult to distinguish with any precision between confirmations issued by a wealthy and well-connected diocesan and acts which are a function of his metropolitan rights. There are a few, however, which seem straightforward expressions of this larger duty— among surviving credible acts Ralph's confirmations for Lewes and St Osyth's (**48, 56**) and William's for Earls Colne, St Benet of Holme, Reading and Thorney (**70, 72, 85, 97**); among lost acts conceivably Lanfranc for St Albans, more probably Anselm for Bath, Ralph for Colchester and William for Thetford (***10, *11, *41, *95***). Whether in Kent or outside it grants of churches were recognised as complex matters in England, at least since Anselm's council of 1102 had denied the capacity of laymen to transfer them without episcopal consent. In this collection only the difficult **34** appears to confirm such a grant without qualification. All the others are grants either by the archbishop or another bishop, or explicitly made with their consent. On the other hand the technical language of later practice, such as references to the *persona*, rights of presentation or grants 'in proprios usus', is notable for its absence—no act of secure reputation refers to any of these.[100]

Five acts were issued either during or after law suits, though only two of these must have involved the archbishop as primate or metropolitan, since they involve proceedings against another bishop (**14, 59**);[101] several others are

---

[100] Brett, *English church* 141–8, though subsequent scholarship has called into question some of the evidence cited there.

[101] 14 concerns the primacy, 59 represents the adjournment *sine die* of an action against bp Theulf of Worcester; 66, 78, 82. Though Professor Brooke's judgement in 'English *acta*' 44–7 that it was an ever-deepening study of the law which shaped both the desire for charters and their form is surely right, these early documents give only a flickering insight into such changes.

records of events at which the archbishop was present, though not necessarily as a principal.[102] There are only four reasonably secure indulgences, and three which are uncertain or highly improbable. If one may argue from the rather tentative and inconsistent drafting of the likely texts, such formal grants were still something of a novelty.[103] The rest more or less defy systematic description; there is a solitary summons to a council,[104] two records of conciliar judgements,[105] an exhortation to the due payment of tithes[106] and so on. Ralph's letter of protection for monks of Abingdon setting off to establish a cell at Edwardstone (**44**) is the one most likely to reflect a larger category of lost correspondence, since such ephemera had only the thinnest chance of preservation in most archives, but are much more common in letter collections where they survive at all.

THE DIPLOMATIC OF THE ACTA: I. EXTERNAL FEATURES

FORMAT

The seventeen probable originals to survive for the period are associated with only four sets of beneficiaries. Christ Church, Canterbury accounts for all three of Anselm's acts, and one each from Ralph and William, Lewes priory for four of Ralph, tenants of the Canterbury estates for seven (including two grants of an archiepiscopal church to Aldgate), and the canons of Calke priory for one. Given the central importance of the beneficiary, this represents a skewed sample at best, yet it remains extraordinarily various. By far the largest is Ralph's great privilege for Lewes (**48**), 282 × 368 mm—the only surviving example to be deeper than it is wide. It is also much more nearly a true rectangle than any other, with almost parallel sides. Three more are virtually square—another Lewes grant, a small act only some 112 × 96 mm, with a deep plica (**47**), and two acts of William for Calke (**63**) and Aldgate (**80**). All the rest are significantly wider than they are deep, and range in size from Ralph's grant to Edward of Cornhill and his wife (**36**, 247 × 117 mm) to his tiny four-line grant to Christ Church (**38**, 162 × 52 mm). This absence of any consistent practice is shown strikingly in **80–81**, two near-duplicates of

---

[102] 9, 42, 92–4.
[103] 13, 50, 73, 96; *+2, *+4, *59.
[104] 79.
[105] 63, 71.
[106] 58; cf 77.

William for Aldgate; **80** is 134 × 129 mm, with a 25 mm plica; **81** has no plica, but is 166 × 106 mm. The methods of sealing and the variety of scripts, discussed below, all confirm this lack of a standard procedure.

SEALING

No seal survives for Lanfranc, and no authentic original. There are explicit references to a seal in the certainly spurious +**7** and +**8**, and the equally spurious +**3** once bore a seal on a tongue, but only the form of **6** might suggest that the archbishop ever applied one to any of his authentic acts. Relatively, given the rarity of impressions of authentic episcopal seals in the period, we are well-informed about his successors. All three of the authentic originals which survive for Anselm bear impressions of his genuine seal in whole or in part, and a fourth is attached to king Henry's charter for Rochester; two apparently spurious ones also survive.[107] The genuine seal has been discussed by Professor Heslop at some length.[108] Only five earlier episcopal seals are recorded in post-conquest England, of which two are lost, that of Odo of Bayeux in the Cotton fire, that of Wulfstan of Worcester during the Second World War, though both are known from earlier drawings or casts; a third survives as a leaden matrix, which has excited some suspicion,[109] and only the seals of Osbern of Exeter and Gundulf of Rochester survive as impressions attached to charters.[110] The seals of Wulfstan and Gundulf are round, and relatively small. The seal of Odo of Bayeux seems to have been a blunt oval, with the bishop standing full-length on one side, but wholly exceptionally as an equestrian figure on the other, apparently a direct imitation of the design on the reverse of the seal of the king his half-brother.[111] Osbern of Exeter too is represented at full-length in simple vestments on an oval seal, while Peter

---

[107] nos 14, 15, 16, 24. The seal has often been reproduced; apart from the references listed under 16 below, see J.H. Bloom, *English seals* (London 1906) 109 (from BL seal cast lv. 72, itself apparently taken from 14 below, Birch, *Catalogue* i no. 1169*), Heslop, 'English seals' pl. IIf, P.D.A. Harvey and A. McGuiness, *A guide to British medieval seals* (London 1996) pl. 57; nos +**26**, +**32**.

[108] Heslop, 'English seals' 12–13; Zarnecki, *Romanesque art* 306–7.

[109] *EEA* xiv p. lxv and n.

[110] *EEA* xi no. 7. In a survey of the sealing of charters in northern France (which excluded Normandy) Ghislain Brunel suggested that the use of seals *en placard* began to spread from *c.* 1040, if slowly, and that pendant seals only survive from *c.* 1080—Parisse, *Actes* 234–8. In England, unlike France, seals on royal acts had been pendant from the outset, though the acts of the Whitsun Council of 1072 uniquely once bore the seal of the Conqueror *en placard*—*Facsimiles of English royal writs to 1100* ed. T.A.M. Bishop and P. Chaplais (Oxford 1957) pl. xxix. There is no evidence to suggest that any English episcopal act was ever authenticated in this way.

[111] L.C. Loyd and D.M. Stenton (eds), *Sir Christopher Hatton's book of seals* no. 431, pl. viii.

of Chester's matrix, again an oval, shows him seated, but with a book raised in his left hand and his staff behind his right—in this respect following a model then familiar in western Francia.[112]

Anselm's seal is also in some sense transitional. From the surviving examples, none perfect, one can assemble a composite image of it. It was a relatively large blunt oval, some 85 × 71 mm,[113] and bore the legend SIGILLVM ANSELMI GRA DEI ARCHIEPISCOPI. He is depicted standing on a small dais at full length (unlike Peter of Chester), but in dalmatic as well as chasuble (unlike Odo or Osbern). Like Wulfstan and Peter of Chester he holds a book in his left hand, with a maniple hanging from it; and holds his staff (the crook turned outwards) in his right, while raising two fingers in blessing—an awkward arrangement both artistically and practically. The evolution of the conventional twelfth-century English iconography for episcopal seals would not be complete until his successor's seal, which places the staff in the left hand, abandons the book and adds a mitre, which became more or less standard afterwards. The wax is natural,[114] except for the brownish wax of **24**, a royal act apparently prepared by the beneficiary.[115]

The method of sealing reveals the same wide and inconsistent practice as the dimensions of the acts. The three surviving originals in Anselm's name, all for the priory and see of Canterbury, were sealed in three different ways, **14** on a tag[116], **15** on a tongue at the foot,[117] **16** on a tongue projecting from the top left-hand side, with the archbishop's head pointing away from the charter. No certainly authentic text contains a sealing clause, though one is found in the forgeries +**27**, +**29** and +**32**; it is yet another aberrant feature of **23** that the reference to sealing is incorporated in Anselm's subscription.

All seven of the surviving credible originals for Ralph seem once to have been sealed, though only two damaged examples of the genuine seal survive.[118] From these an approximate account may be constructed. It is a more narrowly pointed oval than Anselm's, some 82 × 53 mm, and depicts the archbishop standing, with his right hand raised in blessing, his crozier turned

---

[112] Zarnecki, *Romanesque art* 306 no. 338; Heslop, 'Seals' 11, 'Forgeries' 305.

[113] No two impressions appear to have precisely the same dimensions, not only because all are damaged to some extent, but perhaps also because of the behaviour of the wax before and after sealing, and more certainly because all have undergone some restorative work.

[114] nos 14, 15, 16; compare the improbable +32.

[115] The seal attached to +26, which looks like a cast from an authentic original, is in a strange grainy brown-red wax attached by a tongue, perhaps as another gesture towards verisimilitude.

[116] But there is no plica.

[117] cf 24.

[118] nos 35–6; Zarnecki, *Romanesque art* 307 no. 342 from 36, pl. IIa below, Du Boulay, 'Bexley' pl. facing 48 from 35; Birch, *Catalogue* i no. 1170, from a cast of 36.

inwards in his left hand, with the maniple flying beyond it. He wears a low mitre, chasuble and pallium, and stands on a small platform. The legend can be reconstructed as RADVL[FUS] DI GR[A CANTVARIE]NSIS ARCHIEPI[SCOPVS]. The surviving impressions are in natural wax, though the copy preserving the dubious **42**, one of only two texts with a sealing clause, asserts that it bore a green one. The spurious **+43** bears an indecipherable fragment of natural wax applied to a tag on the right-hand side. The seal was applied on a tongue at the foot to **35** and **36**, in the second case upside down by the usual calculation; on a tongue projecting from the middle of the left-hand side of **38** for Christ Church; on a tag for **46–7** and possibly **48**, all three for Lewes, though **49** for the same house may once have had a tongue. **47** is the earliest clear case in this collection of sealing on a tag passing through a *plica*. No genuine original bears a sealing clause, though one is found in the enigmatic **34**.

Of the seven surviving authentic orginals for William five[119] still bear a seal in whole or part, and the remaining two[120] were clearly once sealed. A further detached impression is preserved in the PRO as SC13/F154.[121] The seal resembles that of Ralph in its general dimensions, some 75 × 51 mm, and design. The archbishop stands on a very small platform in dalmatic, chasuble and pallium, wearing a low mitre with long ribbons, his left hand holding his crozier, again turned inwards, but with a maniple hanging behind it, his right hand raised in blessing. The legend is [SI]GILLVM GVILLELMI DI GRA CANTVARIENSIS ARCHIEPISCOPI.[122] Like Ralph's, the impressions are slightly concave. The wax is either natural (**64, 65, 80**) or reddish-brown (**63**). Five were sealed on a tongue, usually with a tie below; two for Aldgate were sealed on a tag; the seal for **80** is applied across the tag rather than along it, as is the usual case. The spurious **+76** is unique in being sealed on green cords, and is the only charter, copy or 'original', to have a sealing clause of any kind.

Only one original (**48**) in this collection might, just possibly, have been issued without sealing, though in principle there might be some lost acts in traditional diploma form comparable to the aberrant **23**. It is the more striking then that no authentic original or convincing copy bears a sealing clause. Though sealing was almost certainly the norm from Anselm's

[119] nos 62, 63, 64, 65, 79.

[120] nos 61, 80.

[121] This is a fine impression in natural wax, now 71 × 51 mm, though chipping round the edges has left only . . .GILLVM . . .. LELMI DI GRA . . . NTVARIENSIS A. . ..of the legend.

[122] Birch, *Catalogue* i nos 1171–2; F. Saxl, *English sculptures of the twelfth century* (London 1954) pl. IIIf.

time, all surviving sealing clauses suggest the intervention of a later hand.[123]

SCRIPT AND SCRIBES, by M. T. J. WEBBER[124]

The scribes and handwriting of the earliest surviving original *acta* of the archbishops of Canterbury are notable for their close correspondence with those of the books of the cathedral priory of Christ Church and of documents issued by the priory. All three original *acta* of Anselm (**14, 15, 16**), three of Ralph d'Escures (**36, 38, 49**), and one of William of Corbeil are written in (or reflect the influence of) the distinctive variety of formal Caroline minuscule that had evolved at Christ Church during the mid-1080s, and had rapidly matured by at least the mid-1090s (see below). Such handwriting appears not only in *acta* concerning property or rights in which the cathedral priory had an interest but also in those in which it did not, such as **63**, in favour of Calke priory, which records William, abbot of Chester's surrender of his claims on the church of Calke. A sharing of scribal resources between the monastic community and the archbishop may also be evident in the work of the scribe who wrote a very different, informal hand: the scribe of **35, 62, 66, 80** and **81**—documents written on behalf of two successive archbishops, Ralph and William. His hand has also been identified in additions made soon after 1124 to Cambridge, Corpus Christi College, ms 19 (see below), a copy of the *Decretum* of Ivo of Chartres, produced by a scribe whose hand has been found in several Christ Church books.[125] The book certainly formed part of the communal book collections in the later twelfth century, since it contains a mark that forms one of a series of symbols and letters added to many of the priory's books during the second half of the twelfth century.[126] Nevertheless, both the main contents and the additions would have been of

---

[123] This is markedly different from the position in the northern French bishoprics, as set out by Ghislain Brunel in Parisse, *Actes* 234–8. She concluded that references to sealing appeared in acts as soon as, or very shortly after, seals began to be applied.

[124] These paragraphs owe much to the identifications and observations of Michael Gullick who commented upon an earlier draft and has, over the years, generously shared with us the results of his research on Christ Church scribes in advance of publication.

[125] Webber, 'Script and manuscript' 154, 154 n. 41 and pl. 16b.

[126] On these marks, found at the top right-hand corner of the first page of each manuscript (some of which are also recorded in a booklist perhaps dating from the 1170s), see N.R. Ker, *Medieval libraries of Great Britain*, 2 ed. London 1964, 29.

special interest to an archbishop, so it is possible that the additions were made at William's request by one of his own clerks.[127]

ANSELM (1093–1109)

The three surviving authentic originals were produced by different scribes all writing a distinctive variety of formal Caroline minuscule that first emerged at Christ Church, Canterbury, during the mid-1080s, and is found in both books and documents produced during the late eleventh and first third of the twelfth century.[128] The hands of two of the *acta*, **14** and **15**, have been identified in other material from Canterbury. The scribe of **14**, a document closely datable to a period of less than two months in 1109, has not been identified in the earliest books written in the new variety of script (which date from the 1080s and 1090s), but copied other material associated with the efforts to secure a profession of obedience from Thomas II, archbishop-elect of York, in 1109, namely the enrolled forms of the petition of the clergy of York and Thomas's profession.[129] This scribe also wrote the first part of a composite manuscript from Christ Church: Oxford, Bodleian Library, ms Bodley 161 (fos 1–110), a copy of Bede's commentary on the Song of Songs. The scribe of **15** has been identified as Eadmer, one of the earliest exponents of this variety of minuscule (Pl. Ib). His hand has also been identified in a number of books and documents (issued both by the community and by the arch-bishop) dating from the mid-1080s until his departure with Anselm in 1097, and from the period after his return in 1100 (he was again absent with Anselm in exile between April 1103 and late September 1106).[130] His hand-writing in **15** corresponds most closely with that of his datable work from the period before 1097.[131] The scribe of **16** wrote in the mature version of the Christ Church script that had already emerged by at least the mid-1090s

---

[127] On the additional material, see R. Somerville, 'A textual link between Canterbury and Lucca in the early twelfth century?', *Christianità ed Europa: miscellanea di studi in onore di Luigi Prosdocimi*, ed. C. Alzati, (Rome/Freiburg/Vienna 1994), i 405–415.

[128] N.R. Ker, *English manuscripts in the century after the Norman Conquest* (Oxford 1960), 25–9; 'Script and manuscript' 145–58; Gullick, 'Eadmer' 173–88; Gullick and Pfaff, 'Pontifical' 284–94. Further precision in dating books and documents from Christ Church written in this distinctive variety of minuscule will be provided by Michael Gullick's forthcoming analysis of the hands of the original and enrolled copies of the Canterbury episcopal and abbatial professions.

[129] Canterbury D. & C. C.A. C 117, nos 21–2; *Canterbury professions* no. 62, Appendix B, no. 10.

[130] Gullick, 'Eadmer' 173–89, with references to identifications made previously by R.W. Southern, T.A.M. Bishop and N.R. Ker.

[131] Gullick, 'Eadmer' 185.

(Pl. Ia).[132] His hand has not been identified in any other document or manuscript book, but its character (in particular its proportions and the treatment of serifs) may reflect a stage of development between that displayed by the hand of the scribe who may have been the first to write expert, mature Christ Church script and that displayed by the hand of **38** (see below).[133]

RALPH D'ESCURES (1114–1122)

Two of the seven surviving original *acta* of archbishop Ralph are written by scribes who employed the distinctive formal Christ Church script (**36** and **38**). One and perhaps both have been identified elsewhere. **38** was written by an expert scribe in the mature Christ Church script, whose hand has been identified in several books and documents, the latter datable to between 1121 and 1123 (Pl. IIIa). He wrote Oxford, Bodleian Library, ms Bodley 160, fos 1–51 (Bede on the Catholic Epistles), additions to Dublin, Trinity College, ms 98 (B.3.6) (a pontifical), Canterbury D. & C. C.A. C 9 (a confirmation charter of Henry I in favour of archbishop Ralph and the monks of Christ Church, datable to 1121), BL Campbell Charter xxi.6 (a confirmation charter of Henry I in favour of archbishop William and the monks of Christ Church, datable to 1123), and the Christ Church entry in the mortuary roll of abbot Vitalis of Savigny (datable to 1122 × 3).[134] The hand of the scribe of **36** (Pl. IIa) bears some similarity to that of the Canterbury, D. & C. C.A. 117 no. 23 (the enrolled profession of Albold, abbot of Bury from 1114–1119), which may be the work of the scribe who wrote Cambridge, University Library, ms Dd.1.4 + Cambridge, St John's College, ms A. 8 (Josephus, *Antiquitates iudaicae* etc.), Cambridge, University Library, ms Dd.8.15 (Haimo of Auxerre on Isaiah),[135] and Oxford, Bodleian Library, ms Bodley 271, fos 15v–112v, 114r–139ra, line 10 (Anselm, *opera*).[136] The proportions of the handwriting in **36**, however, are taller and narrower. The hand of **49**, as yet unidentified elsewhere, also reflects the influence of the formal Christ Church script (evident in the angular backs of the letters **c** and **e** and in the contrast between thick and thin strokes according to their direction) but displays features of less formal handwriting (for example: **d** with an oblique, slightly curving shaft; **f, r** and long **s** with shafts extending below the line of writing).

---

[132] Gullick, 'Eadmer' 175 n. 7; Gullick and Pfaff, 'Pontifical' 285 .
[133] The earlier of the two is Scribe A of the Dublin pontifical: Gullick and Pfaff, 'Pontifical' 285.
[134] Webber, 'Script and manuscript' 152; Gullick and Pfaff, 'Pontifical' 286–7 (on Scribe C).
[135] Webber, 'Script and manuscript' pl. 14b.
[136] Michael Gullick, personal communication.

The earliest of the surviving original *acta* from Canterbury to have been written in an informal hand that displays few of the features of formal hand-writing is **35**. The strokes are written with much less deliberation and with a narrower nib, which permitted more rapid writing; the rapidity of movement is evident in the length of both the common mark of abbreviation and of the descender that forms the shaft of the tironian *nota* for *et* and the limb of **h**. Such handwriting became increasingly common in royal and other *acta* dur-ing the first half of the twelfth century.[137] The scribe of **35** continued to be active during the archiepiscopate of William of Corbeil. He wrote four of William's extant original *acta* (**62, 66, 80, 81**: see below), and made additions to a Christ Church book, Cambridge, Corpus Christi College, ms 19, data-ble to in or after 1124 (fo. i: a list of popes and the dates of their reigns, down to and including the consecration of Honorius II, 1124; perhaps also fos 333v–334r, 2nd col. line 22: extracts from councils).[138]

46–48, in favour of Lewes priory, are in the same hand, but one that is not found in any of the other extant Canterbury originals, and was probably that of a Lewes scribe. The handwriting of the three documents displays varying levels of formality and elaboration, reflecting the status of each. Certain ele-ments of the forms have been elaborated in a manner characteristic of the curial minuscule of papal documents: the shafts of ascenders are exaggerated in length; the ascenders of **f** and tall **s** are ornamented with loops, a few of which are further elaborated with a ruche; the ligatures of **ct** and **st** are also formed with elaborate loops; there is an additional loop in the tail of **g**, and the looped tittle is used as an alternative to the common mark of abbrevia-tion.[139] All of these details are present in **48**, the remarkable general confir-mation of benefactions to Lewes. The two simpler grants, **46** and **47**, each contain the occasional elaboration: **46** contains two instances of the looped **ct** ligature, one of the looped **st** ligature, and a few looped **ss**; **47**, written rather more rapidly, displays just one looped **s** and a couple of looped **gs** (Pl. IIb). These elaborations aside, the handwriting is a rather conservative Caroline minuscule, which, in its generally rounded character and square proportions as well as other small details, is similar to that of other early twelfth-century charters in favour of Lewes.[140]

---

[137] Bishop, *Scriptores* 12–15; Webber, 'Scribes' 147–9.

[138] T.A.M. Bishop, 'Notes on Cambridge Manuscripts I' *Transactions of the Cambridge Bibliographical Society* i (1949–53) 437.

[139] Bishop, *Scriptores* 12, n. 4.

[140] Compare Pl. IIb with *Early Yorkshire charters* viii, pls II–IV, charters of William de Warenne in favour of Lewes, all datable to between 1088 and 1118.

WILLIAM OF CORBEIL (1123–1136)

Of the seven original *acta* of archbishop William only **63** is in the distinctive Christ Church script, albeit a somewhat informal version in which the simpler forms of round-backed **d** and the tironian *nota* for *et* were employed. Four (**62, 66, 80, 81**) are in the hand of the scribe who wrote **35**, on behalf of archbishop Ralph. The handwriting of **62** and **81** (Pl. IIIb) is very similar to **35**; that of **66** and **80**, at first glance, is not, largely because the letter forms and the spaces between them are more compressed. Nevertheless, various small details indicate that all four documents are the work of the same scribe: the similarity is most marked in the script of the archiepiscopal title in which the letter forms and marks of abbreviation are almost identical in all four specimens; the form of more complex graphs, such as **g** and the ampersand is also closely similar. In addition, a symbol of punctuation not commonly found in Anglo-Norman charters is present in both **62** and **80**, namely a *positura* (to denote the end of a section of text), comprising two dots above a comma-shaped mark.

64 and **65**, two related grants, are in hands that lack fluency and display certain peculiarities. **64** exhibits a curious combination of letterforms written in a very regular fashion and others that are not. **65** (Pl. IIIc) has a particularly studied, imitative quality that may indicate that it is later than the purported date. Some of the strokes display features characteristic of formal bookhands of the second half of the twelfth century: curved strokes, such as those forming the arches of **h** and **n**, are in some instances more sharply angled than is usual for the period before 1136; the straight horizontal stroke of the common mark of abbreviation over the **p** of *p*reposito (line 5), which terminates in a sharply angled downwards stroke, is also unusual so early in the twelfth century. There are, however, no obvious anachronisms in the handwriting of **64**.

THE DIPLOMATIC OF THE ACTA:
INTERNAL FEATURES

To discuss the diplomatic of a group of charters which contains a number of manifest forgeries and many more that are thoroughly suspicious presents obvious difficulties. The special features of the forged texts are called to attention in the commentary to them, but are only occasionally noted here. The more probable charters printed below fall into two broad classes. Apart from the quite distinct record beginning 'Hec est conventio' (**9**), a small but not insignificant group of thirteen texts are cast in the form of declarations, beginning usually 'Ego'. Such usage is common in diplomas, and in those *notitiae* which often precede the emergence of the sealed charter in episcopal acts across the Channel, but few of the Canterbury acts in which it occurs are elaborate or formal.[141] Three early ones are in fact additions to royal sealed diplomas, reflecting a development of the long-established *pancarte* form, though one also bears the archbishop's seal at the foot, with that of the bishop who adds a similar declaration, and of the king.[142] Four further acts of Anselm, for Christ Church, for Bec and Chester (founded from Bec) and St Valery are cast in the same way, though it remains uncertain whether the Bec and Chester ones were originally separate documents, since both are copies,[143] and that for St Valery is most unlikely to be genuine.[144] However **16,** for Christ Church, survives as a sealed original. There is no reason to suppose that the convention was either uniquely early, or confined to houses with strong cross-Channel connections, for it continued to influence practice under Ralph and William on a modest scale. Ralph's grants of Saltwood to St Philibert (a priory of Bec), of Aldington to Edward of Cornhill and of Little Malling to the abbey there are all nearer the declaration than the writ charter.[145] William uses the same form for his two grants to Edward of Cornhill and to Gervase his son, and in his more solemn confirmation of the foundation of Reading abbey.[146]

By far the largest group, however, consists of more or less conventional writ charters, in general owing much more to the practice of the Anglo-Norman kings than to earlier forms or the papal chancery. Such a classification conceals enormous variations, from **48,** the grand and elaborate privilege of Ralph for Lewes,[147] which is indeed strongly influenced by papal practice, to **38,** his laconic three and a half line gift to Christ Church priory. Nevertheless, for all this variety they share an underlying structure, and most of what is said of the diplomatic of the texts below draws on their usage.

---

[141] The qualified exceptions are 16 (an original) and 86 (a slightly dubious copy). The study of P. Johanek, *Die Frühzeit der Siegelurkunde im Bistum Würzburg* (Quellen und Forschungen zur Geschichte des Bistums und Hochstifts Würzburg xx, 1969) is an admirable analysis of the transition from *notitia* to sealed charter, with wide citation of the earlier literature.

[142] 5, 8, 24.

[143] 12, 21.

[144] +32.

[145] 34, 36, 51.

[146] 64–5, 86.

[147] If substantially genuine 23 (a copy) would fall into the same class.

CHRISMON

No convincing original bearing the chrismon familiar in Anglo-Saxon royal diplomas or in episcopal diplomatic elsewhere in Europe survives for any of the archbishops, but several copies may suggest that it was used occasionally under Anselm and Ralph. The deeply suspicious +**32** for St Valery bears one, possibly as a reflection of its French origin, and the copyists of **21**, **51**, both for Malling, and **23** for Norwich also included one.

INTITULATIO

Title precedes inscription in every authentic act, with the qualified exception of **34** below, an act for Bec with several other exceptional features.[148]

Since only three texts below attributed to Lanfranc have any serious claim to authenticity, and of these **9** is a record of his action drawn up, presumably, by others, his letters are central to any discussion of his preferred style. These show considerable variety, some of this no doubt a function of the various registers in which he wrote to different recipients. In the forty-eight letters which can be used for analysis, two occur eight times, a bare 'archiepiscopus' (as in **6** below) and 'indignus antistes'; 'Gratia Dei archiepiscopus' occurs in seven cases. The 'non meis meritis sed gratia Dei archiepiscopus' in **5**, a note attached to a royal charter, is not found exactly in those words in the letters, but variations on the theme are common enough to suggest he may have used it more widely.[149] In the conciliar acts of 1072 and 1075 which he subscribed, he appears as 'Dorobernensis archiepiscopus', and it was the dominant form used for professions to him throughout his rule.[150] One might speculate that this form would be more widely attested if there were more acts to work from.

Anselm has left more charters, and more than three hundred letters written in his name as archbishop.[151] Among the charters a simple 'archiepiscopus'

---

[148] Compare too the inauthentic +43, +76.

[149] *Lanfranc letters* 9, 22, 43, 47.

[150] *Councils* i(2) 603, 614. The 1075 council has been identified as the work of one of the archbp's own clerks. For the usage of the professions, below p. lxxii, where 'Dorobernensis' only begins to give way to 'Cantuariensis' from 1086, but vanishes entirely from August 1107.

[151] *EA* nos 165–472; because the collection in ms Lambeth 59, the largest, appears to represent an attempt at a comprehensive set of Anselm's letters, put together soon after 1120, the likelihood of later contamination is slight, though several of the texts have been suggested to represent variant drafts of the same letter. It is also true that a copyist may well be tempted to abbreviate such formal elements in the text. This makes any exact statistical analysis very speculative. For the content and character of Lambeth 59 see Southern, *Anselm* (1990) 458–81, R. Gameson, 'English manuscript art in the late eleventh century: Canterbury and its context' in

appears once in **15**, an original and once in **13**, a copy, but almost eighty times in the letters. 'Archiepiscopus Cantuariensis' appears in **14**, an original, and in two copies (**12, 19**), and some thirty-three times among the letters. Two forms, 'minister ecclesie Cantuariensis' (**14b**), and 'sancte Dorobernensis ecclesie archiepiscopus' (**16**) are found in originals which excite no suspicion, but not in any surviving letter. The added note to an original royal charter for Rochester, recalling Lanfranc's usage in a similar grant, 'non meis meritis sed gratia Dei Cantuariensis archiepiscopus' (**24**), is not found exactly in the charters or letters, but is close to a set of formulations in copies of other charters and in a number of his letters: 'gratia Dei sancte Cantuariensis ecclesie archiepiscopus' (**18, 21**), 'Dei dispositione archiepiscopus Cantuarie' (**25**), 'gratia Dei archiepiscopus' (**31**),[152] 'gratia Dei sancte Cantuariensis ecclesie antistes' (**20**) and 'gratia Dei archiepiscopus Cantuariensis' (**21, 25**).[153] This unstable practice means that there is no cogent reason to reject two forms found only in copies, and not precisely in this form in the letters either, 'sancte Cantuariensis ecclesie antistes' (**17**)[154] and 'Dei dispositione archiepiscopus Cantuarie' (**25**). In view of Anselm's passionate commitment to the cause of the primacy it is very striking that he only once uses the title in his letters, or in any original charter or convincing copy. The one case is highly specialised, the body of the text of his very late letter to Thomas archbishop-elect of York, threatening him with every penalty should he fail to make his profession (**14b**). Two charters which do use it in other contexts, **23** and **+32**, are more or less suspicious on other grounds, and the style contributes to the doubts they inspire. Even if these dubious texts prove eventually to deserve more credit than we give them, at least it may be asserted that neither was the work of the archbishop himself or his own clerks. As will be seen below, the use of the primatial title in authentic documents otherwise is barely known before the time of Theobald outside the professions. It is perhaps modestly surprising that a very common form in the letters, 'servus ecclesie Cantuariensis',[155] is not found at all in the surviving charters.

Canterbury and the Norman Conquest 119–20 and *The manuscripts of early Norman England* (Oxford 1999) no. 581 against W. Fröhlich, whose views are most fully stated in 'The genesis of the collections of St. Anselm's letters', *American Benedictine Review* xxxv (1984) 249–66. Fröhlich was followed by S. Vaughn, *Anselm of Bec and Robert of Meulan* (Berkeley/LA, 1987); the matter was debated further between Southern and Vaughn in *Albion* xx (1988), esp. 192–201, 212–5.

[152] cf *EA* 182, 188–90, 195–6, 203, 208.
[153] cf *EA* 251, 264, 286, 431.
[154] cf *EA* 314, 172, 183, 197, 178.
[155] *EA* 206, 210, 214, 217–20, 234–5, 254, 256, 261–3, 266, 269, 271–4, 279–80, 285, 298, 302, 315, 325, 340, 345, 388–9, 407, 410, 413, 418–9, 421, 425, 427, 429–30, 432, 439, 441, 448, 451, 463, 466.

Archbishop Ralph's acts show a higher degree of regularity. In principle there might be some uncertainty about the way he represented his name, or others represented it. In fact there is a good deal of consistency. In two originals he appears as Rad' (**35, 38**), in four charters for Lewes he appears twice as 'R.' (**46–7**), twice as 'Radulfus' (**48–9**), and only one departs from the expected with 'Radulffus' (**36**), though that was written by a Canterbury priory scribe.[156] His style can be sought in twenty-one apparently genuine texts surviving more or less complete, seven as originals. In two, one an original and both dealing with modest grants on the archbishop's lands, he is simply 'archiepiscopus'(**36–7**). In six, two of them originals, he is styled 'Cantuariensis archiepiscopus'[157] or 'archiepiscopus Cantuariensis';[158] in ten more, of which three are originals, 'Dei gratia' is added.[159] Two or three texts, rather letters than charters, have 'indignus Cant' ecclesie minister'(**44**)[160] or 'sancte Cant' ecclesie debilis minister' (**59**). The one wholly aberrant case is **48**, the great privilege for Lewes, a document which was surely written by the beneficiaries. This provides the quite exceptional 'Dei gratia Cant' archiepiscopus et totius Britannie primas'.

For William twenty-eight reasonably trustworthy acts survive more or less complete, seven again in the original. There can only be the most modest uncertainty about the way his name was represented; in four originals he is 'Will' (**62–3, 66, 80**), in one 'Will's' (**64**), in two 'Will'mus' (**65, 81**). In his time the move to a consistent style becomes much clearer. 'Dei gratia Cantuariensis archiepiscopus', already gaining ground under Ralph, becomes virtually standard; it forms part of his style in all but two of his probable surviving acts.[161] The exceptions are **64**, a problematic original based very loosely on the earlier and similar act of archbishop Ralph, and sharing with it a bare 'archiepiscopus', and the early copy of a summons for bishop Urban to the legatine Council of 1125 (**79**), which has simply 'Cantuariensis archiepiscopus'.

---

[156] 35, 38; 48–9; 36 (see above p. lxiv); the copies show much greater variety.

[157] 34–5, 42 (distinctly dubious), 49. The same form appears in the archbp's long letter to Calixtus II over the primacy, below p. lxxiii n.

[158] 52–3.

[159] 38–9, 46–7, 50–51, 56–8; 'gratia Dei' in 55. The same form appears in the apparently spurious 33.

[160] If the argument in the commentary is accepted, then the spurious +43 also preserves part of a similar authentic letter in the same terms.

[161] There is a minor variant in 73: 'gratia Dei Cant' archiepiscopus', an inversion common enough under Anselm. It is also used in his letter to the monks of Worcester, datable between Oct. 1123 and June 1124, below p. lxxiii and n..

A new element entered the archiepiscopal style after the bull of Honorius II of 25 January 1126, constituting William 'apostolice sedis legatus'.[162] The new legate was back at Canterbury before 29 June, and in the texts below any English or Welsh act containing the legatine title has been dated after mid-1126.[163] Honorius died on 13 × 14 February 1130, and a disputed election meant that England did not recognise his successor, Innocent II, until 13 January 1131. It is possible that Innocent renewed William's legation when he visited Rouen in May, for William of Malmesbury attributes the renewal of the legation to that year, and by March 1132 the pope was again addressing the archbishop as legate.[164] In theory, therefore, William could have styled himself legate at any point between January 1126 and the spring of 1130, when news of Honorius' death reached England, and again from (say) mid-1131 until his death, though we cannot be confident that he did not do so between the death of Honorius and the receipt of a new commission from Innocent. Twenty-one of the twenty-eight acts do in fact use the title. The commonest form is 'sedis apostolice legatus' (eight, including three originals) or 'apostolice sedis legatus' (six, all copies), though 'sancte Romane ecclesie legatus' occurs in six copies and 'Romane ecclesie legatus' in one. Of those that do not use the title only **79** is securely dated before the grant of the legation of 1126,[165] but only **94** was certainly issued after 1127, and probably quite close to **93**, which has it, though both are copies. It is possible that **94** was given after news of the death of Honorius II reached England in the spring of 1130 and before the renewal of the legation by Innocent II in 1131 × 2. The other acts without the legatine style cannot be dated closely.[166] One cannot be sure that its absence is significant, but if it is then they were granted either before the autumn of 1125, when the archbishop set out for Rome on the journey which secured the first grant of the legation or in the same interval of early 1130 to early 1132 .

---

[162] *Councils* i(2) 742–3, JL 7284. In the small number of bulls addressed to the archbp as legate Honorius used this form—*Book of Llan Dâv* 34, 38, 45, *Historians York* iii 50 ('sedis apostolice leg.' in the text, but it is poorly transmitted).

[163] Except for 92 below, an act in favour of a Norman beneficiary.

[164] *Councils* i(2) 755–7; *Book of Llan Dâv* 65; Malmesbury, *HN* 20; C.R. Cheney 'Deaths of popes' 89. Compare too *Historians York* iii 67, JL 7766, of 22 April 1136. There is one undated bull of Honorius for William surviving in a later copy which does not address him as legate, *Mon.* iv 538, JL 7736. This is the grant of Dover to the archbp and Christ Church, and the content is irrelevant to the archbp's special status, which may explain the absence of the title better than a date before the grant of the legation.

[165] And compare his letter of 1123 × 4 cited above, n. 161.

[166] 62, 64–5, 86. The cases of 64–5 are peculiarly complex; see the commentary to those acts.

In the acts the primatial style is as exceptional under William as under his predecessors. There is a solitary text from Leeds priory (**75**, preserved only in a copy of s. xiv) where William is archbishop, legate and 'Anglorum primas'. This is not the only unusual feature of the document, so the suspicions it arouses, and the relative lateness of the copy, make it impossible to have much confidence in the integrity of its text. Rather less direct evidence is found in the detailed record of a plea at Sandwich in 1127 which, in its fullest but latest version, notes the presence of William as 'legatus ecclesie sancte Romane ecclesie et primas tocius Britannie'.[167] The evidence for Anselm, Ralph and William shows that only Anselm's exceptional letter to archbishop Thomas, directly related to the issue of primacy, is a clear case of the archbishop authorising an act in which he is styled primate before the time of Theobald, though the Norwich diploma of Anselm, the great privilege of Ralph for Lewes and the Sandwich plea suggest others might claim it for him.

There is a large and important group of texts which have not been discussed so far, the professions made by bishops-elect between 1070 and 1135. The four professions to Lanfranc, made before the Easter Council of 1072, address him variously as 'sancte Cantuariensis ecclesie . . . metropolitane', 'sancte metropolitane sedis antistes', 'Dorobernensis archiepiscope' and 'Dorobernensis archiepiscope'.[168] After the council the standard form is archbishop and 'Britanniarum primas', occasionally elaborated as 'totius Britannice regionis primas' or 'primas totius Britannice insule',[169] and only three omit the primatial style entirely, none for any obvious reason.[170] Under Anselm, Ralph and William the standard form is 'totius Britannie primas', with only one minor variant, 'Britanniarum primas'.[171] There are only two cases where the style is omitted. One is from bishop David of Bangor, who had arrived with a letter of recommendation threatening that the Welsh would seek a bishop from the Irish 'or some other barbarous region' if Ralph would not consecrate him.[173] The other is even more striking. Seffrid of Chichester was consecrated in the presence of the legate John of Crema, sent to England in part (and a great part as the two archbishops might think) to resolve the furious debate over the primacy which had occurred in Rome in 1123. Seffrid alone does not call William primate.[173] However, the bearing of

---

[167] The shorter version is attested by William as 'sancte Romane ecclesie legatus etc'; below p. 107.
[168] *Canterbury professions* nos 31–4.
[169] ibid. nos 35, 44.
[170] ibid. nos 42 for a bishop of Dublin (but cf nos 36, 51, 69), 43, 45.
[171] ibid. no. 55.
[172] ibid. no. 67; Eadmer, *Historia* 259–60.
[173] ibid. no. 72; Hugh the Chanter xliii, 186–200.

this evidence of the professions on the archbishops' practice in their acts is only remote before 1136. There is a marked contrast between something like universal use of the title in a liturgical context and an almost equally complete absence of it in the *acta*. Here again there is a clean break under Theobald. While only one of the professions made to archbishop Theobald before 1145 omits the primatial title, there is cogent evidence that he did not use it in his acts until he received the privilege of Eugenius III dated 5 May 1145, which confirmed to him whatever primacy had been lawfully enjoyed by his predecessors; after that it became pretty much standard for the rest of his rule.[174]

INSCRIPTIO

The forms of address in this collection take a bewildering variety of forms, just as the substance of the text ranges widely.[175] The 'Ego' group described earlier have no address, but all but three of the formulae in acts of more conventional type appear only once in exactly the same words in acts of solid reputation; one of the three that appears twice is found in two original acts which are virtual duplicates (**80–81**) and another is used rather differently in each (**70, 93**). Correspondingly one cannot speak of any significant development over the period, or of usage particular to any one archbishop. The larger number are cast in more or less general terms—'omnibus fidelibus Cristi' (**17, 55**), 'omnibus ecclesie catholice filiis (**68**),[176] 'omnibus sancte matris ecclesie filiis' (**85**) and the like, at its most developed in **56**: 'omnibus Cristi fidelibus episcopis et clericis, abbatibus et monachis, reliquisque cuiuscumque conditionis sunt ecclesie filiis'. It is striking that variants of the form which was to predominate so much in later years, 'tam presentibus quam futuris' are found in the address of only two acts, though one is an original for Lewes (**47, 97**).[177] Some add 'per Angliam' (**63, 70, 93**), or are addressed to the archbishop's own men or friends (**15, 80–81, 93**), others address a bishop, the faithful of a particular diocese or area, or of the archdiocese (**23, 66, 80–81**), or adapt a formulation more familiar in royal writs, most

---

[174] *Canterbury professions* nos 81–6; *PUE* iii no. 47; C.R. Cheney, 'On the acta of Theobald and Thomas, archbishops of Canterbury', *Journal of the Society of Archivists* vi (1981) 469; Foliot, *Letters* 505–6. It is noteworthy, on the other hand, that the two professions to archbp Thomas do not call him primate.

[175] Compare Saltman, *Theobald* 192–6.

[176] But cf the much more dubious 74–5.

[177] However, in the text of two near-duplicate original acts for Aldgate William announces his gift to the canons 'tam presentibus quam futuris' (80–81), cf too 51.

elaborately in an indulgence for Llandaff, **50**: 'omnibus ecclesie filiis Francis et Anglis atque Gualensibus et cuiuscumque sint nationis hominibus'.[178] Only two have 'in perpetuum' (**47–8**, both originals from Lewes), and one suspicious and eccentric text is more oddly defined as addressed 'omnibus qui volunt scire veritatem de corpore beati Neoti confessoris' (**31**). Theobald sometimes addressed his confirmations to the beneficiary, a practice that recurs very rarely under his successors, but there is no such case in this collection.[179]

There is an interesting group of brief acts, closely resembling secular documents of the period, many of which refer to the estates of the archbishopric, and are addressed to the men of the shire, estate or hundred in question, found under every archbishop before William (**6**, **19**, **21**, **25**, **35**, **37**, **39**, **46**, **52**, **58**).[180] The royal echo is perhaps clearest in **38**: 'Rad' episcopo Cicest' et omnibus hominibus suis Francis et Anglis de Suthsexe', closely followed by **57**, or in **58**: 'omnibus episcopis in quorum parochiis Radulfus Basset ecclesias habuit in dominatu suo'. William used a similar form in **71**, **77** and **78**, mandates issued apparently during a vacancy at Hereford, in **82** for Holy Trinity, Aldgate, and in **94** for Shrewsbury. There are others, however, little if at all different in their apparent subject, which have a general address, so again no rigorous pattern can be discerned.

SALUTATIO

The extreme variety of inscription is not found in the salutation. The great bulk of credible acts cast in writ form use one of two forms. The commonest is a bare 'salutem', found twenty-one times, often but not always in association with the specific addresses discussed above. The second widespread form consists in some modest variation around 'salutem Deique benedictionem et suam', found in some twenty-nine cases.[181] The humility topoi 'quantum valet', 'quantum potest' or 'si quid valet', so frequent in Anselm's letters, are found only twice in the acts, in both cases under Ralph, 'quantum valet' in his otherwise terse **39** for Christ Church, and an altogether exceptional 'salutem et amicitiam et fideles orationes pro posse' in a rather conventional letter to

---

[178] Compare the elaboration of some Scottish royal acts of about the same period—*The charters of King David I* ed. G.W.S. Barrow (Woodbridge 1999) 12–14.

[179] e.g. Saltman, *Theobald* nos 30, 38, 54–5, 90, 111, 190, 259; *EEA* ii p. lviii.

[180] cf the spurious +30.

[181] This is also used in William's letter to the monks of Worcester, below p. lxxiii n.

a fellow bishop in **44**. None for any archbishop includes a version of 'in eternum'or 'perpetuam'.

ARENGA

Almost half of Theobald's *acta* include *arengae*, and the rich variety of their phrasing was subjected to detailed analysis by Professor Saltman. In many respects this was no more than an episode in Canterbury diplomatic, for the *arenga* was to decline steadily under his successors, and owed little to the practice of his predecessors. Only five of the acts below include even relatively modest versions. Of those five, three are attributed to Anselm, but two are thoroughly suspicious (**23** and **+32**, a pseudo-original), and the third, **21**, does not command entire confidence. Yet again **48**, the great privilege for Lewes, stands out among Ralph's acts; its *arenga* follows a general pattern widely found elsewhere in the charters of Cluny, though none offers any very close parallel in detail, and it clearly derives from the practice of the beneficiaries. There is similarly a solitary example under William, **73**, an indulgence for Holme which poses a number of problems of its own, if not of a kind to throw its authenticity into doubt. The *arenga* precedes the *intitulatio* in **21**, cast in the 'Ego' form, and in **48**, but follows the *salutatio* more conventionally in **23**, **+32** and **73**. The *arenga* was thoroughly exceptional, therefore, occurring in only one trustworthy original, and should be explained much more in terms of the tastes of the beneficiary than in the practice of the archbishops.

NOTIFICATIO

The 'Ego' group defined earlier follow no clear pattern in introducing the main text; they begin commonly with a plain indicative—'Concedo',[182] 'Testimonium fero'[183] and so on—though **51** begins 'notum facere curavi', and the curious mixed text of **34** includes 'notum sit omnibus fidelibus'. Of those in writ-charter form, **48** and **73** move from *arenga* to disposition with no transition; several more proceed directly from greeting to disposition, whether they be mandates (**14**, **59**, **66**, **77**, **82**), confirmations (**72**), indulgences (**48**, **97**), grants (**6**, **47**) or records of proceedings elsewhere (**92**). Rather more however are introduced by one of two broad types of formula. The simplest and commonest is 'Sciatis', followed directly by an accusative

---

[182] 36, 64–5, 86, cf 5, 12.
[183] 21.

and infinitive, which occurs in twelve acts, seven of them originals. The alternative of 'Sciatis quod' with an indicative is almost as frequent. Even though none of the nine cases occurs in an original it would require an unusually ruthless or indolent copyist to invent this formulation, given the different grammatical constructions involved. Two variations, 'Scias quia' (**46**) and 'Sciatis pro certo quia' (**31**), also found only in copies, may be explained by the exceptional nature of the acts in which they occur as well as by the transmission. The most elaborate formulation of this family, 'Sciant tam presentes quam posteri quod' is found in **85**, a late copy of an act for Minster-in-Sheppey which may be at least in part corrupt and has several features which appear unusual so early.

A second and less coherent group uses some form of 'Notum sit'. The only original in the group is **63**, 'Notum omnium devotioni sit', but variations on this occur widely in copies which present no particularly suspicious features. 'Notum sit' may be followed by 'vobis' (**18**, **17**) , 'omnibus' (**75**), 'vobis omnibus' (**25**, **55**), 'omnium devotioni' (**97**, cf **71**), 'omnium dilectioni' (**68**, **74**), or transformed into forms such as 'Notum facere volumus quod' (**79**). Forms such as 'Notum sit universitati vestre' or 'Notum sit omnibus tam presentibus quam futuris', so widespread after 1150, are rarely represented in these early acts, and only in copies: the least convincing is the 'Tam presentibus quam post futuris innotescat' of **84**, another act for Minster-in-Sheppey which lies under considerable suspicion; the 'Notum sit omnibus tam presentibus quam futuris' of **53** for Rochester has been called into question recently. However, even if one rejects both as uncertain at best, another Rochester act has the related form 'Noscant presentes et postfuturi' (**87**). This reappears in a quite unrelated Shrewsbury document (**93**), and each goes some way to support the testimony of the other. They may also provide a modest indication that those drafting acts of the archbishop for different beneficiaries were beginning to move towards some agreed conventions.

NARRATIO AND DISPOSITIO

Given the enormous variety of forms found among these acts, it is only possible to give a very general summary of the essential elements of their content. For the most part, any account of the preliminaries to the archbishop's action is infrequent and summary, if present at all.[184] There are rather more significant examples in the dubious **23** and **42**, and in the much better attested

---

[184] e.g. 5. 16–18, 44, 46, 50, 61.

63, 68, 71, 74 and **78**. However, there are a small group in which the heart of the text is the archbishop's testimony to actions at which he was present, at least twice as an actor (**59, 66**); usually this is followed by a brief statement that he confirms or endorses what was done (the dubious **21** and **31**, and the much more secure **66** and **92**), but in **94** the whole text is in effect a narrative, where the archbishop's confirmation is at best implicit.

The bulk of the acts, however, fall into the three groups of precepts, grants and confirmations. The precepts are few, and the dispositive verbs are forms of 'Mando' (**77, 78**), 'Precipio' (**79**) or some combination of these with each other (**14**a, **71, 82**), or with 'volo' (**63**) or 'interdico' (**14**b). The dominant verb in grants is 'Concedo' (widely, and **15, 36, 47, 62, 64–5** are originals), though 'Do' is also common (e.g. the originals **35, 47, 49**), and they are combined in **52, 80–81, 84**. Three restorations (**16–7, 38**, and cf **87**) use 'Reddo'. The confirmations are most commonly forms of 'Concedo et confirmo',[185] though a bare 'Confirmo'[186] or 'Concedo'[187] also occurs Beyond these there are two cases of 'Firmo' (**48, 96**) and isolated forms of 'Confirmo. . . et laudo' (**48**), 'Confirmo . . . et roboro' (**70**) and 'Confirmo . . . et sanctio' (**24**). In three grants and one confirmation the archbishop's action is said to be for his soul and those of his predecessors (**21**) or predecessors and successors (**25, 47, 51**). Only two texts, both in copies, save the rights of the archbishop (**18**) or bishop (**72**).

A feature which is specially characteristic of the whole group of acts is the shifting use of singular and plural throughout the document. Lanfranc in his letters uses singular and plural almost indifferently (though usually consistently). While friends and superiors are generally addressed in the singular, subjects are sometimes addressed in the plural, sometimes in the singular, and without obvious reasons for either. Anselm virtually invariably uses the singular to all correspondents in his letters. The probable acts in his name are in the singular with the qualified exception of the mixed **17–8, 21, 25** and **26**. All of these have one plural form in a text otherwise entirely in the singular, and in **25** one of the two mss has the singular. Only the thoroughly suspicious **+20** and **23** use the plural form consistently. Ralph's usage may have been more uneven. Setting aside the manifestly inauthentic **+43** and **+54**, in five charters, of which **38–9** are originals, he speaks in the singular; in nine, of which six (**35–6, 46–9**) are originals,[188] he uses both singular and plural, while

---

[185] 12, 18, 23, 51, 53, 55–6, 61, 97.
[186] 5, 13, 72, 85.
[187] 26, 86.
[188] cf too +33.

in three, all known only in copies (**44**, **50**, **59**), the whole is cast in the plural. Under William only four charters (of which **80** is an original) use the singular exclusively—though in each case there is only one word to indicate this; in twelve, of which six (**62–6**, **81**) are originals, there is a mixture of both, while in twelve more, none an original, he is made to speak entirely in the plural. While then Ralph and William may well have used the consistent plural form, there is no surviving original in which they do, and in those known only from copies the practice may well be that of the later scribe rather than of the ultimate exemplar. By 1145 there is convincing evidence from originals that Theobald was using plural forms, though still not consistently.[189]

FINAL CLAUSES

In copies the elements following the *dispositio* are more than usually vulnerable to amputation by a scribe with a strictly functional understanding of his task. Nevertheless a number of the acts end abruptly with the *dispositio*, even in originals.[190] Those that are more complex deploy the expected variety of forms. The *iniunctio* clause, derived from royal practice and declining steadily through the century, appears in some form in six acts of William, one an original, but with no consistent formulation. The clearest cases are the ominous **77–8**, both for Leominster, and the more uncertain **84**, all copies. In the other examples the form can barely be distinguished from the admonition element in the sanctions clause (**61**, **63**, **72**, **85**). Clauses comparable to the *corroboratio* are very rare indeed, however liberally one interprets the category. Apart from the sealing clauses discussed earlier, which are virtually confined to texts which are doubtful or worse,[191] the nearest one gets in authentic acts are the half clause in **24** referring to confirmation 'signo dominice crucis Cristi'—the more strikingly since the charter bears the archbishop's seal as well as his subscription—and the thoroughly improbable +**20**: 'scripto hoc corroboramus'.

The sanction clause appears much more widely; two indeed are little more than a sanction attached to a royal grant (**5**, **24**). The three elements of conventional diplomatic analysis can only be applied very imperfectly to this disparate collection, but forms of admonition, cursing and blessing are all found here. One rough parallel to the admonition occurs fairly widely—a request to

---

[189] Saltman, *Theobald* 223–4 shows that the plural became commonplace in Theobald's later years; for originals in the plural without the primatial style, and therefore probably before 1145 see his nos 32, 104, 113 (where the original is now known) and 205, but 151, 161 are mixed, and 29, 38 are entirely in the singular.

[190] For example 14, 38, 46.

[191] With the possibly exceptions of the eccentric 34, and 42 which is very doubtful.

the recipients (**6, 63**) or the archbishop's successors (**17, 21, 25, 51, 85**) to maintain the gift, though only **63** is an original, and only the dubious **85** is followed by a blessing and a curse. A suspiciously conventional admonition ends the enigmatic **23**. Unlike their successors, Anselm, Ralph and William were almost as free with their blessings as their curses.[192] In several cases, none an original, they offered only rewards to those who honoured their decision—while **31** is both dubious and unusual in its context, **44** occurs in a letter to a brother bishop and **50** ends an indulgence, **58** ends a straightforward gift of a church and tithes and **86** a general confirmation. There is a particularly curious case with **81**; although there is nothing there in the surviving original, all three later copies, conceivably from another exemplar, add 'Pax benefactoribus suis', but after the witness-list and place. The two additions to royal charters for Rochester (**5** in an early copy, and the original **24**), and the less secure copies of **18, 21** and **84** confine themselves to curses on those who infringe the grant, the Rochester and Chester acts with an almost gleeful emphasis. The remainder, in the names of Ralph and William, combine both blessings and curses; here too **48**, Ralph's great privilege for Lewes, stands out as the only original, but the apparently credible **56** and **70** as well as the more dubious **85** follow the same pattern.

Cases of a final *apprecatio* are very rare. A treble 'Amen' occurs at the end of Anselm's anathema in **24**, a double one (or more) is said to have ended the lost ***95**, and a single one occurs in the two later copies of **86**, if not in the earliest. Two more elaborate forms, 'Dominus sit vobiscum' and ''Deus pacis et dilectionis sit semper vobiscum' occur in copies of unrelated grants for Hereford and Holme (**71, 73**).

ESCHATOCOL

Those acts which do not end with the *dispositio*, a sanction clause or an *apprecatio* may present any or several of four elements, a farewell, a witness-list, a place or date. A form of 'Vale' or 'Valete' now ends one or more versions of eighteen acts, though only three are originals; in all three cases (**15, 63, 66**) it is not expanded to make it clear whether the form should be singular or plural[193]. Naturally it may have been present in more if the originals had survived, but the opposite is at least possible. In **77** it is only present in the later of the two copies; more strikingly, the first early modern transcriber of **42** omitted it, but his two successors, deriving their texts from his, added

---

[192] Saltman, *Theobald* 212; *EEA* ii pp. lxviii–ix.
[193] The copies are 13, 21, 25, 31, 42, 56, 59, 61, 70, 77, 78, 82, 93–4, 96.

it. While many instances occur at the end of relatively informal acts or letters, six conclude what appear to be more solemn grants, if only **63** is an original.[194] The case of **15,** an original for Christ Church, is more striking, since 'Val.' follows an elaborate witness list. Such a combination is unusual; Saltman found only one original, also for Christ Church, with such a combination, and only ten copies, while Professor Cheney found none, and both were dealing with much larger samples.[195]

A further twenty-four[196] have at least some of a witness-list but no farewell, and ten of these are originals. In two early cases the witnesses are in the nominative, introduced by 'Testes horum sunt' (**15**) or a simple 'Testes' (**16**); in the rest they are in the ablative, preceded by 'T.' (**36, 62, 64–5**), 'Test.' (**35, 49**) or 'Teste' (**80–81**). On this basis one clearly should not expand the 'T.' or 'Test.' of a copy as 'Testibus' without some thought. The copies follow a similar pattern: two in the nominative, 'De hoc testes sunt' (**37**) and 'Testes' (**55**), the remainder in the ablative introduced by 'Testibus' (**52, 53, 74–5**, though one copy of **53** and **74** reads 'Teste'), 'Teste' (**84–5, 92, 97**), 'Test.' (**26, 87**), 'Testante' (**9**) or 'T' (**39**). The very suspect copy of +**88** alone has 'Testimonio' followed by a genitive. The mandates, whether original or copy, have no witness list, though the testimony for Sées in **92** is only a confirmation by implication. If most of the witnessed grants and confirmations deal with the lands and rights of the sees and dioceses of Canterbury and Rochester, there are credible single cases also for Sées and Thorney (**97**), as well as the dubious **23** for Norwich. The numbers of witnesses in the originals range from twenty-seven in **80**, twenty-three in **81** and twelve in **65** down to five in **36**. In copies, where the likelihood of abbreviation is great, the range is from eleven in **53** and eight in **26** to a single witness in **68** and **84**, always excepting the wholly distinct and suspicious **23**, with its twelve bishops and nine abbots, and the otherwise unexampled corporate attestation of **68**. In three originals (**16** and the already long **80–81**) the originals end their list with 'et alii plures' or 'cum multis aliis', so the appearance of similar forms in the copies **53, 75, 87** and **97** does not necessarily imply abbreviation. The witnesses are generally organised with the clergy in order of office, followed by monks preceding canons, and both normally preceding chaplains and clerks,

---

[194] 22, 25, 56, 61, 63, 70.

[195] Saltman, *Theobald* 223; *EEA* ii pp. lxxiii-iv.

[196] For this purpose I assume that the witness list of +88 once stood at the end of an authentic document of 1126 × 8, and so I have used it for these calculations, if not in the rest of the discussion of the charters.

British Library, Campbell ch. vii. 5   No. 16

Canterbury Dean and Chapter C. A. 1193   No. 15

PLATE I

Public Record Office, DL 27/46   No. 36

Public Record Office, E40/6689   No. 47

PLATE II

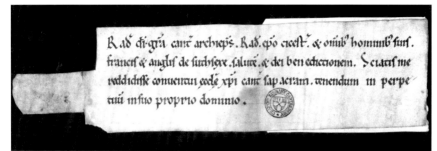

Canterbury Dean and Chapter, C. A. S 250   No. 38

Public Record Office, E40/15739   No. 81

Public Record Office, DL 25/106   No. 65

PLATE III

Canterbury, Dean and Chapter, C. A. L70

Canterbury, Dean and Chapter, C. A. L70   No. 66

PLATE IV

followed by the laity, but there are enough exceptions to impose caution.[197] A comparison of the very similar **80–81**, written by different scribes for the same beneficiary and apparently on the same occasion, offers further warnings; not only does one scribe give four less witnesses than the other, but he distinguishes the chaplains from the clerks, while the other treats them all as clerks.[198]

The difficulty of articulating this restricted group of witnessed charters with other surviving material on the archbishops' inner circle has been discussed above. Some eighty probably distinct persons appear in witness lists commanding some confidence, always remembering the possibility that (for example) not all Alans are one man, and that canon Siward/Simon may not be the only person who used two names, just as Godfrey of Malling might appear also as Godfrey of Thanington or Godfrey the steward.[199] More than half of these appear only once, or only in the two closely related and apparently contemporary versions of the same grant, **80–81**. Occasionally this is rather surprising; of the five known priors of Christ Church of the period only two appear, once each, in charters of good repute, and two more, again once, in texts under grave suspicion.[200] This is scarcely to be explained by the existence of a clear distinction between the archbishop's household and the monastic community, for there an abundant evidence in both the charters and the other evidence that there was no such boundary, even under William, the only canon of the four.

The clerical witnesses who do appear with some regularity are John and Helewise, successively archdeacons of Canterbury. Helewise had also been archdeacon of Rochester, and attests once as such, twice simply as archdeacon and four times as archdeacon of Canterbury. John attests six times as archdeacon, and a further seven times as bishop of Rochester. Of the two others to occur more than three times Alan the clerk (and sometimes chaplain), appears to attest three times under Ralph, three times under William,

---

[197] In 26 the prior of Christ Church and three monks precede the archdn, in 49 laymen and clerks appear mixed together after a prior and two monks, in 80 one chaplain precedes the monks, though more follow them. Ansfrid the steward appears in the witness-lists of 80–81 as if a layman, but in 49, 53, 64 ahead of at least one clerk.

[198] Brett, *English church* 108, 180.

[199] The saintly hermit of Farne called himself, or was called, at one time or another Tosti, William and Bartholomew (Simeon i 296); for Siward/Simon see below, no. 64n. For Godfrey, Urry, *Canterbury* 53–4.

[200] 26, 85; +20, +88 . Ernulf did attest twice as bp of Rochester, however—36, 53.The appearance of Theoderic as prior, when he can have been at best second or third prior, in 49, and of an otherwise unknown Thomas in 97, who may well have been in office in another house, do not really affect the issue.

and may be the same man who appears four times under Theobald,[201] but is clearly distinct from Alan the monk who attests with him in **80–81**. Lastly, William's companion at St Osyth's, Siward, who attests **64** is probably also the Simon, canon and chaplain, who attests **62, 80** and **81**. The most frequent figure among the laity is Ansfrid the steward; under Ralph and William he is addressed in **35** and **62**, and attests nine times.[202] Two other apparent laymen, Robert son of Riculf and William of St Alban (a knight of Ansfrid the steward),[203] attest four times each under Ralph and William, but it is notable that all William of St Alban's attestations, and three of Robert son of Riculf's, concern the church of Bexley. In short, in the surviving acts witness clauses are relatively unusual. Where they occur the bishop of Rochester, the archdeacon of Canterbury and the steward are often among them, but their evidence provides no convincing image of a definable core of household members, regularly occurring whoever the beneficiary. Since there is every reason to suppose that all the archbishops did have members of the household who accompanied them frequently on their extensive travels, and were in close and regular communication with them, the evidence of the witness lists tells one more about the charters than the household, at least in this period.

As with royal acts of the period, a place of grant is sometimes found in the archbishops' acts, but a date very rarely. The only authentic acts with a date are two originals for Lewes (**47–8**), almost certainly written by the beneficiaries, and in both the formulation is thoroughly idiosyncratic, with the grant also having a place of issue and in one case 'Data . . . per manum Iohannis cancellarii et archidiaconi', in the other 'Data . . . in manu filii nostri domni H. . . . prioris'. There is no other evidence for John or anyone else bearing the title of chancellor to the archbishop, and both cases the formulae appear to be derived, directly or indirectly, from the usage of the papal chancery. The only Lewes original which may have been written by a Canterbury scribe, **49**, is also the only one with a form of address and a witness list entirely conventional in royal practice. Four further originals and three credible copies for several beneficiaries do however have a place of issue. For the most part the grants are made close to the beneficiaries: of the two Lewes grants with places given, one was the archbishop's manor of South Malling, almost

[201] 35–6, 39, 62, 80–81; Saltman, *Theobald* nos 55, 86, 161, 310.

[202] Above pp. xlvi–vii.

[203] *Text. Roff.* fos 196v-7r no. 177. R. Eales, 'Local loyalties in Norman England: Kent in Stephen's reign', *ANS* viii (1986) 95–8 provides a useful overview of the changes in Kentish lay society over the period.

within sight of the priory, if the other was rather farther away at Charing. Another grant of land in Lavant is set at Pagham, also a large archiepiscopal estate (**37**); Jordan received the church of Bexley, and Rochester a general confirmation, at Canterbury (**62, 87**); Aldgate received its two grants of Bexley church at the archiepiscopal manor of Aldington in Surrey (**80–81**), and Gervase of Cornhill the confirmation of his wife's inheritance at Lambeth (**65**). On this slight evidence beneficiaries seem to seize their moment to secure charters, rather than seeking them out. The one exception, which may point to a very different future, is William's confirmation for Thorney (**97**), also given at Lambeth, and perhaps to petitioners who travelled there to get it.[204]

PRINCIPLES OF SELECTION AND EDITION

In general these are the same as those in preceding volumes, but the survival of substantial letter collections from Lanfranc and Anselm presents some special problems. The distinction between charters attributed to Lanfranc and his letters seems to be clear, and there is no overlap between the edition by Clover and Gibson and this collection. The editors of Anselm's letters have been more willing to include documents properly described as *acta*, so **16–17, 31** below were also printed by Dom Schmitt, as was **14**, printed here because it survives as a sealed original, though the content would normally have excluded it. Of the surviving letters attributed to archbishop Ralph three are included (**42, 44** and **59**) since they are in varying degrees acts of authority. The fourth is his *Requisitio,* a long and impassioned defence of the rights of Canterbury addressed to pope Calixtus II in 1119.[205] It certainly deserves further study, but in another context. Only one letter of William is known; addressed to the monks of Worcester it is far removed in purpose from an act, is conveniently accessible and has not been reprinted here.[206] There is one special case, a purported document on the primacy dispute, which has been attributed to Lanfranc. As there is no reason to suppose this document existed in any form before the Reformation, it includes no information

---

[204] For the use of Lambeth as a residence by the archbps long before the formal exchange with Rochester at the end of the twelfth century see C.N.L. Brooke, 'London and Lambeth in the eleventh and twelfth centuries', *Report of the Friends of Lambeth Palace Library for 1972* (1973) 11–23; T. Tatton-Brown, 'The beginnings of Lambeth Palace', *ANS* xxiv (2001) 203–14 esp. 204–5.

[205] *Historians York* ii 228–51.

[206] Bethell, 'Black monks' 696–7.

suggesting any earlier unrecognised exemplar and it is far from clear that it is intended to represent an act of the archbishop rather than of one of the councils of 1072, it has been omitted from the main sequence but printed in the Appendix for completeness.

Because this is so early a group, one can be less confident than usual about the expansion of names—for instance, in principle the forms 'Cantuarie' or 'Cantuariensium' might replace the conventional 'Cantuariensis'. Though no original gives proof of such a usage, and **14, 46, 48, 65** do expand in the usual way, the very early copies **25–6** both expand 'Cantuarie'. For this reason the names are represented as they appear in the base manuscript, without expansion. Similarly, in the previous Canterbury volumes Professor Cheney used '+' to indicate both charters which he thought manifestly forged and some he thought suspicious. It should by now be clear that such a convention in this collection would require a whole range of crosses of various sizes and intensities, and only those texts which seem more or less indefensible in their present form have been so marked. The measurements of originals in other volumes in the series are usually signalled as approximate. This is not done here, not because the measurements are more exact but because no original is sufficiently symmetrical to allow precision. Approximation should be understood in every case. Post-medieval copies of surviving documents are not noticed unless they have some importance in the transmission or publication of the act concerned.

LANFRANC 1070–1089

+1. Canterbury: priory of St Gregory

Record of its foundation, the translation there from Lyminge of the bodies of saints Edburga, Mildred and Ethelburga, and of relics of former archbishops, the establishment of six canons with care of the souls of the poor of the hospital, with two clerks to serve each canon. The church may conduct baptisms and offer burial without charge to the clergy and laity, and direct schools of music and grammar for the region within its precinct, and to answer only to the archbishop and his successors. A long list of lands, rents, churches and the tithes of the knights of the see is confirmed as the endowment.   [1085 × 3 Sept. 1087]

B = Cambridge UL Ll. 2. 15 (cartulary of St Gregory) fos 1–2. s. xiii med.

Pd H. Boehmer, *Die Fälschungen Erzbischof Lanfranks* 173–5; J.C. Dickinson, *The origins of the Austin canons* 280–2; *St Gregory's cartulary* 1–3; partial text in *Mon. Angl.* vi(2) 615; M. Bateson in *EHR* xviii (1903) 712.

Lanfrancus Dei gratia Cantuariensis archiepiscopus amicis suis omnibus et fidelibus sed et cuntis Cristi fidelibus, eternam Domini salutem et eius benedictionem. Ad universorum notitiam volumus pervenire nos extra urbis nostre Cantuariensis portam aquilonarem in honorem beatissimi patroni nostri et totius Anglie Gregorii pape construxisse ecclesiam pro redemptione anime mee et domini nostri regis Anglorum Willelmi. In quam deferri fecimus beatarum virginum Ædburgis et Mildrithe corpora, necnon et corpus regine Northanimbrorum Ethelburge prefate sancte Aedburgis sororis germane. Que videlicet corpora aput villam nostram de Limminges ab antiquo in ecclesia ipsius ville tumulata inventa sunt. Sed et plurimam partem de reliquiis sanctorum pontificum qui ante nos ecclesie Cristi prefuere ipsi ecclesie beati Gregorii ad eius honorem et munimen contulimus. In hac autem ecclesia sex presbiteros in ea administraturos constituimus communiter et canonice victuros, quibus curam animarum commisimus pauperum in hospitali e regione ipsius ecclesie constituto degentium, quod et nos construi noviter et ditari fecimus. Ad dictorum autem sex sacerdotum ministerium et ad officium ecclesiasticum tam nocte quam die in ipsa ecclesia horis canonicis rite peragendum presbiteris singulis binos deputauimus clericos, ex prelibato hospitali duodecim cotidianas prebendas ad victus perpetuo percepturos. Sane advenarum et hospitum, civium quoque et aliorum provinciarum prout quisque a suo sacerdote licentiam habuerit, confessionem a prefatis sex presbiteris beati Gregorii suscipiendam penitentibusque iniungendam penitentiam constituimus. Baptismum etiam in ipsa ecclesia celebrari decrevimus. Sepulturam quoque venerabilem et liberam presbiteris et clericis et utriusque sexus laicis absque omni exactione pretii inibi fieri precepimus. Sed et intra septa sepedicte ecclesie scolas urbis et viculorum eius tam grammatice quam musice regi debere statuentes, earum regimen prepositis sacerdotum ipsius ecclesie et eorum dispositioni commisimus. Hanc autem ecclesiam eiusque cuntas pertinentias sed et prepositos eius atque ministros in potestate nostra et successorum nostrorum dumtaxat retinentes, ab omni alterius ecclesiastice secularisve persone manu et ditione liberos esse decernimus. Hec autem sunt que ad sustentamen et usus necessarios ecclesie ipsius et ministrorum eius quiete et libere et absque omni cuiuslibet exactione inperpetuum possidenda^a: terram de Hugifeld cum omnibus pertinentiis eius in bosco et plano cum molendino de Tuniford; terram de Yethinges et de Ritherle cum pertinentiis earum in bos[fo. iv]co et plano et terram de Pinkesteghele cum pertinentiis eius in masagiis et ortis; in urbe autem Cantuaria et eius suburbio redditus quinquaginta quatuor solidorum et sex denariorum; ecclesiam quoque sancte Marie que sita est super portam urbis aquilonalem et ecclesiam sancte crucis que est super portam occidentalem et ecclesiam sancti Dunstani extra eandem portam occidentalem, ecclesiam etiam sancti Bartholomei de Waltam cum pertinentiis eius et cum terra de Yocclete; ecclesiam sancte Margarite de Beatrichesdenne cum masagiis et bosco ipsius denne. Has ecclesias cum earum pertinentiis in usus proprios ipsi ecclesie beati Gregorii contulimus inperpetuum possidendas; aput Fordwich autem unum masagium trium circiter iugerum cum duobus molendinis in domo una. Preterea dedimus eidem ecclesie decimas de dominiis militum nostrorum quos in Cantia feodavimus, scilicet: totas decimas dominii de Tanintune quam villam Godefrido contulimus, et dominii de Gosehale et de Golstanestune quas villulas Aernoldo dedimus, et dominii de Fliete quod feodum dedimus Osberno, et dominii de Bereham quam villulam Rogero dedimus, et dominii de Wedetune quam Radulfo dedimus, et dominii de Watekere et de Wadehale et de Langedene et de Denstede quod [totum]^b unum feodum duobus militibus contulimus Nigello et Roberto, et decimas totas dominii de Lenham quam Godefrido donavimus, et dominii de Leueland et de Godintune quas villulas Ricardo contulimus et Roberto, et dominii de Plukele quod Willelmo dedimus, et dominii de Einesford, quam villam alteri Willelmo dedimus; aput Wingeham vero decimam terre que appellatur Herteslande. Has omnes decimas totas et integras prefate ecclesie beati Gregorii libere et quiete percipiendas et in perpetuum possidendas contulimus; ceterum in Risseburnia de ducentis acris a possessoribus earum totidem garbas, apud Sulliford de quinquaginta acris totidem garbas, aput Herebaldune de ducentis acris garbas totidem. Volumus ergo et auctoritate qua largiente Deo fungimur districte precepimus quatinus prelibata ecclesia beati Gregorii nostri et totius Anglorum terre patroni, ministri quoque eius in ea perpetuo Deo annuente servituri prefatas possessiones et redditus quas ei concessimus libere habeant et inperpetuum absque omni cuiuslibet exactione quiete possideant. Statuimus ergo et sub interminatione anathematis inhibemus ne quis hanc nostre confirmationis paginam infringere vel ei aliquatenus temere contraire presumat. Omnibus autem augmentum aliquod seu bona quelibet prefate ecclesie iuste [fo.2] conferentibus aut in posterum collaturis omnipotentis Dei gratiam et benedictionem hic et eternaliter ab eodem summo bonorum omnium largitore conferri deposcimus. Huius vero statuti nostri et confirmationis nostre testes esse voluimus Gundulfum Rofensem episcopum, Scolandum abbatem sancti Augustini Cantuarie, Guidonem et Esbernum monachos, magistrum Ebroinum, magistrum Lefwinum clericos, Godefridum, Ærnoldum, Rogerium, Nigellum, Robertum, milites cum aliis quampluribus.

ᵃ A verb seems to be missing. Boehmer supplied dedimus.   *ᵇ* B *obscured;* totum *conjectured by Boehmer*

For Lanfranc's foundation at St Gregory's, and the hospital of St John, Northgate see Eadmer, *Historia* 15–16, Gibson, *Lanfranc* 186–90, 228, T. Tatton-Brown, 'Beginnings' 41–52. As it stands, this text cannot be authentic. The use of the first person plural throughout, the gift of churches 'in proprios usus', the reference to the charter as 'hanc paginam', the occurrence of two otherwise unrecorded 'magistri' among the witnesses and the phrasing of the text throughout are wholly improbable before the later twelfth century, or even later. The salutation reappears in the charter of Stephen Langton (*Acta S. Langton* no. 40, *St Gregory's cartulary* no. 11), and the text we have may well have been drawn up after 1200. Apart from the equally unlikely charter in the name of Anselm (below 20) the earliest document in the cartulary to command any confidence is 68 below, and even that is problematic. That is not to say that some of the information here lacks early support. The translations of SS. Mildred, Edburga and Ethelburga are said to have occurred in 1085, and the claim that St Mildred had been at Lyminge 'ab antiquo' was already being advanced by St Gregory before 1100, though hotly contested; Colker, 'Polemic' 60–4, D. Rollason, *The Mildrith legend* 21–25. Many of the knights in the witness-list, and tenants whose tithes are granted, can be identified from the documents in the *Domesday monachorum*, though the tenant of Eynsford under Lanfranc seems to have been Ralph fitz Ospac, not William (*Domesday monachorum* 46–7, 88, 105; Du Boulay, *Lordship* 342). The reference to St Gregory the Great as 'totius Anglie terre patronus' is characteristic of claims being made at Christ Church in just these years (P. Hayward in *Journal of ecclesiastical history*, forthcoming).

+*2.   Canterbury: hospital of St John the Baptist, Northgate

Grant of indulgence of forty days.   [15 August 1070 × 28 May 1089]

> Mentioned only, as the first in a list of indulgences for the hospital, in letters patent prepared for the hospital on 29 June 1375. Pd in Duncombe, *History* 254–5 from the muniments of Northgate, destroyed in June 1942. See also *EEA* ii no.*7: 'Lanfrancus archiepiscopus fundator hospitalis xl dies relaxationis concessit.'

> The scale of the indulgence is quite improbable for the supposed date. For the foundation see the note to the last charter. Lanfranc established it as a house for men and women: 'Ordinavit ... eis de suo vestitum et victum quotidianum'. No charter in his name survived into the eighteenth century, and it is possible that this indulgence was never recorded in a charter, genuine or forged.

+3.   Durham cathedral

Confirmation, at the command of pope Gregory (VII) and king William (I) and request of bishop William in a council at London , to the church of Durham of the whole diocese from Tees to Tweed with the ancient sees of Hexham and Lindisfarne, with Carlisle, Teviotdale and their territories. As pope Gregory had commanded him and archbishop Thomas of York and the king by letters brought by bishop William, he has ordered the removal of the canons from the church of St Cuthbert and the establishment of monks in the cathedral. He records that the pope has put the community under the protection of St Peter, and granted the prior the seat of an abbot on the left side of the choir, with free disposition of all the affairs of the community by the assent of the king and bishop, with the first voice in the election of a bishop and the first place in his counsels. The prior is to dispose of all his churches, or appoint proper clergy to them, in whatever diocese they may be, free of interference from any bishop, and to enjoy the same rights in his diocese as the dean of York does in his. The prior is to be elected by the brethren, not to be removed without good cause, and to deal with all pleas, within and without, by their counsel. No bishop is to exact any aid from their lands or churches. All these rights are set out more fully in charters of bishop William and archbishop Thomas (I).

London 'in concilio' [1082 × late 1085]

> A = Durham UL, Durham Cathedral muniments, 1. 1. Archiep. 3. Endorsed, s. xii, with s. xiii addns: [carta] Lanfranci archiepiscopi [Cantuar'] secundum cartam Willelmi primi [Dunelm' episcopi]. 93 × 327, with tongue and tie. Seal lost.
> B = ibid. Cartuarium I (priory cartulary) fo. 197 s. xv in. C = ibid. Cartuarium III (priory cartulary) fo. 66r-v s. xv in.
> Pd from B in *Historiae Dunelmensis scriptores tres* (Surtees Soc. ix 1839) Appx. x-xi, from A in *Feodarium prioratus Dunelmensis* ed W. Greenwell (Surtees Soc. lviii 1872) lxxv-lxxvi.

Lanfrancus Dei gratia Dorbonensis[a] archiepiscopus omnibus Anglie episcopis tam presentibus quam futuris, salutem. Noveritis nos hoc scriptum ex domni pape Gregorii septimi, et ex precepto domini nostri regis Anglorum Gwillelmi, petente Gwillo[b] fratre nostro Dun' coepiscopo, in concilio[c] Lundoniensi conscripsisse. Presenti igitur carta subscribimus, testificamur et auctoritate nobis a Deo collata perpetuis temporibus confirmantes roboramus quatinus episcopalis sedes, una cum beati Cuthberti corpore, cum omni integritate[d] sue diocesis inviolabiliter permaneat, et cum omni parrochia que est inter Tese et Twede, cum ecclesia Hagustaldensi, et Lindisfarnensi ubi antiquitus episcopales sedes fuerant, et Carleolo, et Tevietedale et omnibus provinciis adiacentibus inviolabiliter eternis temporibus perseveret. Domnus enim papa prefatus Gregorius nobis et fratri nostro Th' Ebor' archiepiscopo et regi Gwillelmo in vi obedientie hoc nobis iniunxit, quatinus eius susceptis litterarum decretis, que deferente Gwillelmo Dun' episcopo venerabili nobis direxerat, nos eadem que sua et beati Petri auctoritate statuerat nostris scriptorum munimentis confirmaremus, et omnibus per Angliam futuris episcopis rata fuisse statuta et sanxita a sede apostolica testificaremur. Quare scire vos volumus, quia omnia que supra meminimus tam a domno papa quam a nobis inviolata et inconcussa eternis perseverare temporibus, una cum rege prefato Gwillelmo et Thom' Eboracensi, in concilio[c] apud Lundonias definivimus, et sub anathematis interdictione prohibemus. Volumus itaque, concedimus atque decrevimus quatinus, remotis canonicis de beati Cuthberti ecclesia, monachi ibidem Deo servituri introducantur, et ordo monasticus ibidem canonice observetur. Testificamur etiam quia domnus papa omnes fratres ibi Deo congregandos sub beati Petri et sua protectione suscepit. Prioribus vero ipsius ecclesie sedem abbatis in choro sinistro concessit, et liberam eis in omnibus dispositionem, concedente rege et Gwillelmo episcopo, contulit quatinus primam vocem cum capitulo in episcopi electione habeant, et primi dextere episcopi ipsius ecclesie collaterales existant. Ecclesias vero suas in quacumque diocesie fuerint libere pro voluntate sua disponant, vel in manu sua teneant, seu honestis personis de eis tenendas absque omni episcoporum fatigatione vel inquietatione distribuant, et quicquid honoris vel potestatis decani Ebor' sub archiepiscopo possident apostolica et nostra auctoritate conservent. Prior vero communi consilio fratrum eligatur, et nisi rationabili causa exigente et conventu ipsum meritis suis exigentibus refutante minime deponetur, et tam interius quam exterius omnis causa cum ipsius et fratrum consilio libere disponatur, et nullum omnino auxilium de ecclesiis eorum vel terris ab aliquo episcoporum exigatur. Que omnia carta[f] Willelmi episcopi et Tome archiepiscopi plenius et perfectius contestantur. Hec igitur omnia plene concedimus et sub anathemate inconcussa permanere precipimus. Val'. Teste Gundulfo Rofensi episcopo, et Remigio Lincolniensi episcopo, Paulo abbate Sancti Albani, et Thuroldo abbate de Burh, et multis aliis personis in concilio^g Lundoniarum.^{h}

^{a} Dorobornensis B; Dororbosien' C ^{b} Gwillelmo BÇ ^{c} consilio B ^{d} omni (*superscript*) integtate A; omni integritate BC ^{e} dioscesi A ^{f} carta ABC ^{g} consilio BC ^{h} etc *add.* B

Were it genuine, before the news of the death of pope Gregory VII, who died on 25 May 1085, could reach England, since he is mentioned as apparently still living. A forgery of the second half of the twelfth century, to which the script clearly belongs. G.V. Scammell, *Hugh du Puiset, bishop of Durham* (1956) Appx IV 300–7, identified the hand of this forgery with that of the charters in the names of bp William and archbp Thomas noted below, and Offler in *Durham episcopal charters* 21–25. Offler and D. Bates. 'The forged charters of William the Conqueror and bishop William of St Calais' in *Anglo-Norman Durham* 111–24 at 115 rejected that identification, and Bates at 120 proposed a period in the early 1170s for the main campaign of forgery, to which this document is linked by script and content. The spurious charter of bp William, Offler's no. 3a dated '1082', contains the substance of the earlier section to 'nostra auctoritate conservent'. The text of the equally spurious act of archbp Thomas, *EEA* v no. +3 , cites the charter of Lanfranc, but is generally more remote from it until the passage near the end from 'Prior vero communi consilio' to 'episcoporum exigatur', which is virtually identical. There is no reason to suppose that the forgery here is an adaptation of any earlier and authentic act. See too the forgeries in the name of kg William I printed as Bates, *Acta* nos 108–11. The discussion of *EEA* xx no. 15 calls the related act of archbp Roger of 1154 × 64, defended by Bates, into new doubt, but without affecting the probable date of the confection of the Lanfranc act.

*+4. Glastonbury abbey

Grant of an indulgence of thirty days for visitors to the house.

[15 August 1070–28 May 1089]

Mentioned only in Trinity College, Cambridge ms R. 5. 33 (James no. 764) fos 77–87, an inventory of the charters of Glastonbury compiled in the mid-thirteenth century. On fo. 78 (pd in *Iohannis . . . Glastoniensis chronica sive historia de rebus Glastoniensibus* ed. T. Hearne (1726) ii 378–9) occurs the section:

Dies indulgentiarum Glaston', unde cartas non habemus, licet habuerimus. De sancto Dunstano c. dies indulgentie. De sancto Lanfranco archiepiscopo Cantuariensi xxx dies. . . . . .Innocentius papa iii hec omnia confirmavit.

The indulgence from Dunstan is plainly a fiction, and the claim that Lanfranc gave so large a grant at this date is scarcely more credible. There is no other surviving trace of the bull of Innocent III (C.R. and M.G. Cheney, *The letters of pope Innocent III concerning England and Wales* no. 1161). The manuscript is described in detail in Crick, 'Antiquity' 217–43, esp. 223, 242.

5. Rochester cathedral priory

Note attached to William II's grant of the manor of Haddenham (Bucks.) in which he confirms his gift to the church as the king has ratified it, and excommunicates any who seek to infringe the grant. [Sept. 1087 × 28 May 1089]

B = Strood MALSC DRc/ R 1 (Textus Roffensis) fo. 213 no. 206. s. xii in.
Pd *Text. Roff.* 215–6; cal. *Reg. regum* i no.301, Flight, *Bishops and monks* 261 no. 201.

Ego Lanfrancus, non meis meritis sed gratia Dei archiepiscopus, hoc donum meum quod regia auctoritate confirmatum est confirmo, et auctoritate Dei omnipotentis et omnium sanctorum excommunico omnes illos qui prędictum manerium de prędicta ęcclesia vel abstulerint vel auferre temptaverint vel ablatum ab aliis cognita veritate receperint vel retinuerint. Ęterna pęna cum Iuda proditore sit eis nisi ad satisfactionem venerint.

For Lanfranc's style here compare *Letters of Lanfranc* nos 9, 22, 43, 47. Lanfranc's extensive holding at Haddenham, formerly land of earl Tosti, is recorded in *DB* i 143d. The royal charter exists in two versions. The first is found only in the Textus Roffensis, and excites no obvious suspicion. By c. 1200 Rochester had produced a second by conflating this with William II's grant of Lambeth (*Text. Roff.* fo. 211r-v no. 202, *Reg. regum* i no. 302). Here Lanfranc's note was incorporated in the main text in a slightly modified form:

A = BL Campbell charter vii.1 (*Facsimiles of national manuscripts*, 1865–8, i no. 4), a single sheet version of ? s. xii ex., without any indication that it ever bore a seal. B = BL Cotton Domitian x (Rochester cartulary) fos 107–8. s. xiii in. C = Maidstone CKS DRb/ Ar2 (Registrum Temporalium, formerly DRc/ R 3) fo. 11v. s. xiv. There are royal confirmations in PRO Charter Roll of 50 Henry III C53/55 m. 1 (original in Strood MALSC DRc/ T 60), PRO Charter Roll 3 Edward I C53/63 m. 2 (thence *Cal. Ch. Rolls* ii 194–5), PRO Charter Roll 9 Edward III C53/122 m. 8 no. 36, PRO Charter Roll 10 Edward III C53/123 m. 25 no. 51, PRO Patent Roll 2 Henry VI pt. 2 C66/413 m. 27, PRO Patent Roll 12 Edward IV pt. 2 C66/530 mm. 14–9 (original in Strood MALSC DRc/ T 65), PRO Confirmation Roll 1 Henry VIII pt. 8 C56/32 no. 2 (original in Strood MALSC DRc/ T 66). The text below is from A.
Cal. Flight, *Bishops and monks* 261 no. 202.

Ego Lanfrancus non meis meritis sed gratia Dei *Cantuar'* archiepiscopus hoc donum *regium et hanc regalem concessionem et confirmationem quantum in me est* confirmo et auctoritate Dei omnipotentis et omnium sanctorum excommunico omnes illos qui *hanc regiam munificentiam in aliqua sui parte infringere vel infirmare* temptaverint *vel aliquid de libertatibus ecclesie sancti Andree Roffensis concessis subtrahere* vel auferre cognita veritate *presumpserint,* eterna *sit eis* pena cum Iuda proditore nisi ad *congruam* satisfactionem venerint. *Amen.*

Passages in italics are adaptations of the original. The changes are intended to establish that the grant was a royal one confirmed by the archbp, rather than the reverse, and to incorporate a grant of every exemption from royal exactions. Another spurious act in the name of a kg William, surviving only in a copy of s. xiii² (Strood MALSC DRc/ T58/ 1), is printed as

Bates, *Acta* no. 228. It is a general confirmation of rights to Rochester 'sicut unquam melius habuit ecclesia Christi Cant' istas libertates et consuetudines', a clause reminiscent of the equally improbable *Reg. regum* ii nos 936 (from a copy of *c.* 1200), and 1867, known from a wholly unconvincing 'original' and copied into the early-thirteenth-century cartulary C (Flight, *Bishops and monks* nos 523–4). At the end appears the same confirmation clause in Lanfranc's name. The clause is surely intended to refer to a specific gift, as above, and not to a more general confirmation, so was presumably taken from the modified text here and applied to a quite different text afterwards. The general problem of Rochester's enduring enthusiasm for forgery is discussed by Brett, 'Forgery'.

6. Rochester cathedral

Grant of the manor of Haddenham for the feeding of the monks for the soul of the late king William (I) who gave the manor to him, for the soul of king William his son and for his own.   [Sept. 1087 × 28 May 1089]

B = Maidstone CKS DRb/ Ar2 (Registrum Temporalium, formerly DRc/ R 3) fo. 17v. s. xiv.
Pd Brett, 'A supplementary note on the charters attributed to archbishop Lanfranc' 525;
Flight, *Bishops and monks* 92 n. 7, cal. ibid. 262 no. 205.

Lanfrancus archiepiscopus Remigio episcopo, Hugoni de Bellocampo vicecomiti et ceteris amicis suis de Buchingehamscire et Roberto preposito suo de Hedenham, salutem. Sciatis me concessisse manerium meum quod vocatur Hedenham ecclesie sancti Andree infra civitatem Roffen' site ad victum monachorum Deo et eidem sancto inibi serviencium pro anima defuncti regis Willemi, qui mihi hoc dedit, et pro anima regis W. filii eius et pro mea. Et rogo[a] ut huius concessionis testes sitis si quando necessitas expostulaverit et c'.

[a]rego B

The absence of this charter from the Textus Roffensis is surprising, though not in itself a decisive objection to its authenticity. Flight 92 provides good arguments for supposing that 'Donum Lanfranci archiepiscopi de Hedenham', listed as no. xiv in the *capitulatio* to BL Cott. Dom. x, refers to this text, which probably stood on a leaf after fo. 106 which was later removed. Unlike the manipulated version of the last text, this is unambiguously a grant by Lanfranc, it is cast as one would expect in the first person singular, and it contains no obvious anachronisms. The bare 'archiepiscopus' of the *intitulatio* is paralleled in *Letters of Lanfranc* nos 28, 42, 48, 53–5, 60. The final clause is of a kind commoner in early texts than later (above pp. lxxviii–ix. and cf 17 below). By around 1200 Rochester preferred to claim that Haddenham was a direct gift of the king, as the later modification of 5 above reveals.

+7. Rochester cathedral

Notification to Thurstan the bailiff of Freckenham and his men of the hundred of Lackford that he has restored to the church and bishop Gundulf the manor of Freckenham with Isleham and the advowsons of their churches as free and quit as king William gave them to him, and as he holds the lands of Canterbury. Here and in all its other manors Rochester is to be free of all exactions (listed) secular or ecclesiastical, and answer to none but the church of Canterbury and the archbishop. [1087]

B = BL ms Cotton Vespasian A xxii (Rochester register) fo. 123v (formerly 127), s. xiii. C = BL Cotton Faust. B v (Historia Roffensis) fo. 68r-v, s. xv, a copy of an inspeximus by prior Richard and the convent of Christ Church, Canterbury, dated 5 Feb. 1333, which once apparently included three versions of this text, two in a spurious inspeximus in the name of Hubert Walter (*EEA* iii no. + 592) which inspects both the charter itself and the grant by Anselm (below, +28) purporting to inspect Lanfranc's text, and a third in an inspeximus in the name of archbp Boniface dated 19 July 1259 at Lambeth. Only the first of these is transcribed in the ms. D = Cotton Charter Vitellius B 3 (destroyed), another suspect inspeximus by archbp Boniface, dated 15 May 1254 at Lambeth, which includes Anselm's inspeximus. The charter is noticed briefly in Smith's catalogue of the Cotton charters before the fire of 1731 in Bodl. ms Smith 90 p. 37. E = Maidstone CKS DRb/ Ar2 (Registrum Temporalium, formerly DRc/ R 3) fo. 17v. s. xiv.

Pd *Reg Roff.* 359 (from B), 441 (from C), *Mon Angl.* (1673) iii 3, (1817) i 176 (from D). Cal. Flight, *Bishops and monks* 261 no. 203.

Lanfrancus Dei gratia archiepiscopus Cant' Thurstano preposito de Frekeham et ceteris hominibus liberis et servis in hundredo de Lacforde in Suffolchia salutem. Sciatis me sursum reddidisse ecclesie sancti Andree et Gundulpho episcopo Roffe manerium de Frakeham cum Iselham et ecclesiarum advocacionibus que appendent, quia de antiquo dominico et ordinaria subieccione illius ecclesie olim fuerunt, adeo libere et quiete sicut Willelmus rex illud mihi concessit, et sicut ego omnes terras ad ecclesiam Cant' spectantes teneo in dominico, in feodis, libertatibus, iusticiis, rectitudinibus, consuetudinibus in*a* omnimoda lege diocesana, toln and theam, land and stream, et omnibus aliis serviciis et iuribus novis et antiquis ita quod nulli alii in regno Anglie, in spiritualibus et*b* temporalibus ecclesia Roffensis vel clerus et*c* populus in Frekeham et Iselham vel in omnibus maneriis suis sit subiecta vel respondere teneatur nisi ecclesie Cantuariensi et archiepiscopo eiusdem. Huius autem concessionis*d* et restitucionis rogo quod testes sint, Herbertus episcopus Suffolchie et Baldewynus abbas sancti Eadmundi et clerus et populus totus in comitatibus Suffolchie et Kantebreggie, et omnes alii Cristi*e* fideles ad quorum notitiam futuris temporibus hoc factum perveniat. Acta sunt hec ad perpetuam rei memoriam *f*et sigilli mei impressione roborata anno incarnationis dominice*f* MLXXXVII°.

*ᵃ*et D   *ᵇ*aut C   *ᶜ*vel C   *ᵈ*constitutionis D   *ᵉ*om. D   *ᶠᶠ*Anno Domini E

There is an apparently genuine charter of William I granting Freckenham to archbp Lanfranc in Bates, *Acta* no. 226, *Reg. regum* i no. 47, and Lanfranc was staying at his manor there when he wrote *Letters of Lanfranc* no. 44. Nevertheless this charter is clearly spurious, from the attestation of bp Herbert, who did not become bishop until after Lanfranc's death, and from such anachronistic terms as 'ordinaria subiectio' and 'lex diocesana'. It appears to belong to the long series of charters forged at Rochester to defend the monks' title to these lands and churches, of which numerous examples are found below (+8, +27, +28, +54, +89). The inspeximus texts in the name of Hubert and Boniface appear themselves to be spurious (*EEA* ii nos +591–2). For Lanfranc's recovery of Freckenham and subsequent grant of it to Rochester, and for Gundulf's arrangement with his monks whereby he retained these distant holdings in his own hand see Textus Roffensis fos 171–172v no. 86. For a plea over Isleham as a dependency of Freckenham between Gundulf and Picot the sheriff of Cambridgeshire before Odo of Bayeux of 1077 × 1082 see ibid. fos 175–6v no. 91. Lanfranc's charter is cited in the equally untrustworthy Saltman, *Theobald* no. 221, also only known from the inspeximus of prior 'Richard'. A charter of Lanfranc is cited without further details by bp Walter (*EEA Rochester* forthcoming, no. 55, itself suspicious) and by Gilbert de Glanville (*EEA Rochester*, no. 104, also suspect).

+8.   Rochester cathedral

Note attached to forged charter of king Alfred granting rights in Freckenham and Isleham, confirming the gift at the request of bishop Gundulf.   [1086]

> There is a spurious charter of Alfred, written in s. xii/xiii, in BL Cotton Charter viii. 19 (P. H. Sawyer, *Anglo-Saxon charters* no. 349), printed in Birch, *Cartularium Saxonicum* i no. 571; facsimile in S. Keynes, *Facsimiles of Anglo-Saxon charters* pl. 41, with commentary at 11–12; cal. Flight, *Bishop and monks*, 262 no. 204. The text of this in the spurious inspeximus by Hubert Walter (*EEA* iii no. +592) has an added note, printed from BL Cotton Faust. B v fo. 68, s. xv, in *Reg. Roff.* 441:

Et ego Lamfrancus gracia Dei archiepiscopus Cant' post carte huius probacionem et eius habitam veritatem hanc donacionem, concessionem et augmentacionem regis Aeluredi factam ecclesie Roffe consigno et rogatu Gundulphi episcopi signaculo sancte crucis signo et sigilli nostri apposicione consigno, anno gracie millesimo octogesimo sexto. Testibus ad hiis consenciend' vocatis Herberto episcopo Tesford et Ernulpho priore Cantuar'.

> That this is a late concoction is clear both from the crude script and anachronistic phrasing of the charter to which it is said to have been attached and from the impossibility of the witness clause. Lanfranc died in 1089, Herbert did not become bp of Thetford/Norwich until 1090–1, and Ernulf did not become prior of Canterbury before 1096. The motive appears the same as for +7 above, since pseudo-Alfred's charter contains a grant directly to Rochester of rights in Freckenham and Isleham, although it seems clear that these rights were derived ultimately from a grant to Lanfranc by William I. For the *Historia* in which this text is embedded see R. Haines in *Journal of ecclesiastical history* xliv (1993) 586–609.

9. Rochester cathedral

Agreement in the presence of the archbishop between bishop Gundulf and Gilbert of Tonbridge, whereby Gilbert is to pay the bishop fifty shillings yearly for the land of St Andrew he holds until he provides lands to the same annual value.   [July 1085 × 12 March 1088]

B = Strood MALSC DRc/ R 1 (Textus Roffensis) fo. 175 no. 90. s. xii in.
Pd *Text. Roff.* 149, van Caenegem, *Lawsuits* no. 136; cal. Flight, *Bishops and monks* 292 no. 801.

Hęc est conventio quę facta est Cantuarię in presentia domni archiepiscopi Lanfranci, atque eo precipiente scripta, inter Gundulfum episcopum et Gislebertum de Tunebrigge. Iudicio ipsius domni archiepiscopi debet Gislebertus unoquoque anno dare .l. solidos domno episcopo Gundulfo pro terra sancti Andreę quam ipse Gislebertus habet, quoadusque dabit ei tantum de alia terra sua unde habeat per singulos annos .l. solidos vel valens. Testante eodem archiepiscopo Lanfranco, et episcopo Will'o de Dunhelma, et abbate Gisleberto Westmonasterii, et abbate Paulo sancti Albani, et Haimone vicecomite de Cantorberia, et Bertramno de Virduno, et maxima parte de familia ipsius domni archiepiscopi.

Gilbert Crispin died on 6 Dec. 1117, after ruling the abbey for thirty-two years. His predecessor's obit was celebrated on 19 June, and was presumably followed by a vacancy of unspecified length, but Gilbert is unlikely to have taken office before July 1085—see *Heads* i 76–7, 257, citing esp. J. Armitage Robinson, *Flete's History of Westminster abbey* (Cambridge 1909) 141–2, in turn drawing on *Lanfranci opera* Appx. 54. Kg William II took bp Williams' lands into custody on 12 March 1088—*De iniusta vexatione* 74. Abbot Paul was Lanfranc's nephew; Bertram of Verdun was a royal servant (*DB* i 151c) who is found acting with bp William in the summer of 1086 or Sept. 1087 × March 1088 on behalf of York in Hampshire (Bates, *Acta* no. 352). The exchange provided for here was part of the process of creating the lowy of Tonbridge, for which see Ward, 'The lowy' 125 and W.V. Dumbreck, 'The lowy of Tonbridge', *Arch. Cant.* lxxii (1958) 138–47. Gilbert's father Richard is treated as lord of the honour of Tonbridge in *DB*, but took the monastic habit, very possibly at St Neots, perhaps in 1087. By the time of the rebellion of 1088 his son already controlled Tonbridge—*Domesday monachorum* 39–41.

*10. St Albans abbey

Confirmation of rights in the wood of Northaw (Herts.).
                                                   [15 August 1070–28 May 1089]

According to the *Gesta abbatum monasterii sancti Albani* from BL Cotton mss Nero D i (s. xiii med.) and Claudius E iv (s. xiv ex.) i 164, in the course of a long dispute between abbot Robert (1151–66) and the Valognes family over the wood at Northaw the abbot sought out kg Henry II as he returned from the campaign of Toulouse late in 1159. The kg commanded Robert of Valognes to answer 'iuxta tenorem charte L. Cantuariensis archiepiscopi et aliarum chartarum'. This presumably was the 'Scriptum Lanfranci

Cantuarien' archiepiscopi super convencione prenotata' listed in the unfoliated index to a second volume of the cartulary, which is found at the end of Trustees of the Chatsworth Settlement ms 73A (s. xiv ex.). The preceding entry concerns the agreement between abbot Robert (1151–66) and Peter de Valognes the younger (d. 1158), by which Peter was to hold the wood for life only. One would expect rather a charter of Theobald in the case, but no such text is known. The second volume in question is now divided between BL Cotton Otho D iii, very badly damaged in the fire of 1731, and BL Add. 40734 fos 18–30, but no text of Lanfranc can be identified there. For the Chatsworth cartulary see J.R. Hunn in *Medieval Archaeology* xxvii (1983) 151–2. In Michaelmas Term 1200 Robert fitz Walter renewed the claim to the wood before the kg's court in the right of his wife Gunnora, daughter of Robert of Valognes. Among the texts proffered in the abbey's defence were Lanfranc's charter and the agreement between abbot Robert and Peter of Valognes, by which Peter was to hold the wood 'per xxv. solidos et duos ancipitres [*al.* austuros]' each year for life (*CRR* i 291). See further van Caenegem, *Lawsuits* no. 396.

ANSELM 1093–1109

*11. Bath cathedral priory

Confirmation to the priory of the gift of Dunster church.

[Dec. 1093 × 21 April 1109]

Mentioned in a charter of Theobald, printed from Cambridge, Corpus Christi Coll. ms 111 (cartulary of Bath) p. 122 s. xii as *Two chartularies of the priory of St Peter at Bath* ed. W. Hunt no. 65, Saltman, *Theobald* no. 8, citing confirmations to Bath of the gift of Dunster church in the names of Anselm and William II.

12. Abbey of Le Bec-Hellouin

Confirmation of the grant of Clare church with all its appurtenances to Bec by Gilbert fitz Richard, with the assent of king Henry and bishop Herbert of Thetford.

[1099 × 21 April 1109]

B = Paris BN lat. 12884 (the 'Chronicon Beccense' of Dom Thibault) fo. 109 (p. 207). s. xvii. Mentioned only in Paris BN lat. 13905 (collections of J. Jouvelin) fo. 22v (p. 44). s. xviii. Listed in the inventory of Bec charters made in 1670 in Paris BN ms Cinq cents de Colbert 190 p. 64.
Pd (imperfectly) by Porée, *Histoire du Bec* i 444 n.4.

Ego Anselmus archiepiscopus Cantuariensis concedo et confirmo, quantum ad me pertinet, donationem Gisleberti filii Ricardi filii comitis Gisleberti quam fecit de ecclesia sancti Ioannis de Clara et de omnibus appendiciis eius ecclesie sancte Marie Becci. Quam donationem concessit et confirmavit Henricus rex Anglorum et Herebertus*ᵃ* episcopus Tiefordensis.

ᵃ two or three letters added and cancelled.

As the text stands, it could represent an entry at the foot of a pancarte rather than a free-standing confirmation, and it is far from clear that the last sentence should be linked to Anselm's note directly. That there were in fact once at least two separate confirmations in the name of the kg and the archbp is suggested by the 1670 inventory, which lists consecutively 'Confirmation de Henry roy d'Angleterre de la donation faite a l'abbaye du Bec de l'eglise de St Jean de Claire [not in *Reg. regum* ii] cotté LL' and 'Autre confirmation de St Anselme archevesque de Cantorbie de la donation faite a l'abbaye du Bec de l'eglise de St Jean Baptiste de Claire avec ses dependences, cotté MM'. In B and C this passage is cited immediately after the grant by Gilbert with the assent of bp Herbert dated 1099, copied in full in the margin of B fo. 79v. The charters of Clare give either 1090 or 1099 as the date of foundation: *Stoke by Clare cartulary* i nos 70, 137.

13. Bury: abbey of St Edmunds

Confirmation of the ten-day indulgence granted by cardinal John and grant of
a further three days to those who visit St Edmund and make gifts for the church.

[late 1101 × August 1107, ? April – June 1107]

> B = Cambridge UL Mm. 4. 19 (cartulary of Bury St Edmunds) fo. 106. s. xii/xiii. C = ibid.
> fo. 162r-v.
> Pd in D.C. Douglas, *Feudal documents from the abbey of Bury St Edmunds* 153 no.171;
> compare ibid. xliv-v.

Anselmus archiepiscopus domno priori Ae[lfero] et toti*a* conventui sancti
Ædmundi, salutem et benedictionem. Sciatis quod ego confirmo decem dies
remissionis quos dominus Iohannes cardinalis Romane ecclesie concessit hiis*b*
qui sanctum Ædmundum requirendo ad opus sue ecclesie sua*c* ponunt, et
ipsis decem diebus ex mea parte sicut petistis tres adicio. Valete*d*,

> *a om.* C   *b* iis C   *c om.* C   *d* val' B

> The cardinal is almost certainly John, cardinal bp of Tusculum, who was legate in England
> late in 1101 (*Councils* i (2) 667–8). The address of this charter to the prior suggests that the
> abbey was vacant, as it was between Sept. 1102 and August 1107 (John of Worcs. iii 321–2,
> explaining to some extent the otherwise puzzling mathematics of the Bury annals in
> *Memorials of St Edmund's abbey* ii 4). Anselm was at Bury from soon after Easter until the
> week after Whitsun in 1107 (Eadmer, *Historia* 185). In a letter probably written a little
> earlier to the same recipients the archbp had absolved penitent monks—*EA* 382. This may
> well be the earliest surviving authentic English episcopal indulgence; see the valuable survey
> by N. Vincent, 'Some pardoners' tales: the earliest English indulgences', *TRHS* 6s xii (2002)
> 23–58, esp. 36–7.

14. Canterbury: bishops of the diocese

Letter to bishop Sampson of Worcester, enclosing a copy of his letter to
Thomas (II) archbishop-elect of York denying him permission to exercise any
priestly function in his parochia, *and forbidding him to accept consecration*
without making his profession to Canterbury.   [March–21 April 1109]

> A = Canterbury D. & C. C.A. Y 57. 160 × 85 mm, the foot slit for a narrow tag with a seal
> in white wax, but with no plica; only ..CHI.. of the legend is now visible; see above p. lx.
> Endorsed, s. xii: Anselm archiep'; s. xii/xiii: S. Wigorn' ne man' imponat Tome Eborac'
> donec prof' faciat Cantuariens' ecclesie; s. xiii: Anselmus archiepiscopus episcopo
> Wigorn' ne manus imponat Eboracensi priusquam prof' faciat eccl' Cant'. The text is
> written in a small book-hand which leaves almost no margins at all, and the seal slit is
> dangerously near the foot of the charter; some of the text is difficult to read.
> B = BL Cotton Domitian v (collection of Canterbury primacy documents) fo. 15v. s. xii/xiii.
> Pd in part from A in *HMC Fifth Rep.* Appx 452b; the letter survives in several forms; versions
> with other addresses are printed as *EA* 471–2.

A. archiepiscopus Cantuariensis dilecto amico suo reverendo episcopo Wigorniensi S*a*. salutem. Mando et precipio vobis*b* per sanctam obędientiam quam ęcclesię Cantuariensi et mihi debetis ut secundum quod in subiectis litteris quas Thomę electo ęcclesię Eboracensi destinavi scriptum est vos erga ipsum Thomam amodo tenea[tis].

A. minister ęcclesię Cantuariensis Thomę electo archiepiscopo Eboracensi. Tibi Thoma in conspectu*c* omnipotentis Dei ego Anselmus, archiepiscopus Cantuariensis et totius Brittannię primas, loquor. Loquens ex parte ipsius Dei sacerdotale officium quod meo iussu in parrochia mea per suffraganeum meum suscepisti tibi interdico, atque precipio ne te de aliqua cura pastorali ullo modo presumas intromittere, donec a rebellione quam contra ęcclesiam Cantuariensem incepisti discedas, et ei subiectionem quam antecessores tui Thomas videlicet et Girardus archiepiscopi ex antiqua antecessorum consuetudine professi sunt profitearis. Quod si in iis que cępisti magis perseverare quam ab eis desistere delegeris, omnibus episcopis totius Brittannię sub perpetuo anathemate interdico ne tibi ullus eorum manus ad promotionem pontificatus imponat, vel si ab externis promotus fueris pro episcopo vel in aliqua Cristiana communione te suscipiat. Tibi quoque Thoma sub eodem anathemate ex parte Dei interdico ut nunquam benedictionem episcopatus [Ebor]acensis suscipias, nisi prius professionem quam antecessores tui Thomas et Girardus ęcclesię Cantuariensi fecerunt facias. Si autem episcopatum Eboracensem ex toto dimiseris, concedo ut officio sacerdotali [quod] iam suscepisti utaris.

a Sams' B *b marked for corr. to* vobis et precipio B *c* spectu B

The passages in square brackets are effectively illegible in A, and are supplied from B; the presence of a tailed 'e' in A is particularly difficult to determine. A has been in the priory archives at least since the twelfth century. It seems most unlikely that this version was ever sent, and it may not have been intended for sending. The physical characteristics of the single sheet and its archival history suggest that it was a 'file copy'. Hugh the Chanter 38–9 seeks to cast doubt on its authenticity, though there is little reason to follow him; the act was written by a scribe known to have been active at Christ Church in these years (above, p. lxiii). Other surviving versions are addressed to bp William of Winchester, William of Exeter and a bp R. For the circumstances see Eadmer, *Historia* 186–206, Southern, *St Anselm* (1963) 138–42; (1990) 340–4; the letter was written shortly before Anselm died.

15. Canterbury: lands of the see

Grant to William Calvellus and his heirs of lands by the castle outside the city of Canterbury in return for an annual rent of 52 shillings to the cellarer of Christ Church, excepting the murdrum fine, and penalties for theft or offences

against the prior. the monks or their servants. Half is to be paid in mid-Lent, the rest at Michaelmas. His heir shall pay 20 shillings in relief.

[11 June 1096 × Nov. 1097, Sept. 1101 × April 1103, Sept. 1106 × 1107]

A = Canterbury D. & C. C.A. C 1193. 177 × 86 + 18 mm seal tongue. Endorsed, s. xii/xiii: De terra W. Caluel; s. xiii/xiv: Cant'. Sealed on a tongue with seal in white wax; the legend has gone. Written in a handsome bookhand in a script which runs very close to the sides and top of the sheet (Plate Ib).
Pd in Urry, *Canterbury* 386 no. II.

Anselmus archiepiscopus omnibus fidelibus et amicis suis, salutem. Sciatis me concessisse Will' Calvello et herede*ᵃ* sui*ᵃ* extra civitatem Cantuariam circa castellum novem partes terrę inter terram arabilem et prata, ea conventione ut ipse Calvellus et herede*ᵃ* sui singulis annis dent celarario fratrum lii solidos pro omni re praeter tres forisfacturas, id est murdrum et furtum si ipse Calvellus vel herede*ᵃ* sui fecerint, et praeter si verecundiam ipse sive herede*ᵃ* sui fecerint monachis ęcclesie vel servientibus eorum. Horum vero denariorum una medietas dabitur in media Quadragesima et altera in festivitate sancti Michaelis. Calvello autem mortuo, pro redemptione quam herede*ᵃ* facere solent, herede*ᵃ* sui xx solidos dabunt et censum quem pater prius dederat, ipsi deinceps similiter dabunt. Testes horum sunt, Godefridus de Tanit', Ælfredus filius Godwini, Gotsoldus, Radulfus frater ipsius Calvelli, Radulfus Wastecarn, Edwinus filius Pitegos. Val'.

ᵃ an erasure following in each case.

The hand has been identified as that of Eadmer (above, p. lxiii; Gullick, 'Eadmer' 183–5). Eadmer shared the archbp's periods of exile between Nov. 1097 and Sept. 1100, and again from late April 1103 to late Sept. 1106, and this text is unlikely to have been written outside England. Gullick believes this to represent a stage in the evolution of Eadmer's script characteristic of the period before 1100. Urry, *Canterbury* no. III is a related grant in the name of prior Ernulf and the monks, with Anselm's consent, which is possibly in the same hand, and is assumed to have been issued at about the same time in the dating above—though there is no overlap in the witness-lists. As here the prior's text has been altered, incompetently, with the apparent object of making it a grant to William and one heir, not in perpetuity. The seal shows the archbp with his pallium. For William Calvellus, traditionally founder of the nunnery of St Sepulchre in Canterbury (though William Thorn in the fourteenth century attributed the foundation to Anselm) and portreeve of Canterbury, see Urry, 'Normans' 133–5 and *Canterbury* 62ff, 385, citing esp. *EA* nos 356, 358–9, Somner, *Antiquities* 36, Thorn in Twysden, *Scriptores* col. 1893, *Valor* i 30; Leland, *Collectanea* i 89; also Thompson, *Women religious* 36–7.

16. Canterbury: Christ Church

Restoration to the monks of half the proceeds of the high altar of the cathedral as granted by Lanfranc, and grant of the other half, and restitution of the manor of Stisted. [27 May 1095 × 21 April 1109]

A = BL Campbell Charter vii. 5 (formerly owned by T. Astle). Endorsed, s. xii/xiii: De altari Cristi et Sti.; s. xiv/xv: Carta Anselmi archiepiscopi de medietate altaris et de manerio de Stistede. 240 × 118 mm, sealed on a tongue at the top left hand corner; the seal in white wax, with much of the legend damaged, is applied with the archbp's feet towards the text: the legend is . . .LVM A. . .SE. . . GRATIA DEI ARCH. . . . In a square bookhand (Plate Ia).
B = Lambeth Palace ms 59 (collection of Anselm's letters) fo. 101v. s. xii[1] (and in a number of related copies). C = Cambridge, Corpus Christi Coll. ms 189 (cartulary of Christ Church, Canterbury) fo. 202, s. xii/xiii, a small fragment of a leaf containing part of the text. D = Lambeth Palace ms 1212 (cartulary of the archbpric of Canterbury) p. 334 'e veteri libro'. s. xiii ex. E = Canterbury, D. & C. Register P fos 26v-7 (damaged). s. xiii in. F = Canterbury D. & C. Register I fo. 82. s. xiii ex. G = Canterbury, D. & C. Register A fo. 21v (28v) no. 64. s. xv. H = Canterbury D. & C. Register B fo. 159. s. xv. J = Canterbury D. & C. C.A. S 317 (paper copy of the charters of Stisted). s. xv. CDE seem to be copies of an earlier lost cartulary of the priory, chiefly containing Anglo-Saxon diplomata, of which this charter was the latest element. The text below is from A and B only.
Pd in Somner, *Antiquities* Appx. to Supplement 49 (no. xxiiia); from A and B in *EA* 474; from A with quasi-facsimile and engraving of the seal in A.C. Ducarel, *Anglo-Norman antiquities considered' in a tour through England and Normandy* (1767) p. v and pl. VIII; from C in Twysden, *Scriptores* col. 2226; from C and D in C. Hart, *The early charters of Essex. The Norman period* 27–8; from CDE in R. Fleming, 'Christ Church Canterbury's Anglo-Norman cartulary' 152. Transl. from A and B as W. Fröhlich, *Letters* iii 268 no. 474, *Anselmo d'Aosta* iii 502. Seal described in Birch, *Catalogue* no. 1169, figured in pl. 6, and see above p. lx.

Ego Anselmus sanctę Dorobernensis ęcclesię archiepiscopus reddo monachis eiusdem ęcclesię[a] medietatem altaris Cristi[b], quam in manu mea habebam post mortem prędecessoris mei Lanfranci archiepiscopi, qui eis aliam medietatem cognita veritate quod ad illos pertineret in vita sua reddiderat. Similiter manerium quod Stistede vocatur eisdem monachis reddo, quoniam hoc ad res eorum pertinere et pertinuisse scitur. Testes: Will' ecclesię Cristi[b] archidiac', Haimo vicecomes, Haimo filius Vital', Robertus filius Watsonis, Wimundus homo vicecomitis, Raulfus[c] nepos episcopi Gundulfi, et alii plures.

[a] Cristi *add.* B   [b] xpisti A   [c] *corr. to* Radulfus B[2]

The curious practice of sealing on a tongue projecting from the left-hand edge, as here, occurs widely in the s. xii archive of Christ Church, in documents in the name of the prior and the kg as well as in 38 below. Precariously this has been placed in or after 1095 since the seal shows a pallium. Stisted is entered in *DB* ii 8 among the Christ Church estates 'ad victum monachorum'. Compare Du Boulay, *Lordship* 21. The original gift is attributed to Wluid/Wlfgidus in Fleming, 'Lists' 127, 136; cf D. Whitelock, *Anglo-Saxon wills* nos 32, a bequest of Wulfgyth the widow 'for the sustenance of the monks in the community' subject to a life interest for her two sons, and 34, a similar bequest by Ketel, one of the sons, both in the reign of kg Edward. The rights of the priory here remained contentious; it seems to have been held at farm by Ansfrid *dapifer* in the time of archbp William, and Saltman, *Theobald* no. 44 records an effort to evict Ansfrid's son John; the family remained largely in possession, however, long after that; see A.E. Conway in *Arch. Cant.* xxix (1911) 9–13; Du Boulay, *Lordship* 373, Colvin, 'List' 39. Eadmer, *Historia* 220 notes the grant of the proceeds of the altar. N. Brooks, *Canterbury* 102, 323 and Fleming, 'Christ Church cartulary' identify CDE as copies of a lost earlier cartulary of Christ Church, attributed to the late eleventh or early twelfth century, in which this grant was the last to be entered.

17. Canterbury: Christ Church

Grant for the feeding of the monks of the lands of Saltwood and Hythe, after they had reverted to the archbishop on the death of Robert de Montfort on the road to Jerusalem. [1107 × 21 April 1109]

B = Lambeth Palace ms 59 (Collection of letters of Anselm) fo.189v. s. xii in.
Pd in A.Wilmart, 'La tradition des lettres de S.Anselme; lettres inédites de S.Anselme et de ses correspondents', *Revue Bénédictine* xliii (1931) 52–3, *EA* 475. Transl. as Fröhlich *Letters* iii 269 no. 475, *Anselmo d'Aosta* iii 502–4.

[A]nselmus sanctę Cantuariensis ęcclesię antistes omnibus fidelibus Cristi, salutem et benedictionem Dei et nostram. Notum vobis sit quod nuper mortuo Rodberto de Morteforti in via Ierusalem hę terrę Saltuude et Hetha venerunt mihi in dominium, et ego eas reddidi ęcclesię Cristi et monachis ad victum eorum. Rogo ergo successores meos omnes videlicet archiepiscopos ut permittant prenominatas terras in ęcclesia ita permanere sicut ego eam saisivi*a*.

a suasivi B.

This is the only example of use of the first-person plural in a salutation in Anselm's letters and acts. A writ of William I which is either interpolated or of uncertain authenticity, since the kg is styled 'Dei gratia', restored Saltwood (held before 1066 by earl Godwin) to Lanfranc 'ad profectum ecclesie': Bates, *Acta* no. 70. In Domesday i 4c, *Domesday monachorum* 93, Hugh de Montfort held lands at Saltwood from the archbp, though it is listed among the manors of the monks at *Domesday monachorum* 81. Anselm's grant took effect for only some of the land, for after Robert de Montfort died in 1107 × 8, having surrendered his estates to the kg, he was succeeded by Henry de Essex (Orderic vi 100, 104). The land at Saltwood may already have been a cause of contention, if the dispute with Robert de Montfort touched on in *EA* 299 concerned this estate; it became a *cause célèbre* under Becket; compare Du Boulay, *Lordship* Appx 366–8, Colvin, 'List' 14–15; Crosby, *Bishop and chapter* 75. For a confirmation of the gift of the church by Robert de Montfort to Bec see below 34 and Saltman, *Theobald* no. 297. The De Veres later granted land in Saltwood to Monks Horton (*EEA* ii no. 138), presumably through rights derived from the marriage of Robert de Vere to Robert de Montfort's sister, but the Montforts still had interests there in the time of Hubert Walter (*CRR 9–10 Henry III* 301 no. 1466 cited by N.H. MacMichael in *Arch. Cant.* lxxiv (1961) 1–3).

18. Canterbury: Christ Church

Confirmation to the monks of all their lands and possessions as confirmed by king William with the same freedom of disposition of their estates as he enjoyed on his. [4 Dec. 1093 × 21 April 1109]

B = Canterbury D. & C. C.A. C 204 (copy of the privileges of the priory) dorse no. 2 s. xiii¹.
C = Vatican, Archivio Segreto, Reg. Vat. 18 (Register of Pope Gregory IX) fo.177r-v, confirmation of the charter of Anselm, dated 1 July 1236 at Terni. D = BL Additional ms 6159 (cartulary of Christ Church) fo. 9v. s. xiv in. E = Canterbury D. & C. Register I (in copy of the bull of Gregory IX) fo. 50. s. xiii ex. F = Canterbury D. & C. Register A (cartulary of Christ Church) fo. 21r-v (28) no. 62. s. xv (copy of the bull of Gregory IX). G = Canterbury D. & C. C.A. C 204 (copy of the privileges of the priory) s. xii/xiii. H = BL Additional ms 6159 fo. 8v. s. xiv in. J = Ibid. fo. 285v. K = Canterbury D. & C. Register I fo. 82. s. xiii ex. L = Canterbury D. & C. Register E fo. 60v. s. xiv in. M = Canterbury D. & C. Register A fo. 164 (186). s. xiv in.
Pd from C in *Les Registres de Grégoire IX* ed. L. Auvray ii 440–1 no. 3233. Cal. in *Calendar of entries in the papal registers relating to Great Britain and Ireland* i 155.

Anselmus gratia Dei*ᵃ* sancte*ᵇ* Cantuar' ecclesie archiepiscopus*ᶜ* omnibus eiusdem ecclesie filiis et fidelibus, salutem et benedictionem. Notum sit vobis me concessisse et confirmasse monachis in ecclesia Cantuar'*ᵈ* mihi commissa Deo servientibus omnes res et possessiones suas sicut rex Willelmus concessit eis*ᵉ* et confirmavit, honorifice, libere et integre possidendas in perpetuum. Concedo insuper ad meam*ᶠ* et successorum meorum et illorum quietem et perpetuam pacem*ᵍ* ut ipsi libere disponant et ordinent de rebus que ad eos pertinent, sicut eis melius et utilius visum fuerit de communi consilio capituli sui, quatinus sicut easdem habemus in possessionibus nostris *ʰ*secundum cartas regum*ʰ* libertates, similem habeant*ⁱ* in portionibus singulis*ʲ* potestatem, salva in omnibus*ᵏ* mihi et successoribus meis regulari disciplina. *ˡ*Quod si quis hec vi vel fraude violare presumpserit, anathema sit*ˡ*.

ᵃ gratia Dei BCGHM; Dei gratia DEFJKL   *ᵇ* om. LM
ᶜ archiep. BCDEF; antistes GHJKLM   *ᵈ*Cant. BCDEF; om. GHJKLM
ᵉ eis BCDEF; om. GHJKLM   *ᶠ*meam] m'am C
ᵍ perp. pacem BDGHJKLM; pacem perp. CEF
ʰ⁻ʰ sec. cartas regum BCDEF om. GHJKLM
ⁱ habeamus BCEFGKLM; habeant DHJ   *ʲ* singulis BCDEF; om. GHJKLM
ᵏ in omn. om. BCDEF   *ˡ⁻ˡ* Quod si quis—sit BCDEF; Valete GHJKLM.

This is the only act of Anselm apparently listed in the inventories of the archbpric and priory. In the inventory for the archbpric in PRO E36/137 printed by Irene Churchill in *Camden Miscellany xv* 13 occurs 'Transcriptum Willelmi Henrici et Henrici regum Anglie et archiepiscopi Anselmi et confirmacio Allexandri pape' in 'vas xviii'. PRO E36/138, the s. xvi Christ Church inventory, p. 2 lists 'Littera Anselmi archiepiscopi super omnibus possessionibus et libertatibus ecclesie nostre ubi habetur quod easdem habemus cum eo in possessionibus nostris libertates, salva sibi et successoribus suis regulari disciplina', apparently a single-sheet version of this text. Ibid. p. 17 lists as Cista sexta no. 26 'Transcriptum regum et sancti Augustini et de Ffeversham abbatum et N. prioris sancti Gregorii Edwardi, Willelmi H. I, H.

2, H. 3 et Ricardi regum Anglie, Anselmi archiepiscopi et Gregorii pape super libertatibus Cant' ecclesie, videlicet de saca et sokne, gelde et denegelde etc', presumably an enlargement of C.A. C 204. The presence of two copies of the same charter close together in C.A. C 204 and BL Add. ms 6159, and the consistent agreement of BCDEF against the other copies, suggest that there were two versions of this grant at Canterbury, at least by the mid-thirteenth century. It is curious that the distracted variant 'habeamus' for 'habeant' occurs in all copies of the first form and some of the second. Given its manifest absurdity the reading of DHJ may be merely a scribal correction. The text in both forms presents no obvious difficulties, and there is good evidence that Anselm did confer some such freedom on his monks. According to Eadmer, *Historia* 219: 'res monachorum posuit in dispositione eorum', and *EA* 327 notes in passing that the clergy of the churches on the priory estates were installed with the consent of the prior, not the archdn. However, the subject was much contested later, Eadmer does not speak in terms of a charter conveying such rights and the authenticity of the grant, at least in its present form, must remain in doubt. The mixture of singular and plural here is more characteristic of later texts, though far from decisive, the saving clause is very rare in these early acts and the reference to the common counsel of the chapter in a monastic context is equally unexpected so early. Given the apparent desire of the compiler of Lambeth Palace ms 59 to gather up every record of Anselm's action *c.* 1120, including 16–17 above for the priory, and the apparent substance of this act, it may be significant that it was not copied there. The text is not treated in the valuable discussion by Du Boulay in *Lordship* 18ff or by Crosby, *Bishop and chapter* 66–77 in his discussion of the evolution of the early privileges of the priory.

19.   Canterbury: hospital of St Nicholas, Harbledown

Grant to the lepers of land at 'Hegham' by 'Croydene' next to their house, free of rent and custom.   [4 Dec. 1093 × 21 April 1109]

   B = (lost; destroyed in 1942) Harbledown muniments no. 65, a medieval roll-rental of the
   hospital, no. 31. C = Lambeth Palace ms 1131 (part 2), (transcription of B by Henry
   Hall, rector of Harbledown, in 1763) p. 42.

Anselmus archiepiscopus Cant' hundredo de Westgate, salutem. Sciatis quod ego concedo lazaris hospitalis de Herbald' terram illam que iuxta illos est, et vocatur Hegham apud Croydune [que]*a* iacet in campo qui vocatur Burnefelde, liberam et quietam de auro et gablo et omni alia consuetudine.

   a suppl. ed.

   Saltman, *Theobald* no. 34 records a further grant of a mark of silver from land at
   Bishopsbourne made by Anselm. Ducarel had given an earlier sketch of the muniments in
   1761, preserved in Lambeth Palace ms 1169, noting two 'very ancient' rolls, one of which presumably was B, as nos 38–9. Duncombe, *History* 237 records the hospital's later holding in
   Upfield in 'Croydene' in the parish of Harbledown and at 'Hegham alias Hyham in Tonford
   field'. Neither name can be found on a modern map. A render of gold from this small holding is sufficiently odd to suggest that perhaps 'auro' replaced 'opere' at some point in the
   transmission—compare 47 below.

+20.   Canterbury: priory of St Gregory

Confirmation of the gifts of lands and tithes made by Lanfranc, who founded the church, and of the grant made by Anselm at its consecration of the annual harvest of eight acres of the best land at Northfleet.

[9 August 1108 × 21 April 1109]

B = Cambridge UL ms Ll. 2. 15 (cartulary of St Gregory, Canterbury) fo. 2. s. xiii med.
Pd in *St Gregory's cartulary* 3 no. 2.

Anselmus Dei gratia sancte Cantuariensis ecclesie antistes omnibus fidelibus suis, salutem et benedictionem. Notum sit omnibus vobis nos concessisse et hac carta nostra confirmasse ecclesie beati Gregorii extra portam Cant' aquilonarem site omnia que venerabilis predecessor noster Lanfrancus illius fundator eidem ecclesie contulit in ecclesiis et decimis, in terris et bosco et pratis et molendinis et in omni maneria donarum et possessionum et reddituum. Sed et quod prefate ecclesie in illius consecratione quam auctore Deo peragentes eius intuitu et amore donantes adauximus, hac eadem carta nostra in perpetuam eidem confirmamus elemosinam, videlicet octo acras succise messis annuatim apud Northfliete, quattuor acras de tritico et quattuor de ordeo, in terra scilicet meliori post fimatam*a*. Sed et omnia que a bonis catholicis eidem ecclesie de cetero iuste et pie conferenda sunt, providentis omnia Dei auctoritate et nostra, scripto hoc corroboramus, omnibus ipsi ecclesie benefacientibus et benefacturis eternam a Domino salutem obtinere desiderantes. Huius carte testes sunt R. episcopus Roffensis, Hugo abbas ecclesie sancti Augustini, Conrad prior, Petrus monachus, Willelmus senescal.

a The previous ed. here reads 'funatam'

There is no conclusive objection to the substance of this charter. However, like the charter of Lanfranc (above, +1), it is cast in the plural throughout, contrary to Anselm's near invariable practice both in his letters and in his more probable charters. The phrase 'omni maneria donarum', apparently a macaronic 'all manner of gifts', with the minor correction of 'donorum', could just be a very rare but occasional twelfth-century usage, but is unlikely to have crept into the text of a genuine charter in the early twelfth century. A corroboration clause of this kind is equally unexampled in Canterbury acts before 1136.

21.   Chester abbey

Confirmation of all the gifts made to the abbey by earl Hugh of Chester and his men at its foundation, quit of toll and all other custom. The men of the monks are to answer to none but abbot Richard, the monk of Bec appointed by the archbishop's consent when he was abbot. With the agreement of Anselm and bishop Robert (of Chester) the earl has provided that the prebends of the existing canons are to revert to the monks on the death of their holder.

[4 Dec. 1093 × 21 April 1109]

B = Duke of Westminster, Eaton Hall ms 1 (original charter of Earl Ranulf II of Chester, perhaps of 1151 × 1152, incorporating Anselm's record). C = Windsor, St George's Chapel Archives XI E 5 (inspeximus of the abbey charters by Guncelin Badlesmere dated 31 July 1280). D = BL Harley 1965 (register of Chester abbey) fos 4v-5. s. xiv in.

Pd from B by J.R.Planché in *Journal of the British Arch. Assoc.* vi (1851) 321–2, trans. in *Journal of the Chester Archaeological Association* (o.s. i 1849–51) 294–5; *Chart. Chester* i 38 from BCD.

Decet quemque Cristianum de his quę ad honorem Dei in futurum stabilia esse decerni[a] presens audivit testimonium perhibere, ne aliquis Deum minus amans ea possit quavis occasione in sequenti tempore pervertendo mutare. Unde ego Anselmus gratia Dei sanctę Cantuariensis ęcclesię archiepiscopus[b] testimonium fero quod quando Hugo Cestrensis comes[c] posuit monachos in ęcclesia sanctę Werburgę, concessit et confirmavit ut eadem ęcclesia et omnes res eius quas habebat et quas ipse vel homines sui tunc dederunt vel postmodum darent ita libere essent et quiete[d] a theloneis et omnibus operibus et omnibus aliis consuetudinibus ut nichil in eis sibi aliquatenus retinuerit. Statuit etiam ut homines ad ipsam ęcclesiam pertinentes nulli pro qualibet causa nisi dompno Ricardo, quem de abbatia Beccensi monachum unde ego tunc abbas eram rogatus ab ipso comite abbatem ibi fieri concessi, et successoribus eius respondeant. De prebendis autem canonicorum constituit ipsis concedentibus, et me et Rodberto episcopo et baronibus suis testibus, ut post discessum[e] uniuscuiusque eorum prebende eorum libere sine ulla contradictione in dominium monachorum ad usum eorum venirent. Si quis autem aliquid horum infringere voluerit anathema sit, et cum Iuda traditore Domini[f] perhenniter dampnetur et cum Symone mago et demonibus in inferno crucietur.

[a] decerni BC; *corr. to* decernuntur D   [b] archiepiscopus CD; archiepiscopatus B
[c] Cest. comes B; comes Cest. CD   [d] quieta C   [e] discessum B; decessum CD
[f] trad. Dom. BC; Dom. trad. D

B also contains Saltman, *Theobald* no. 68. Chester was established late in 1092 when Anselm was present as abbot of Bec (R.W. Southern, 'St Anselm and Gilbert Crispin, abbot of Westminster' 87–8, *EA* 231). The earl's charter, of which all but Anselm's confirmation is printed as *Chester charters* no. 28, is itself suspicious, and may have been produced a little later than its supposed date; compare T. Webber, 'Scribes', 141. For C see *Chart. Chester* i no. 34. D includes a full text of Anselm's grant as a separate document and an abbreviated text of B.

22. Malling abbey

Grant of the vill of Little Malling.   [4 Dec. 1093 × 21 April 1109]

B = PRO C53 / 134, Charter roll for 21 Edward III, m. 11 (confirmation of numerous charters of Malling, dated 8 May 1347).
Pd *Cal. Ch. Rolls* v 61.

+ Anselmus gratia Dei archiepiscopus Cantuariensis Haimoni vicecomiti et Gilleberto de Tonebrigge et omnibus hominibus Francigenis et Anglis de lesto de Eylleford*ᵃ*, salutem. Sciatis quod ego concedo sanctimonialibus que in parochia episcopi Hrofensis apud Mcallingas Domino Cristo famulantur villam nostram que Parva Mellinges vocatur, et prope illas sita est, omnibus diebus. Hoc autem eis concedo pro elemosina ut prosit anime mee et animabus predecessorum meorum. Et volo ut successores mei hoc ipsum eis concedant et confirment ut retributionem inde recipiant in vita eterna. Val'.

ᵃ after corr.

This grant was confirmed by kg Henry I in a charter of 1100 × 1105 (*Reg. regum* ii no. 635), but the archbp's charter need not be so early. The grant was apparently confirmed by archbps Ralph and William (below 51, *83). It has no improbable characteristics, for even the rather odd 'omnibus diebus' seems unlikely to be the work of a later forger. It is noticed in the rather suspicious Saltman, *Theobald* no. 173.

23. Norwich cathedral priory

Confirmation of the grants of king William (II) and king Henry (I) at the request of bishop Herbert, which have established Norwich as the cathedral church of the diocese with a monastic chapter there. The monks are to appoint the same officers as are found in the churches of Winchester and Canterbury.

[July 1101 × 18 June 1102; prob. Windsor, 3 Sept. 1101]

B = BL Cotton Charter ii. 21 (original inspeximus by archbp Pecham of Canterbury dated 15 May 1281). C = Canterbury D. & C. C.A. N 26 (original inspeximus of B by prior Henry de Eastry and the chapter of Canterbury, dated 5 April 1302, but with no trace of sealing). D = Cambridge UL Ee 5. 31 (Register of Henry de Eastry) fo. 89, a copy of C. s. xiv in. E = Norwich, Norfolk RO DCN 40/ 1 (Registrum I of the cathedral priory) fo. 19v. s. xiv in. F = Norwich, Norfolk RO DCN 40/ 2 (Registrum II.ii of the cathedral priory) fo. 13r-v, a copy of E. s. xiv.
Pd from E in *Mon. Angl.* iv. 20 (no.12) and *First Register of Norwich priory* ed. Saunders 40–42, from E and F in *Norwich charters* i 163–4 no. 260. Cal. as *Reg. regum* ii no. 549.

+ In nomine Patris et Filii et Spiritus Sancti Amen. A. Cantuariensis archiepiscopus et maioris Britannie atque Hybernye primas summique pontificis Paschalis vicarius fratribus et filiis secularibus et ecclesiasticis

Francis et Anglis de Northfolch et Suthfolch, salutem. Quanto amore et obsequio vestram matrem Norwicensem ecclesiam*a* diligere et honorare debetis ipsius Redemptoris et Salvatoris Ihesu Cristi exemplo instruimini, qui sanctam ecclesiam suo sanguine redemit et lavit et suo spiritu donavit et insignivit sueque carnis alimento cibavit et satiavit. Norwicensem sancte Trinitatis ecclesiam rex Willelmus et rex Henricus frater et successor suus capud et matrem omnium ecclesiarum de Northfolch et de Suthfolch constituerunt, et regie dignitatis cartis et sigillis confirmaverunt, consenserunt*b* voluntati et petitioni fratris et filii nostri Herberti episcopi [m.2] ut in predicta sancte Trinitatis ecclesia monachi constituerentur et loco canonicorum haberentur, vi aut ingenio nullo inde eiciendi aut amovendi, set et regia et nostra auctoritate per decendentes et succedentes generationes usque ad consummationem seculi ibidem servituri et perseveraturi. Hec concedimus et ut in eternum rata permaneant nostra et omnium comprovincialium fratrum et coepiscoporum nostrorum necnon et abbatum atque religiosorum clericorum auctoritate confirmamus. Igitur iuxta voluntatem et petitionem fratris et filii nostri Herberti episcopi Norwicensis ecclesia habeat monachos in officiis et obsequiis suis ad exemplum Wintoniensis ecclesie et nostre que omnium ecclesiarum totius Anglie prima est. Quod concedimus et confirmamus nulla persona, nullus successurus episcopus infringere aut*c* mutare presumat, set constitutionem nostram vere dilectionis et venerationis sinu complectatur et custodiat.*d*

Ego Ansselmus*e* archiepiscopus consensi et presenti sancte crucis signo nostreque auctoritatis subiecto sigillo confirmavi +
Ego Gundulfus Rouecestrensis episcopus subscripsi +
Ego Mauricius Londoniensis*f* episcopus subscripsi +
Ego Radulphus Cicestrensis episcopus subscripsi +
Ego Willelmus Wincestrensis episcopus subscripsi +
Ego Saresbyryensis episcopus subscripsi +
Ego Sampson Wygrecestrensis episcopus subscripsi +
Ego Iohannes Bathoniensis episcopus subscripsi +
Ego Osbernus Execestrensis episcopus subscripsi +
Ego Robertus Cestrensis episcopus subscripsi +
Ego Robertus Lyncolensis episcopus subscripsi +
Ego Ranulphus Dunelmensis episcopus subscripsi +
*g*Ego Gislbertus abbas de Westmonasterio subscripsi +
Ego Serlo Gloecestrensis subscripsi +
Ego Ricardus abbas de Hely subscripsi +
*h*Ego Ricardus abbas de sancto Albano subscripsi +*h*
Ego Stephanus abbas Eboracensis subscripsi +

Ego Hynricus abbas de Bello subscripsi +
Ego Rycherus abbas de Holma subscripsi +
Ego Guntardus abbas de Torney subscripsi +
Ego Aldewinus abbas*ⁱ* Rameseye subscripsi +

ᵃ Norwicen (*sic*) eccl. B; eccl. Norw. F   *ᵇ* consentierunt EF   *ᶜ* et EF
ᵈ Nomina archiepiscoporum et episcoporum *add.* EF   *ᵉ* Cant' *add.* F   *ᶠ* -ensi B
ᵍ Nomina abbatum *add.* EF   *ʰ⁻ʰ om.* D   *ⁱ* de *add.* EF

This confirmation, of unusual form, is one of three charters for the cathedral apparently all
granted on the same occasion. The kg's charter (*Reg. regum* ii no. 548) and bp Herbert's are
printed as *Norwich charters* i nos 3, 112–13; compare *EEA* vi no. 11 for difficulties with the
bp's grant. The kg's is dated in the text to 3 Sept. 1101 at Windsor. Henry of Battle d. on 18
June 1102 (*Heads* i 29); Ranulf of Durham was in gaol or exile from Henry's accession until
July 1101, and the abbots of Ely, Thorney and Ramsey were deposed at the Council of
Westminster at the end of Sept. 1102 and not restored, if at all, until after the death of
Osbern of Exeter in 1103. Salisbury had been vacant since 1099, and bp Roger was formally
invested at about the time of the Council. If one imagines the attestations of the bishops in
the original being laid out in two columns, with Gundulf's heading the second, the first three
of the left-hand column would be Canterbury, London and Winchester, according to the provisions of the Council of 1075 (*Councils* i (2) 612–13), though the remainder would not be in
order of consecration. The two emphatic references to the primacy might suggest that a
Canterbury hand played some part in its drafting, and there are no apparent inconsistencies
in the long witness list. However, the freakish *invocatio, intitulatio* and *arenga* are without
parallel in Anselm's other surviving letters or charters. Indeed Anselm never expressly
asserted primatial claims in Ireland, though several of his letters clearly imply that he
believed he had authority there, as does a poem attributed to abbot Gilbert of Westminster
c. 1105 (*EA* 366). At around this time also the queen addressed an extravagantly fulsome letter to 'Anglorum primae sedis archiepiscopo, Hibernorum omniumque septentrionalum
insularum quae Orcades dicuntur primati', *EA* 242. While the close connection between the
charters of kg, bp and archbp suggests that they were prepared at Norwich, which may
explain the many peculiarities of the text, including its consistent use of a plural form, it was
dismissed as a forgery by Cheney in *EBC* 65 n. 2. It is less than reassuring that in the fourteenth century the monks of Norwich presented a late twelfth-century single sheet version of
the bp's charter, the earliest witness to any of the three grants, as the original.

24. Rochester cathedral

Confirmation attached to charter of Henry I for Rochester.

[?6 March] 1103

A = Strood MALSC DRc/ T 50 (formerly Rochester D & C B 778). 260 × 650 mm, with
  three seals on tongues at foot; Anselm's, in brown wax, is on the left. SIGILLVM
  ANSELMI CAN. . . . .CHIEPISCO. . . is legible. Fragments of Henry I's 'second' seal
  remain on the centre tongue, and Gundulf's seal, well-preserved, is on the right.
  Endorsed, s. xiii: Carta Henr' reg' primi, Anselmi archiepiscopi et Gundulphi Roffen' de
  maneriis et aliis; s. xiv: et Gundulphi de imposicione pensionum.
B = Strood MALSC DRc/ R 1 (Textus Roffensis) fos 218–20 no. 211. s. xii in. C = BL Cotton
  Domitian x (cartulary of Rochester) fos 101–3 no. 2. s. xiii in. D = Maidstone CKS

DRb/ Ar2 (Registrum Temporalium, formerly DRc/ R 3) fo. 12. s. xiv. E = Maidstone CKS DRb/ Ar 1/13 (Reg. Fisher) fos 65v-6r (formerly DRc/ R7 fos 6/82v-3r). s xvi in. A has been tampered with, by the erasure of several signa to make room for an additional confirmation by Gundulf of pensions due to the priory from a number of churches (for which see *EEA Rochester* forthcoming no.+7A). E follows A after its alteration, BCD represent the earlier form of the text; Anselm's confirmation, however, is unaffected by these manipulations.

Pd *Text. Roff.* 224–7 (from B), *Reg. Roff.* 33–4 (from B), *Mon. Angl.* i 163 no. viii (incomplete). Cal. as *Reg. regum* ii no. 636, Flight, *Bishops and monks* 262, 272, 285, nos 206, 303–4, 516.

Et ego Anselmus non meis meritis sed gratia Dei Cantuariensis archiepiscopus hanc confirmationem regia auctoritate confirmatam confirmo, et ut^a ipsi prędictę ęcclesię et monachis prędictis atque post illos inperpetuum victuris firmiter stabilis et stabiliter firma et illibata permaneant sancio, et sancitam signo dominicę crucis Cristi^b consigno. Et auctoritate Dei omnipotentis Patris et Filii et Spiritus sancti et omnium sanctorum eius excommunico omnes illos qui de prędicta ęcclesia aliquid horum omnium quę hactenus ei sunt concessa et donata, et a rege Henrico et a me nunc confirmata, abstulerint vel auferre temptaverint, vel ab aliis ablatum cognita veritate receperint vel retinuerint. Hoc etiam ad ultimum superaddo. Ęterna cum Iuda proditore sit illis pęna, nisi ad satisfactionem venerint. Amen. Amen. Amen.

^{a} ut et B ^{b} om. E

For a similar note added in the name of Gundulf see *EEA Rochester* no. 7. The charter presents difficult critical problems, quite apart from the later alteration of A. As seems to be the norm for such confirmations in diploma form, it was apparently drafted and written locally: Chaplais, 'Seals' 260–75, esp. 270; Bishop, *Scriptores* no. 658. The phrase 'non meis meritis sed' is also found in 5 above (and 28 below), another indication of Rochester drafting. No obvious objection can be made to the impressions of the seals of the kg and archbp; the impression of Gundulf's seal is now apparently unique, but again not evidently suspicious. Though the end of Gundulf's first confirmation clause, the *signa* and the date occur on a leaf added to the Textus later in the century, and are written in a curious imitative hand, the bulk of the charter is in the original hand of the Textus, and that much at least must have existed by *c.* 1124. Rochester also possessed a verbatim repetition of the royal confirmation in the name of kg Stephen, and this is sealed with Stephen's first seal which is found on a number of other documents, all treated as suspect in *Reg. regum* iii xvi–xvii and no. 718, iv 5 and pls. I-II, X, XXIII, but defended by Darlington in *Cartulary of Worcester* lxvii–viii, A. Heslop in Zarnecki, *English Romanesque art 1066–1200* 303, and Flight, *Bishops and monks* 115–6. Even at Rochester it would be odd for a forgery to exist solely to repeat the terms of a genuine earlier grant. On the other hand, the estates of the grant were contentious, Rochester was skilled in the manipulation of seals, and it is unexpected that Anselm's seal should be in brown wax; all other impressions of his seal attached to documents which present no difficulties are uncoloured, as are all known impressions of the king's genuine seal applied in England (Chaplais, 'Seals', 269; above p. lx). Such considerations do not however amount to a pressing case against the text, the forms of which are not suspicious.

25. Rochester cathedral

Grant to the monks of Northfleet church, and perpetual remission of all additions to the rent from the fishery of New Weir beyond the long-established five shillings a year. [4 Dec. 1093 × 21 April 1109]

B = Strood MALSC DRc/ R I (Textus Roffensis) fos 181v-2 no. 98 (of which 182 is a replacement leaf). s. xii. C = BL Cotton Domitian x (Rochester cartulary) fo.120r-v no. 30. s. xiii in.

Pd. from B in *Text. Roff.* 158–9, and from C in *Reg. Roff.* 505. Cal. Flight, *Bishops and monks* 262 no. 207

Anselmus Dei dispositione archiepiscopus Cantuarię Hamoni vicecomiti et^a toti hundret de Tolcetreu^b et toti hundret in quo est Gillingeham et omnibus fidelibus Cristianis, salutem et benedictionem. Notum sit vobis omnibus quod ego Anselmus gratia Dei archiepiscopus Cantuariensis concedo congregationi monachorum que in ęcclesia Rofensi Deo servit et in praesenti tempore et in futuro ęcclesiam de Northflete, cum omnibus pertinentibus ad ean[fo.182]dem ęcclesiam in terris et in decimis et in oblationibus et in omnibus aliis rebus. Et remitto de censu piscarię qui census vulgo ferma dicitur quicquid additum est super antiquum censum a praepositis de Gillingeham, ad quod manerium pertinet eadem piscaria quę est in mari. Erat autem praedictus census olim quinque solidi denariorum tantum^c. Hanc summam constituo ut nullus successorum nostrorum^d vel praepositorum eiusdem manerii in futuro transeat, nec plus aliquid a praedictis monachis pro eadem piscaria per singulos annos, quantumcumque ipsa piscaria proficiat, unquam requirat. Et hanc parvam largitionem facio pro animabus eorum qui me in archiepiscopali^e sede Cantuariae praecesserunt et eorum qui successuri sunt, quatinus ipsi hanc ipsam concessionem inviolabilem et ab omnium malivolorum hominum concussione quietam conservent, insuper et pro anima mea, si Deus sua gratia michi aliquam partem in hac ipsa elemosina concedere dignatur. Valete.

^{a} et *repeated* B ^{b} de Tolectreu B; Toltetri C ^{c} tant. den. *before corr.* C
^{d} nostrorum B; meorum C ^{e} archiepali C

A group of four Northfleet charters was entered on replacement leaves in the Textus, including this one, and 26, 53 and +88 below. Flight, *Bishops and monks* 34–5 thought that this was probably substantially authentic, though noticing that the text from the turn of fo. 182 may have been altered, while rejecting the remaining three. There is nothing inherently unlikely about the text, the Northfleet section of which is all in the original hand, though the rights of Canterbury and Rochester in the church remained topics of serious contention. Rochester priory's rights there were confirmed in a royal charter by Henry II (*Reg. Roff.* 45–6), of dubious authority, and were listed in a series of spurious charters in the names of archbps Richard, Baldwin and Hubert Walter (*EEA* ii nos 194–5, 304–5, iii nos 592–4); in 1240 Rochester sent Robert the monk to Rome to seek justice on their claims against the archbp over Northfleet, but he died there—*Flores historiarum* ed. H.R. Luard (RS 1890) ii 243–4. By the end of the thirteenth century the church was a rectory in the gift of the archbp (*Taxatio* 7) and was still described so in *Valor* i 76. However, revenues at Northfleet were assigned to the priory by Gundulf in Textus Roffensis fo. 196 no. 176, also part of the original text. In *Cust. Roff.* 33, a list of revenues compiled *c.* 1230, the priory was receiving a third of the tithe of grain, possibly as the result of a later agreement.

26. Rochester cathedral

Confirmation of all scot, castle and bridge work and episcopal rights to Rochester as granted to Gundulf and the monks by Lanfranc, with a grant of the church of Northfleet, land worth twenty shillings a year in Hayes and remission of 35 shillings rent from New Weir.   [1096 × 1107]

B = Strood MALSC DRc/ R 1 (Textus Roffensis) fo.179 (a replacement leaf) c. 93. s. xii. C = BL Cotton Domitian x (Rochester cartulary) fo.119v no. 29, s. xiii in. with first four witnesses only. D = Strood MALSC DRc/T 57, suspicious inspeximus by bps Walter of Exeter and Hugh of Ely, dated May 1260.

Pd. from B in *Text. Roff.* 154 and from C in *Reg. Roff.* 32. Cal. Flight, *Bishops and monks* 262 no. 208.

Anselmus gratia Dei archiepiscopus Cantuarie Haimoni vicecomiti et omnibus baronibus regis Francigenis et Anglis de comitatu de Chent[a], salutem. Sciatis quod ego concedo ecclesie sancti Andree et episcopo Gundulfo de Rovecestria omnes illas consuetudines et leges quas habuit de antecessore meo Lanfranco archiepiscopo in scoto et in opere castri et in ponte, et omnia iura episcopalia illi pertinentia in maneriis[b] nostris et clericis et laicis sui episcopatus, sicut unquam melius vel honorabilius habuit ea. Et monachis eiusdem ecclesie do de meo dominico ecclesiam de Northfliete[c] et quicquid ad eam pertinet, in terris et in decimis et in oblationibus et in omnibus aliis rebus. Et de piscaria de Gillingeham, unde monachi solebant dare xl solidos per annum antecessori meo, perdono eisdem monachis xxxv solidos ut habeant eos ad victum eorum. Et eidem supradicto episcopo G.[d] concedo quandam terram valentem viginti solidos per annum in nostro dominico manerio de Heisa quod est in Middelsexa. Test'[e] Ernulfo priore, Ioseph, Eadmero monacho Cantuar', Baldewino de Tornac' monacho Becc'[f], Willelmo archidiacono Cantuar', Aschetillus Roffensi archidiacono, Willelmo de Einesford', Godefrido de Falchenham.

[a] Kent D   [b] maniis C   [c] *corr. fr.* -lete B   [d] Gundulfo C   [e] Teste C
[f] et cetera *and ends* C

This follows immediately on 25 in B, and so is the second of the charters bearing on Northfleet to be entered on a replacement leaf in the Textus, and the first to be entirely so. One at least (below +88) has clearly been tampered with. This one presents no manifestly suspicious features, differing as it does from 25 in including the customs of the archbpric and land in Hayes but not in its account of Rochester's rights in Northfleet. It may well represent an authentic grant, though Flight, *Bishops and monks* 34–5, 262 thought it a conflation of 25 above, which he broadly accepted, 53 and +88. For Baldwin and Joseph see above, pp. xxxvii–viii.

+27. Rochester cathedral

Confirmation to Rochester of rights in the diocese as in the preceding charter, adding all rights in Freckenham and Isleham. [4 Dec. 1093 × 1108]

A = Strood MALSC DRc/T 49, supposed original. Endorsed, s. xiii: Carta A. archiepiscopi; s. xiv: Carta Ancelmi archiepiscopi. Approximately 173 × 96 + seal tongue 18 mm wide. Sealed on a tongue with a seal in coarse red-brown wax. The impression of Anselm's seal is close enough to the real thing to suggest either that it is taken from a cast of the seal attached to an authentic text or that it has been detached from one. It has been repaired too comprehensively to allow for certainty. Of the legend ..LVM AN... CHIEP... survives.

B = Maidstone CKS DRb/ Ar2 (Registrum Temporalium, formerly DRc/ R 3) fo. 17v. s. xiv. C = BL Cotton Faustina B v (Historia Roffensis), fo. 72v. s. xv, inspeximus by prior Richard and the convent of Christ Church Canterbury, dated 5 Feb. 1333, of a number of spurious or interpolated charters for Rochester, including a charter in the name of archbp Boniface, dated 19 July 1259, which in turn inspects Lanfranc's charter, no. +7 above, this text and an interpolated version of Bates, *Acta* no. 226.

Pd. from A and C in *Reg. Roff.* 359–60, 446. Cal. Flight, *Bishops and monks* 262–3 no. 209.

Anselmus gratia Dei archiepiscopus Cantuar' *vicecomitibus de Kent et de Suthfolchia* et omnibus baronibus regis Francigenis et Anglis, salutem. Sciatis quod ego concedo ecclesie sancti Andree et episcopo Gundulpho de Rovecestria omnes illas consuetudines et leges quas habuit de antecessore meo Lanfranco archiepiscopo, in scoto et in opere castri et in ponte, et omnia iura episcopalia in maneriis *suis, tam* in clericis quam in laicis sui episcopatus *quam in locis de Frekeham et Iselham sibi subiectis que sunt in partibus Suffolch' et Kantebregg',* sicut unquam melius vel honorabilius habuit ea. Et monachis eiusdem ecclesie do^a de meo dominico ecclesiam de Northflete et quicquid ad eam pertinet in terris,^{b} in decimis et^c in oblacionibus et in omnibus aliis rebus. Et de piscaria de Gillyngham unde monachi solebant dare quadraginta solidos per annum antecessori meo perdono eisdem monachis triginta quinque solidos ut habeant eos ad victum eorum. Et eidem supradicto episcopo Gundulpho concedo quandam terram valentem viginti solidos per annum in nostro dominico manerio de Heisa quod est in Middelsexia. ^{d}*Et ut hec concessio stabilis et firma in perpetuum habeatur, sigilli mei^e munimine roboratur.*^{d} Teste Ernulfo priore *Cantuar' et aliis.*

^{a} *after* dominico C ^{b} et *add.* B ^{c} *om.* C $^{d-d}$ *om.* B ^{e} nostri C

This charter is essentially a version of the preceding text interpolated with references to episcopal rights in Freckenham and Isleham; the additions are in italic type. The script is clearly of the mid-thirteenth century or later, with no pretence at archaism. For a number of comparable manipulated texts on the same topic see above, +7, below +28, +54, +89. The form of the seal is unexceptionable, though the colouring and texture are curious; it may well have been taken from a cast of an authentic impression, as suggested by A. Oakley in *Arch. Cant.* xci (1975) 55–6.

+28. Rochester cathedral

Confirmation of the rights of Rochester in the diocese and of Freckenham and Isleham as granted by Lanfranc by his charter, which is recited.

Canterbury [1096 × 1107]

B = BL Cotton Faustina B v (Historia Roffensis) fo. 68v. s. xv. C = Lost, and spurious, charter of archbp Boniface, dated 1254, formerly Cotton Charter Vitellius B 3. (For B and C see above, +7).

Pd. from C in *Mon. Angl.* (1673) iii 3, (1817) i 176 (l), from B in *Reg. Roff.* 441–2. Cal. Flight, *Bishops and monks* 263 no. 210.

Anselmus Dei gratia*ª* archiepiscopus Cantuar' vicecomitibus de Kent et Suffolch' et omnibus baronibus regis Francigenis et Anglis et omnibus fidelibus*ᵇ* et amicis meis, salutem. Sciatis quod ego concedo ecclesie Sancti Andree et episcopo Gundulpho de Rovecestr' omnes illas consuetudines et leges quas habuit*ᶜ* de antecessore meo Lamfranco archiepiscopo, et omnia iura episcopalia in maneriis nostris que in episcopatu suo sunt situata, et in manerio de Frekenham cum membro suo in Iselham quod Lamfrancus aliquamdiu*ᵈ* tenuit in manibus suis, utens in eis omnimoda lege episcopali*ᵉ*, et post ita sursum reddidit adeo libere sicut et ipse tenuit, per cartam suam habentem hunc tenorem:

Lanfrancus Dei gratia etc ut supra*ᶠ* [*above* +7]

Et ego Anselmus, non meis meritis sed gratia Dei Cant' archiepiscopus, hanc reddicionem et restitucionem pontificali auctoritate et regio consensu factam concedo, et confirmo ut imperpetuum firmiter stabilis et stabiliter firma et illibata permaneat, et auctoritate Dei omnipotentis Patris et Filii et Spiritus sancti et omnium sanctorum eius excommunico omnes illos qui aliquid de iuribus temporalibus aut spiritualibus*ᵍ* manerii de Frekenham et Iselham ab ipsis rege et archiepiscopo concessis et*ʰ* redditis et restitutis, et a me nunc confirmatis abstulerint, auferre aut diminuere temptaverint, vel ab aliis ablatum cognita veritate receperint vel retinuerint. Hoc etiam ad ultimum superaddo, eterna cum Iuda proditore sit illis pena, nisi ad satisfactionem venerint. Amen.

Teste Ernulpho priore apud Cant', qui hanc cartam consignavit.

a gracia Dei C   *b om.* B   *c* habuit B; habent C   *d* aliq. Lan. C   *e* -ati C
f C *has text of* +7, *but* B *does not*   *g* spir. aut temp. C   *h om.* C

This is the earliest surviving inspeximus charter by many years. The charter of Lanfranc is so obvious a forgery that it is difficult to see how it could have been produced before Anselm's death. Compare the opening passage with 26, +27 above and the end with 24.

+29. Rochester cathedral

General confirmation of all the (specified) lands and rights recovered by Lanfranc in the shire court of Kent before king William I's justiciars and restored to Rochester, and others granted by William II and Henry I, to be held as fully and freely and as quit of toll as in the time of those kings and as Christ Church Canterbury holds its own, since the two churches were both founded by king Ethelberht. London 'in concilio prelatorum', 1101

A = Strood MALSC DRc/ T 48 (formerly B 790), supposed original. Endorsed, s. xiv: Confirmacio Anselmi archiepiscopi. 194 × 222 mm, with no clear evidence of sealing, though the left hand of the foot of the charter is ragged, as if a tongue might have been torn from it.

B = Spurious inspeximus of archbp Boniface of 1254 (as above, +5). C = BL Cotton Faustina B v (Historia Roffensis) fos 68v-69v, s. xv, in inspeximus attributed to Hubert Walter, *EEA* iii no. +592.

Pd from B in *Mon. Angl.* (1673) iii 2-3, (1817) i 175-6 (l), from C in *Reg. Roff.* 442. Cal. Flight, *Bishops and monks* 263 no. 211.

Anselmus gratia Dei archiepiscopus Cantuar' Hamoni vicecomiti et Gileberto de Tonnebregg' ac ceteris hominibus Francigenis et Anglis, salutem. Sciatis quod ego, de mandato domini nostri Henrici regis*a* Anglie et rogatu Gundulfi episcopi Roffe, concedo et confirmo ecclesie sancti Andree Roffe et eidem Gundulfo episcopo omnes terras et ecclesias, libertates et consuetudines, rectitudines et omnia maneria que et quas Lanfrancus archiepiscopus tempore Willelmi regis magni de ipsius mandato in pleno comitatu de Chent coram Godefrido et Egelrico Constanciensi et Cicestrensi episcopis et Hamone vicecomite, iusticiariis regis assignatis, diraciocinando evicit et recuperavit. Et postquam illa recuperaverat, ecclesie Roffe et episcopo Gundulfo sursum reddidit et restituit, nominatim scilicet: Stokes cum ecclesia, Frendesberiam cum ecclesia, Eslyngham, Bromheye et Wicham, Borstalle cum ecclesia, Kuckelstane cum ecclesia, Woldeham cum ecclesia, Hallyngas cum ecclesia, Snodelondes cum ecclesia, Mallyngas cum ecclesia, Trottesclyve cum ecclesia, Langefelde cum ecclesia, Faukeham cum ecclesia, Bromlegham cum ecclesia, Stanes cum ecclesia, Litlebroke et

Hiltone, Suthflete cum ecclesia, Denyntunam*b* cum ecclesia in comitatu de Chent, cum omnibus membris, feodis et pertinenciis suis, que sunt ex donacione antiquorum regum Anglie; in Surreya Lamhetham cum ecclesia quod dedit Goda comitissa, et Willelmus rex filius regis Willelmi ecclesie Roffe deinde restituit; in Suthfolchia Frekeham et Iselham cum ecclesiis, quod Willelmus rex magnus Lanfranco concessit et Lanfrancus ecclesie Sancti Andree Roffe et episcopo Gundulfo sursum reddidit; in Buckynghamshire Haderham quod rex Willelmus rogatu Lanfranci ad victum monachorum apud Roffam Deo famulancium dedit; in Gloucestreshire Astonam*c* quod dedit Willelmus rex ecclesie Roffe et Gundulfo episcopo, que omnia data sunt libere ab omni exactione et subiectione regali in perpetuam elemosinam; et ecclesiam de Retherfeld quam Gilebertus de Tonebregge dedit ecclesie Roffe, ecclesias de Boxele, de Derteford, de Wolewych', et de Chiselherst quas Henricus rex ecclesie Rovecestrie in elemosinam donavit. Et volo quod ecclesia Sancti Andree Roffe et episcopus Gundulfus ac successores sui ista teneant ita libere sicut tempore Willelmi, Willelmi et Henrici *d*regum Anglie et*d* Lanfranci archiepiscopi ecclesia Roffensis melius et plenius tenuit et habuit, et ecclesia Cristi Cantuar' sua maneria tenet, cum soka et saka, toln and theam, grithbreche, hamsokne, forstall', infangenethef, flemenesferme, et de toln de terra et de aqua in civitate Roffe, et de transitu aque, fracto ponte, et de hundredo quartum denarium, et de omnibus exitibus que pertinent ad preposituram civitatis quartam partem, excepto gablo*e* regis; et quod omnes episcopi et eorum tenentes ubicunque in regno Anglie sint liberi*f* a prestacione telonei, sicut homines et tenentes ecclesie Cristi Cantuar', et easdem in omnibus habeant*g* libertates et consuetudines. Hec autem feci, concessi et confirmavi in testimonium veritatis quod ecclesie Cantuariensis et Roffensis ab uno et eodem rege Cristianissimo*h* Ethelberto sunt fundate, et antiquorum regum Anglie possessionibus et donacionibus dotate fuerunt. Acta sunt hec London' in concilio prelatorum et sigilli nostri impressione communita ad maiorem evidenciam veritatis. Anno Domini MC primo. Testibus Girardo archiepiscopo Eboracensi, Mauricio episcopo London', Osmundo episcopo Sar', Gualchelino episcopo Wynton', Stigando episcopo Cicestren', Hereberto episcopo Tefforden', Baldewyno abbate Sancti Eadmundi, Radulpho abbate Sagien', Ernulfo priore Cantuar', Alano comite, Hugone comite, Hugone de Montforti et aliis.

a reg. Hen. C   *b* Denynt- AC; Nevynt- B   *c* Ast. *om.* B
d-d regum Anglie et A; et B; regum Anglie C   *e* galbo C   *f* et *add* C
g in omn. hab. AB: hab. in omn. C   *h* et *add* C

The supposed 'original' is in a thirteenth century hand, similar to that of +27 above but apparently distinct. The witness list is comprehensively impossible for the supposed date or any other, for Baldwin of Bury died in 1097/8, Walkelin of Winchester in 1098 and Osmund of Salisbury in 1099, while Gerard was not translated to York until Jan. 1101 (Hugh the Chanter 20–1). The list of churches Anselm is made to confirm includes Boxley, which was granted by Henry I in 1130 (below +88), as well as Freckenham and Isleham. The reference to an episcopal council in 1101 may derive from a misdating of the council of Westminster 1102, which is common in thirteenth-century annals, including those of Rochester in BL Cotton Vespasian A xxii fo. 28.

+30. Rochester cathedral

Confirmation of the grant by Gilbert of Tonbridge, earl of Hertford, of an annual pension of two marks of silver from the church of Rotherfield to be paid by Alured the parson and his successors, by consent of bishop Ralph of Chichester. [c.1096 × 1107]

B = Strood MALSC DRc/ L 5/1, in s. xiii ex (?) sealed charter of archbp Pecham, reciting the title deeds of Rochester to Rotherfield, dated at Lambeth 1 Oct. 1282.
Pd from B in *Reg. Roff.* 592. Cal. Flight, *Bishops and monks* 263 no. 212.

Anselmus gratia Dei archiepiscopus Cant' Gilberto de Tonnebregg' comiti Hertfordie et omnibus hominibus in lasto de Ailesfordia, salutem. Omnibus vobis notum facio quod de consensu Rad'i episcopi Suthsexie donum et annuum censum duarum marcarum quod Gilbertus de Tonnebregge fecit monachis Rovecestr' et Aluredo persone ecclesie de Retherfeld et successoribus suis imposuit confirmo imperpetuum pro elemosina. Test' Radulfo episcopo Suthsexie, Ernulpho priore Cant' , Gilberto de Tonebreg' et Hamone vicecomite de Chent.

The original gift by Gilbert to Rochester was confirmed by William II in *Reg. regum* i no. 450 (Textus Roffensis fo.182v no. 100, also in B). A charter of Gilbert I, which makes no mention of a pension, survives in the apparent original Strood MALSC DRc/ T 373, attested by Anselm and Godfrey, prior of Winchester. This was printed in *Reg. Roff.* 590–1, from the Domitian cartulary, which also includes a charter of Gilbert III (cr. earl in 1138, d. 1152) recording his grant of the church to Alured, the son and heir of Herbert, who had held the church in the days of his father and grandfather (*Reg. Roff.* 590). The mention of Alured in the charter of Anselm, and its anachronistic reference to Gilbert I as earl of Hertford, show that it is a forgery. In B the Anselm act is followed by two charters, one in the name of bp Seffrid II of Chichester (*EEA* xxiii Appx 5 no. 11, Flight, *Bishops and monks* 281 no. 409), the other of Gilbert of Tonbridge (*Reg. Roff.* 592, at the request of Anselm but with a wholly improbable witness list). The Seffrid act, which is already found in the Domitian cartulary and presents no formal difficulties, claims that bp John (1173–1180) instituted Herbert (or Hubert) to Rotherfield at the presentation of prior Ernulf and the monks of Rochester. Priors Ernulf flicker in and out of the history of Rochester, and *Heads* i 254 cites *Cust. Roff.* 28 for an otherwise unknown one in 1148 × 82. It is quite possible that a Hubert or Herbert succeeded Alured son of Herbert, and that prior Ernulf is indeed to be inserted as occurring after 1173 but before Silvester, who first occurs in 1180 (since *Reg, Roff.* 410–1, *EEA* ii no.

194 is spurious); compare Greatrex, *Biographical register* 602, 637. The dossier in B was probably assembled in the course of the quarrel between Rochester and the Clare family over the patronage of Rotherfield, which reached a peak in 1258, again in 1294, and was in full swing once more at the time of the compilation of the Liber Temporalium (*Reg. Roff.* 595–6). In 1320 the king's agents were apparently claiming at the papal curia that the right of presentation alternated between the bp and the heirs of the earl of Gloucester (*Cal. Chancery Warrants* 505–6). The charter of archbp Pecham is almost certainly not genuine either. There is no record of this plea, or any other, touching Rotherfield in his Register, and the itinerary which can be extracted from that text shows that he was at his Sussex manor of Slindon on 1 Oct. 1282, and seems not to have been near London between August 1282 and March 1283. The seal at the foot is too fragmentary to establish its character with confidence. At the Dissolution the sacrist of Rochester was still receiving a two-mark pension from Rotherfield, *Valor* i 103.

31. Priory of St Neots

Record of his examination of the bones of St Neot at the priory there when abbot of Bec, his transfer of a relic to Bec, and exhortation to the faithful to support the priory. [Feb. 1094 × 21 April 1109]

B = Lincoln, LA Bishop's register I (register of bp Sutton) fos 122v-123 in contemporary copy of inspeximus by bp Sutton dated 8 May 1295.

Pd in G.C. Gorham *History and antiquities of Eynesbury and St Neots* Appx no.vi, *EA* 473, *The rolls and register of bishop Oliver Sutton* ed. R. Hill v (1965) 79–80; partial text in Eadmer, *Vita Ans.* 57n; translated by Fröhlich, *Letters* iii 266–7 no. 473, *Anselmo d'Aosta* iii 500–02.

Anselmus gratia Dei[a] archiepiscopus R.[b] reverendo episcopo Linc' et omnibus qui volunt scire veritatem de corpore beati Neoti confessoris, salutem. Sciatis pro certo quia ego ipse cum abbas essem Becci requisivi in Neotesberia in scrinio quod vocant feretrum, et inveni ossa sancti et pretiosi confessoris Neoti, et statim reposui ea in eodem scrinio, excepto[c] uno brachio quod dicitur esse in Cornu Gallie et excepto[c] modico quod mecum propter memoriam et venerationem eiusdem sancti retinui, et diligenter serato scrinio intus clausis eisdem ossibus, et tuli mecum clavem ad ecclesiam Becci ubi usque in hodiernum diem studiose servatur. Precor autem ut omnes quibus Deus opportunitatem dabit et requisiti fuerint aliquod auxilium prout Deus illis inspirare dignabitur aut in facto aut in verbo ad construendam eiusdem sancti confessoris ecclesiam impendant, et nullus eis qui opus eiusdem ecclesie procurant vel ad hoc auxilium querunt aliquo modo molestus existat, quatinus unicuique Deus in vita eterna retribuat, et idem sanctus pro illis apud [fo.123] Deum sicut illis scit expedire intercedat. Nos quoque quantum possumus Deum suppliciter exoramus ut omnibus qui eidem ecclesie aliquod auxilium impendent suam tribuat benedictionem et peccatorum eorum absolutionem. Valete.

^a corr. fr. Dei gratia B   *^b a small letter, but a capital*   *^c* ex'to B. *Hill expanded as* extracto

Addressed to bp R. who must be Robert I of Lincoln, nominated in March 1093 but not consecrated until the next year. The last sentence, from 'Nos quoque quantum. . .', is the only one in the plural, and this might be part of an enclosing text (though, if so, it is part of an earlier document than Sutton's). The syntax of this text is erratic, and sometimes ambiguous, and much of its formulation differs from that of better attested acts—but the circumstances are not parallelled either. The history of the relics of St Neot is a tangled one. They were said to have been carried from Cornwall to St Neots by the early eleventh century, but Orderic Vitalis around 1115 and William of Malmesbury ten years later accepted that they had been translated from there to Crowland during the Danish wars and had remained there. Crowland still claimed to have the bulk of them in 1213—*Analecta Bollandiana* xx (1901) 464–6. St Neots, a dependency of Bec since *c.* 1080, seems to have asserted that the relics had been returned later, and Henry of Huntingdon in the late 1120s (ed. Greenway 690, followed by Torigni ed. Delisle i 118) simply assumed they were there. The story is conveniently surveyed in *Annals of St Neots with* Vita prima sancti Neoti eds D. Dumville and M. Lapidge, lxxxvi-xcvi; compare too M. Chibnall, 'History of the priory of St Neots', *Proc. Cambridge Antiquarian Soc.* lix (1966) 67–74 and 'The relations of Saint Anselm with the English dependencies of the abbey of Bec', repr. from *Spicilegium Beccense* (1959) 521–30 in *Piety, power and history in medieval England and Normandy*. However, these accounts all accept the authenticity of Anselm's letter. Given the complexities of the case, the apparent function of the text as proof that St Neot rested entire (except the relics at Bec and in Cornwall) at the priory and not in Crowland and its absence from all the earlier collections of Anselm's remains, however comprehensive their ambitions, its authenticity though possible remains uncertain. The uncertainty is if anything increased by the much later claim of Dom Thibault (d. 1684) that, even after the depredations of the wars of religion, Bec still had the jawbone of St Neot, 'cuius integrum corpus olim asservabatur in hoc Beccensi sacrario', but that no relic of him had been listed in the detailed inventory of Bec's relics made on the occasion of the Empress Matilda's magnificent donation of 1134 (Porée, *Histoire du Bec* i 655).

+32. Abbey of Saint-Valery

Confirmation by apostolic authority at the request of abbot Arnald of all the abbey's possessions in England by virtue of gifts made by king William I and his men, being twelve hides in Essex and two and a half hides in Cambridgeshire with twenty acres given by Guy de Reincourt.   [4 Dec. 1093 × 21 April 1109]

> A = Oxford, New College Archive no. 13152 (formerly Takeley 300). Endorsed, s. xiii: Anselmuu; s. xiii/xiv: H Horton. 167 × 154 mm, the foot slit to carry a leather thong bearing an elliptical seal in white wax, heavily varnished and very badly chipped. Ruled in dry point. Written in an awkward, and possibly imitative, hand.
> Pd from A by L. Delisle, *Bibl. de l'École des chartes* lxix (1908), 574 no. v; H.E.Salter, *Facsimiles of early charters in Oxford muniment rooms* no. 27.

+ Quoniam edax oblivio et temporum volubilitas solet exterminare et de medio tollere quod bene caniniceque patratum est, curavimus aliquid memorie tradere quod sancte valeat ęcclesię prodesse. Ego igitur Anselmus, Dei gratia Cantuariensis archiepiscopus et Anglię primas, volo et auctoritate apostolica confirmo quidquid monachi sancti Walarici habent in Anglia, ex dono regis Willelmi, illius scilicet Willelmi qui Anglos sibi subiugavit et baronum eius qui secum venerunt, et in elemosina aliquid eidem sancto dederunt, vel Deo annuente habituri sunt. Habent siquidem prefati monachi in Exsexia xii hidas, scilicet ex dono Willelmi regis, et in Cantebrugescir' ii hidas et dimidiam et xx acras ex dono Guidonis de Reimecurt. Hoc inquam ita confirmo ut quicumque istud donum amaverit, servaverit et defenderit cęlestem obtineat benedictionem. Et econtra si quis inminuerit aut contra monachos insurrexerit, et aliquam violentiam eis pro hoc intulerit, nisi ab hac resipiscat presumptione, cuiuscumque conditionis dignitatisve sit, maledictionem cum Dathan et Abiron sortiatur et anathema sit. Hoc quoque feci domni Arnulfi abbatis supradicti sancti humili petitione et multorum sancte ęcclesię fidelium consilio, prece et ammonitione. Et ut istud ad quoscumque hęc carta pervenerit ratum habeatur, proprio sigillo signavi et munivi.

> This charter has unusual features, particularly in *arenga, intitulatio* and method of sealing. No other letter or authentic charter of Anselm uses the primatial style, with the exception of the wholly aberrant 14 and 23 above; the style only became standard under Theobald. All these features, and especially the sealing technique, might be explained by its being drawn up at Saint-Valery, for the use of a leather tag seems to have been much more frequent at this time across the Channel (Chaplais, 'Seals', 268–9). The much less problematic Saltman, *Theobald* no. 137 is also sealed on a leather thong, though the arrangement is distinct. However the impression of the seal casts much more serious doubt on its authenticity; it bears no relation to that found on more trustworthy documents. Most notably the archbp is represented wearing a mitre with prominent ribbons, but without the pallium which figures so prominently on the other examples of his seal; his staff is in his left hand, while his maniple falls from his right hand, presumably itself once raised in blessing though that part has been lost. There is no other reason to suppose that Anselm used a first seal between 1093 and 1095, when he received the pallium, and it seems unlikely such a first seal would have shown him with a mitre while a second did not. The Essex estates mentioned here seem to be the holding recorded for Saint-Valery in Domesday for the county. The Cambridgeshire estates are not identified in Domesday, but seem to have lain in Melbourn, where Saint-Valery long retained claims (*VCH Cambs.* viii 72). All these lands are confirmed to the abbey in two charters attributed to Henry I, Salter, *Facsimiles of charters in Oxford muniment rooms* nos 28 and 29, *Reg. regum* ii nos 797, 1480 (noticed as spurious in Bishop, *Scriptores* nos 613–4). Both in script and phrasing these are clearly the product of the mid-twelfth century or later; the opening lines of Salter no. 28 are in a curious and rather laboured script not wholly unlike that of Anselm's charter. By the sixteenth century Saint-Valery had become a byword for the diligence and scale of its forgeries, and Clovis Brunel in his study of the more striking examples (*Le moyen âge* 2s xiii (1909) 98) prefaced his examination with the sweeping judgement: 'toute présomption devra être pour leur imposture quand les titres examinés ne seront pas absolument réguliers'. Regularity is far from the best guarantee of authenticity at this date, but the context does impose extreme caution. Salter, who argued that the forms were more consistent with an early date than with a forgery, suggested that it was granted when Anselm may have visited the abbey late in 1097.

RALPH D'ESCURES 1114–1122

+33.   Battle abbey

Confirmation, generally addressed, of grants of tithe by named benefactors in Rewbridge, Buckwell and Oleford, dependencies of the abbey manor of Wye, with free disposition of the proceeds, and permission for future benefactors to make similar grants.   [26 April 1114 × 20 Oct. 1122]

> A = BL Harley charter 43 G 18. Endorsed, s. xii/xiii: Rad' archiepiscopus de decimis. 178 × 97 with 10 mm step for sealing tongue, now gone. The top of this step has been slit horizontally for a narrow tie, fragments of which survive.

Radulf' Dei gratia Cantuar' archiepiscopus omnibus fidelibus, salutem et Dei benedictionem et suam. Sciatis me concessisse et confirmasse omnes decimas quę datę sunt ęcclesię sancti Martini de Bello in elemosinam, et nominatim decimam Bald' filii Toke de Beyardregg', decimam Norm' de Essetesford de Bechewelle et decimam Ansfr' dapiferi de Oleford, quę date sunt eidem ęcclesię in manerio suo de Wi. Hoc quoque nostra auctoritate super sententiam anathematis precipio, quod nullus eosdem monachos prępediat vel calumniando fatiget, sed ut predictas decimas suas integre, libere et quiete in pace colligant ac possideant, vel ut melius eisdem visum fuerit ad proprios usus utiliter sibimet in perpetuum procurent. Insuper et hoc concedo et presenti scripto confirmo, ut quicumque voluerit suas decimas det ipsi ęcclesię de Bello quas iuste dare potuerit, et dantibus Dei benedictionem et nostram concedo in perpetuum. Valete.

> This is a peculiarly troubling document. The bizarre arrangement for an apparent wrapping tie attached as a tag is odd enough for any period, but certainly easier to accept early in the century than late. Yet suspicion naturally attaches to any early charter of Battle, and the subject matter of this charter was certainly involved in controversy later in the century. Around 1176, as part of a settlement with Godfrey de Luci as vicar of Wye, abbot Odo confirmed what was said then to be a long-standing arrangement by which these tithes were assigned to the sacristy according to *Chron. Battle* 334, a text now to be read in the light of N. Vincent, 'King Henry II and the monks of Battle: the Battle chronicle unmasked' in *Belief and culture in the middle ages. Studies presented to Henry Mayr-Harting* ed. R. Gameson and H. Leyser (Oxford 2001) 264–86; compare too *EEA* ii nos 52–4. A bull of Alexander III dated 16 March 1174 confirmed the revenues and tithes of the church of Wye 'sicut . . . . ad cereum iugiter arsurum coram reliquiis ipsius monasterii . . . deputata et assignata esse dinoscitur' (*PUE* iii no. 212). More decisively, the script of this supposed original is identified by Dr Webber as characteristic of the period after 1150, pointing particularly to the long trailing-headed 'a' in medial as well as initial position, the 'de' monogram and a 'g' with a bold horizontal tail

traced from left-to-right as features individually rare and collectively unknown in charters before the second half of the century. It is the more remarkable that most of the forms of this text seem straightforward. Grants of tithe were not the issues for which the known abbey forgers went to work, the terms of the confirmation, though striking, show no decisive anachronism (though 'ad proprios usus' provokes concern); and the title, salutation, movement from singular to plural and back, and valediction are all well-attested in Ralph's other genuine documents. On all these grounds it is probable that the compiler of this charter had access to a genuine charter of Ralph, but there can be no confidence that the exemplar was cast in these terms, concerned these tithes, or indeed was directed to Battle, though the latter is likely.

34. Abbey of Le Bec-Hellouin

Confirmation to Bec and St Philibert-sur-Risle of the church of Saltwood as granted by Robert de Montfort. [26 April 1114 × 20 Oct. 1122]

> B = Windsor, St George's Chapel Archives XI G 29 (Inspeximus by bp Guy of Lisieux 1267–85) of six charters for Bec, the latest dated 1254; the single sheet is presumably a copy since it lacks final clauses and seal. s. xiii.
> Cal. *HMC Various coll.* vii 30.

Notum sit omnibus fidelibus quod ego Rad' Cantuariens' archiepiscopus concedo ecclesie sancte Marie Becci et ecclesie sancti Philiberti que est iuxta Montem Fortem sita et monachis ibi Deo servientibus perpetuo iure possidendam ecclesiam sancti Petri de Saltoda cum omnibus capellis ad eam pertinentibus, quas omnes, videlicet ecclesiam sancti Petri et capellas ad eam pertinentes, Robertus de Monteforti cum terris et decimis ad eam pertinentibus supradictis dedit ecclesiis. Hoc sicut dixi concedo, et ut in perpetuum firmum permaneat sigillo meo confirmo.

> The form and phrasing of this charter are clumsy; the reversal of intitulatio and inscriptio, and the corroboration and sealing clause are all most unusual so early in the century, though the first person singular would be equally rare later. Saltman, *Theobald* no. 297, from the same source, confirms Ralph's gift, for which see also M.Morgan, *The English lands of the abbey of Bec* 24, 143. For the history of Saltwood compare above 17 and references there. In the *Taxatio* of 1291, 2 Saltwood was a rectory, paying a pension of £10 annually to Bec.

35. Bexley church

Grant to William the priest of Bexley and the church of St Mary of pasture for eight cattle and ten pigs free of pannage, and of tithes of the archbishop's pannage in beasts and coin. [27 June 1115 × 20 Oct. 1122]

> A = PRO Ancient Deeds E 40/ 5005. Endorsed, s. xii: Rad' archiepiscopus de octo animalibus in dominico herbagio et de decem porcis sine pannagio et de decima pannagii in Bixle que ipse contulit ecclesie et Willemo presbitero; s. xii: Bixle. 183 × 70 mm (lhs),

52 mm (rhs) mm, with 10 mm tongue and a 3 mm wrapping tie, one end of which is now knotted across the tongue and the main document, apparently to strengthen the junction. There is no step below the tongue for the tie to have been in the more conventional position earlier. Seal in natural wax, of which most has survived, though only '. . .RCHIE. . ...DI GR. . .' of the legend is still visible.
Pd Du Boulay, 'Bexley' 50 no. I, with facs. facing 48.

Rad' Cant' archiepiscopus Anfrido dapifero et toti parrochie de Bix, salutem. Sciatis me dedisse Willelmo presbitero et ecclesie sancte Marie de Bix octo animalia in dominico herbagio nostro, quatuor boves et quatuor vaccas, et decem porcos in bosco nostro, sine patnagio, et totam decimam de patnagio nostro, de porcis et de denariis. Test' Iohanne arch' et Ricardo Norwic' arch' et Anfr' dapifero et Waltero et Alano et Hosberto clericis, Willelmo calvo et Willelmo de sancto Albano, Rodberto filio Riculfi.

> Compare 62, 80–81 below, and on the same topic in the same hand, which is also found in 66 for Christ Church and at least one cathedral priory book (above p. lxv). It is possible that William calvus is William calvellus (above 15), the portreeve of Canterbury, or one of his kin. This is almost certainly an English act, and so probably after Ralph's assumption of the pallium, which Eadmer places before the appointment of archdn John (*Historia* 231), but before 16 Sept. 1116 or between Jan. 1120 and 20 Oct. 1122.

36. Canterbury: lands of the see

Grant to Edward of Cornhill and Godelif his wife of Wulfsi's land in Addington, given to Edward as his wife's dower, for which he has become the archbishop's man, paying 20 shillings rent to the archbishop's treasury.

[24 Sept. 1114 × 20 Oct. 1122]

> A = PRO Duchy of Lancaster Ancient Deeds DL 27/ 46. Endorsed: s. xii: Car' Rad' archiepiscopi de Adintune; s. xiii: fact' Eadward' de Cornhulle; s. xii on face of tongue: Edinton'. 247 × 117 mm (lhs), 95 (rhs) with a 22 mm tongue and a 5 mm step for a wrapping tie. Seal in white wax, heavily varnished, much repaired and upside down. Of the legend only ' . . .NSIS ARCHIE. . .' is legible. Written in a large bookhand (Plate IIa).
> Noticed and partially pd in Round, *Geoffrey de Mandeville* 306–7.

Ego Radulffus archiepiscopus concedo Æadwardo de Cornhelle et uxori eius Godelif et heredibus suis ter[r]am de Eadintune que fuit Wlsini, quam Æ. de Sudwerc dedit cum filia sua Æ. de C[o]rnhelle pro viginti solidis denariorum quos inde dabit in thesaurum meum singulis annis, unde est Æ. noster homo et mihi et successoribus meis in placitis nostris serviet, et nulli pre[p]osito nisi ipsi archiepiscopo inde respondeat. T. Ærn' episcopo Rof', Normanno abbate dein[a], Seinfred' magn', Lu[p]ello capellano, Alano clerico.

[a] *or* dem *or* deiu

Here, and in all succeeding cases, an attestation by bp Ernulf is taken as possible from his investing with the bpric rather than his installation on 10 Oct. or consecration on 26 Dec. 1115 (Eadmer, *Historia* 225, 236–7). The witness list is far from easy to interpret. An abbot Norman of Ivry, a former monk of Bec, was listed in 1154 by Torigni ii 204 as fifth of the six abbots after its foundation in 1076. While this suggests a rather later date for him, he is presumably the 'Normannus abbas' who professed at Bec under abbot William in Porée, *Histoire du Bec* i 633, though ibid i 103 says he was a pupil of Lanfranc at Bec—perhaps because the only other early Norman in the Bec list occurs as no. 27 under Herluin, i 629. There seems to be no other candidate in our surving evidence. If Seinfred magn' is the archbp's half brother he became abbot of Glastonbury in 1120 × 1. The scribe, whose work is familiar in Christ Church works of the period, certainly does appear to mean one witness by the term. For Lupellus and Alan see above p. xlvii.

37. Canterbury: lands of the see

Confirmation addressed to the reeves and hundreds of Pagham and Lavant to Wulnoth son of Seman of his father's holding as his father held it from Lanfranc for an annual rent of one hundred cuttlefish.

Pagham [26 April 1114 × 20 Oct. 1122]

B = BL Cotton Claudius A vi (cartulary of Boxgrove priory) fo. 150v (formerly 145v). s. xiii.
Partial trans. (as an act of archbp Richard of Dover) *Chart. Boxgrove* no. 399.

R. archiepiscopus W. preposito et toti hundredo de Pagah' et W. preposito et toti hundredo de Loventona salutem. Sciatis quod ego concessi Wulnodo filio Semanni terram patris sui ut ipse in hereditate libere eam teneat, sicut ipse Semannus eam de antecessore meo Lanfranco archiepiscopo tenere solebat, et ad recognitionem quod libere tenet omni anno dabit michi et sucessoribus meis centum sepias. De hoc testes sunt Rob' de Ceresio et W. de Witsant et Balld' apud Pagah'.

This is clearly an act of Ralph, not Richard. It is in the first person singular. The archbp refers only to his two predecessors, whereas later grants by Theobald and Thomas refer to Lanfranc, Anselm and their other predecessors. If Seman held the land from Lanfranc, his son is unlikely to have received a confirmation of title after 1162. Robert of Cerisy also attests 49. Compare *EEA Canterbury 1139–61* forthcoming (*Chart. Boxgrove* 172 no. 398), and *EEA* ii nos 5, 71.

38. Canterbury: Christ Church

Perpetual restitution of Sapacre to the convent.

[25 April 1114 × 20 Oct. 1122]

A = Canterbury D. & C. C.A. S 350. 162 × 52, with tongue for seal 20mm wide projecting from the left. No trace of a seal. Four lines of text written in a large book-hand.

Endorsed, s. xii/xiii: Carta Rad' archiepiscopi de Sapacra quod reddidit conuentui in Sutsesse; s. xiii/xiv: Sapacra; s. xiii/xiv: in Sutsesse; s. xiii/xiv: .II. (Plate IIIa)
B = Canterbury D. & C. Register I fo. 86v (127v). s. xiii ex. C = Canterbury D. & C. Register E fo. 6ov. s. xiv in. D = Canterbury D. & C. Register A fo.164 (186). s. xiv in.
Pd from A in L. Delisle, *Bibl. de l'École des chartes* lxix (1908) 574 no. vi.

Rad' Dei gratia Cant' archiepiscopus Rad' episcopo Cicest' et omnibus hominibus suis Francis et Anglis de Suthsexe, salutem et Dei benedictionem. Sciatis me reddidisse conventui ęcclesię Cristi Cant' Sapacram, tenendum in perpetuum in suo proprio dominio.

'Sapacre' is unidentified, and is listed in CD among the archiepiscopal charters, not under the place where it lay.

39. Canterbury: Christ Church

Grant of all customs and services of Tridhirste, *free from all obligations to Aldington, confirming that the gable is due to the high altar of Christ Church.*
[27 June 1115 × 20 Oct. 1122]

B = Canterbury D. & C. Register I fo. 86v (127v) s. xiii ex. C = Canterbury D. & C. Register E fo. 6ov s. xiv in. D = Canterbury D. & C. Register A, fo. 164 (186) s. xiv in.

Rad' Dei gratia Cant' archiepiscopus Ernulfo episcopo Roff' et omnibus hominibus suis Francis et*ᵃ* Anglis Cantie et toti hundredo de Aldintone, salutem et Dei benedictionem et suam quantum valet. Sciatis me concessisse inconcusso iure altari ecclesie Cristi Cant' omnes consuetudines et servitia de Tridhirste soluta*ᵇ* et quieta ab omni dominio et exigitione ministrorum de Aldintone et omnium aliorum exceptis ministris altaris ecclesie Cristi ad quod altare gabulum*ᶜ* suum de supradicto Tryndhirste semper reddiderunt et semper reddere debent. Test' Iohanni Cant' archidiacono, Silvestro monacho, Godefrido capellano, Rodlando medico, Alano clerico, Ranulfo preposito de Aldintone.

ᵃ om. D   *ᵇ* sola BCD   *ᶜ* gablum B

PRO E36/138, the s. xvi Christ Church inventory, p. 2 lists 'Carta Rad(ulp)hi archiepiscopi ut Tridherste libera sit ab omni dominio et exigitione ministrorum de Aldington' et solum altari ecclesie Cristi Cant' et eiusdem ministris imperpetuum quietum ad quod altare gablum suum semper reddere debent' in 'Cista viia'. Though Aldington with Lympne was by far the most valuable of the archiepiscopal manors in *Domesday monachorum* 98–9, it was placed in Bircholt hundred ibid. 83, though later in Street, and the reference to a hundred of Aldington is unexpected. 'Tridhirste' appears to be a lost name, perhaps the Tryndhurst noticed by J. K. Wallenberg, *The place-names of Kent* (Uppsala 1934) 334. In CD it too appears under the archiepiscopal charters of the priory, not under the estate. The same arguments for dating apply here as for 35 above.

*40. Canterbury: hospital of St Nicholas, Harbledown

Grant of a penny a day from the farm of Lymminge in perpetuity for the buying of drink. [26 April 1114 × 20 Oct. 1122]

> A charter of Theobald (*EEA Canterbury 1139–61*, forthcoming) from Lambeth Palace ms 1131 (2) p. 42, a s. xviii transcript of no. 28 in a roll-rental of the hospital which was destroyed in 1942 (cf above, 19), confirms 'unaquaque die unum denarium super antiquam elemosinam de firma nostra de Limminges ad potum emendum eisdem leprosis sicut Radulfus predecessor noster bone memorie eundem denarium eis dedit'. Somner, *Antiquities* (1640) 242, (1703) 123 cites the same source.

*41. Colchester: abbey of St John the Baptist

Confirmation of rights. [26 April 1114 × 20 Oct. 1122]

> Mentioned only in charter of bp Henry de Sandford of Rochester (*Cart. Colchester* i 120), and possibly in Saltman, *Theobald* no. 73.

42. Abbey of La Croix St Leuffroy

Letter to the sons of Robert, count of Meulan, recording their father's deathbed confession to the archbishop and the bishop of Lescicestra*, particularly of his depredations on La Croix, and his gift to them of all his holding in the vill except the vineyard. Ralph urges them to confirm the gift.*

[5 June 1118 × 20 Oct. 1122]

> A = lost original, 'sigillo reverendi in Cristo patris ac domini (*repeated*) Radulphi miseratione divina archiepiscopi Cantuariensis in cera viridi, ut apparebat, sigillata'.
> B = lost vidimus of A, dated Feb. 21 1467, in Latin and French. C = lost copy of B in cartulary of La Croix St Leuffroy D = Paris, BN Coll. du Vexin IV p. 227, copy by Francois de Blois from C, s. xvii. Two s. xviii copies, E = BN Coll. du Vexin VIII p. 573 (fo. 295r) and F = Ib. XIII fo. 38, present the document as an independent text, but it is unlikely that they had any source other than D. E has a marginal cross-reference to D, and F similarly to E.
> Pd D. Crouch, *The Beaumont twins* (Cambridge 1986) 216.

Radulphus Cantuariensis archiepiscopus filiis comitis de Mellento, salutem et Dei benedictionem et*a* suam. Sciatis quod pater vester, cum in extrema infirmitate sua laboraret, a me concilium*b* de salute animae suae requisivit, et inter caetera quae mihi et episcopo de Lescicestra*c* confessus est peccata, haec quoque quae in ecclesia de Cruce sancti Leufridi deliquit in praesentia nostra*d* lachrimabiliter conquestus est, unde concilio*e* nostro quicquid in eadem villa tenebat praeter vineam sub testimonio nostro pro remissione peccatorum suorum*f* ipsi ecclesiae concessit, et poenitentiam ex hoc quod in praefatam ecclesiam delequerat[g] humiliter requisivit. Nos itaque, qui huius rei testes sumus, laudamus et consulimus vobis ut vos animam patris vestri sicut boni filii diligentes, ea quae ipse concessit eadem concedatis, et qui corpus quae[h] dum viveret amastis, amate nunc animam, eadem bene custodiendo quae pro salute sua[i] constituit[j].

[a] *om.* E   [b] consilium E   [c] Lescestra F   [d] nostra praes. E   [e] consilio E   [f] *om.* E
[g] deliq- EF   [h] eius EF   [i] *om.* E   [j] Vale *add.* E²F

Crouch argued that this is not an authentic letter of the archbp on the grounds that it is unlikely so small a house should have pre-occupied either the count or the archbp, and that there was no bp of Leicester. However, we are scarcely in a position to determine the special concerns of the dying count at such a distance. Henry of Huntingdon in his *De contemptu mundi* (Huntingdon 598) describes Robert on his deathbed being urged by an unspecified archbp and priests to make restitution for all he had seized from many churches. Though Henry claims he refused, this charter might represent one modest success. 'Lescicestra' would be an unusual form for Leicester at this date, for it occurs much more commonly as 'Legr. . .' or 'Leir. . .'. The reading is probably corrupt, although the French version on p. 228 reads 'Licestre' here. Since Robert died on 5 June 1118, apparently at Préaux (Orderic, iv 302, vi 188), and the archbp had been in Normandy since the end of the previous year, it is possible the original letter may have referred to the bishop of Lisieux; the transition from 'Lex..' to 'Lesc. . .' is an easy one, particularly for a copyist who knew earl Robert's territorial title from other texts in the cartulary. An alternative suggestion is that 'episcopo' is an error for 'archidiacono', though there is no other reason to suppose that the archdn of Leicester was in Normandy at the time. While the suggestion that the seal was in green wax is unexpected, the style and *salutatio* are found in a number of Ralph's charters, as is the shift from singular to plural forms. On balance, there seems no decisive objection to the text's substantial authenticity, particularly if it was drawn up by the beneficiary.

+43.   Earls Colne priory

Exhortation to the faithful to assist the monks of Abingdon proposing to establish a priory in a church in Essex granted by Aubrey de Vere with the assent of king Henry. Confirmation of all gifts (listed) to the priory of Earls Colne by Aubrey and Beatrice his wife, as confirmed by the king's charter, and grant of protection.   [26 April 1114 × 20 Oct. 1122]

A = Colne Priory estate archives, deposited at Chelmsford, Essex Record Office D/DPr 150 (supposed original). Endorsed, s. xii/xiii: Rad' Arch' Cant'; s. xiv (?): Confirmatio possessionum et decimarum. 309 + 18 × 137 mm, the right hand side folded and slit to take a doubled seal-tag, to which a indecipherable fragment of a seal in white wax remains attached. Slightly damaged at head and foot.

B = Chelmsford, Colne Priory estate archives, deposited at Essex Record Office D/DPr 149 (cartulary of Colne) fos 4v-5v. s. xii ex. BL Cotton Tiberius E ix, fos 5–17 contain extracts from the 'Liber maior ecclesiae', an apparently lost cartulary which contained documents at least as late as 35 Edward III; on fo. 7 is what appears to be an English summary of this charter.

Pd from B in *Cart. Colne* 5–6.

Omnibus Cristiane religionis cultoribus frater Rad' indignus Cantuariensis ecc[lesie minister][a], salutem et Dei benedictionem. Hortantes oramus et orantes hortamur karissimam vestre fraternitatis dilectionem ut gratia Dei cuius servi et nostri cuius confratres sunt fratribus istis de Abe[ndonia][a] consilium et auxilium amicabiliter prebeatis. Ortatu enim nostro et consilio Deo auctore, et Henrici regis assensu, et obedientia Abendonensis abbatis comitante, volunt in quadam ecclesia in Essexa ab Alberico de Ver sibi in elemosina collocata Deo servire, et ibi domos et edificationes monachis habiles construere. Ad quod quicumque Deo inspirante eos adiuuerint, vel consilium et auxilium prebuerint, prebeat illis Deus partem in omnibus beneficiis et orationibus nostris, et mereantur ęternę beatitudinis remuneratione gloriari. Preterea auctoritate officii nostri inviolabiliter confirmamus, et in eternum permanere precipimus omnes donationes terrarum, ecclesiarum, decimarum, reddituum, libertatum vel aliarum rerum quas Albericus de Ver et uxor eius Beatrix eorumque heredes vel homines cum posteritate sua iam fecerunt uel facturi sunt Deo et eius gloriose genitrici virgini Marie et[b] monachis Abend' apud Colun in Essexa Deo famulantibus, scilicet: in Colun ecclesiam sancti Andree cum terra Rannulfi presbiteri et cum omnibus ad ecclesiam pertinentibus, et sexies xx acras de dominio et viridiarium quod est ultra aqua cum vivario et terram quam Serlo habuit, sicut melius et largius unquam habuit, in pascuis et silvis et campis, et duas silvas scilicet Dodepolesho et Nordwude, et silvam de Litlehaie cum xx acris terre, et terram Gode x solidorum de gablo, et terram Eadwini v solidorum de gablo, et xx acras de dominio que cambite fuerant pro terra Blachemanni, et unum hominem cum v acris, et terram Elmeri longi, et terram Wulfuuini forestarii, et molendinum et grangias[c]; ecclesiam de Duvrecurt cum xxx acris terre et cum omnibus sibi pertinentibus, et ecclesiam de Bonecleia cum omnibus pertinentibus, et ecclesiam de Bellocampo cum omnibus pertinentibus, et ecclesiam de Campis cum omnibus pertinentibus, in maneriis scilicet Haingeham, Belcheham, Laureham, Aldeham, Duvrecurt, Bonecleia, Roinges, duas partes decime de dominio de omnibus rebus, et unum hominem cum v acris[d]; in Haingeham duo molendina que Alduuinus molendinarius tenebat, de terra Adelelmi de Burgate x solidatas; apud Scaldeuuellam xl solidatas terre, dimidiam decimam de dominio de Miblanc de Colun; apud Buras totam decimam Ricardi filii Hadeline et Gileberti vicini sui, excepta parte presbiteri; apud Caneuellam tertiam partem decime Aluredi vicecomitis et duas partes decime Radulfi in eadem villa; apud Haingeham tertiam partem decime Rannulfi Mengui et tertiam partem decime Roberti Balci, et [e]tertiam partem decime[e] Guihumari et tertiam partem decime Willelmi Grosvassal. Presenti etiam scripto communimus et corroboramus omnia quecumque aliorum fidelium donatione vel aliis piis modis predicti monachi possederunt vel possessuri sunt, Dei et domini papę et nostra auctoritate prohibentes ne quis contra hanc institutionem et Henrici regis confirmationem, sicut eius carta testatur, has donationes sive possessiones predictorum fratrum infirmare, subtrahere aut exactionibus aut indebitis consuetudinibus onerare presumat. Quod si quis presumpserit, et huius decreti contradictor, convulsor et temerator extiterit, cum Iuda proditore ęterno anathemati subiaceat, nisi Domino nostro [Ihesu]*a* Cristo et eius gloriose genitrici virgini Marie digna penitentia satisfecerit. P[ax Dei]*a* et benedictio omnibus benefactoribus suis. Amen. Val'.

a A *damaged; suppl. from* B   *b* predictis *add.* B   *c* et *add.* B
d in Walde et Wadenho' medietatem decime de dominio de omnibus rebus, et unum hominem cum quinque acris *add.* B   *e-e* tertiam partem decime A; de terra B

The script of this charter belongs to the mid-twelfth-century at best, and is probably later. Its diplomatic is equally unsatisfactory. The opening section, to 'remuneratione gloriari', is unexceptionable as a general letter of protection for monks of Abingdon intending to establish an unnamed cell in Essex (diocese of London), and shows some marked similarities to the comparable letter Ralph wrote to Herbert of Norwich, probably for the Abingdon monks sent to Edwardstone (below 44); the monks of Edwardstone were transferred to Colne later in the century. The reversal of inscription and *intitulatio* here, and the style 'Frater Rad' indignus Cantuariensis ecclesie minister' are without parallel in Ralph's other charters, but the *intitulatio* is comparable to his use in two other letters of less solemn form (44, 59). The reference to 'istis fratribus' also fits the context of a letter better than that of a charter. The second section however, from 'Preterea auctoritate officii', with its elaborate list of donations which Ralph is made to confirm, reads oddly after the opening section, for it presupposes a well-established community, while the opening concerns little more than a project. More strikingly, the whole section from 'in eternum permanere' to 'Willelmi Grosvassal' is found in a thoroughly suspicious confirmation by Henry I, *Reg. regum* ii no. 981, apparently the royal charter cited in the text. This exists in three forms. The first, and shortest, occurs in *Hist. Abingdon* ii 86–8, the only version to include a date. The second, with a distinct witness-list and a further paragraph of exemptions from all secular burdens, including *infangenetheof,* was entered on an added leaf at the beginning of the Colne cartulary *c.*1400. The third, which was the first charter of the original cartulary of Colne, has the witness-list of the Abingdon version but the grant of exemptions also found in the first Colne version, and is substantially re-organised and rewritten. This third version is also found in BL Cotton Vespasian B xv fo. 59 (s. xvi), from 'Colne monast' Registrum in com. Essex'; the source is untraced and may be from another cartulary now lost, though notes to many of the succeeding charters show that they were copied from single sheets. Ralph's charter follows the central section of the third form closely. The passage inserted in B is most easily understood as omitted from A by homoioteleuton, for it occurs in all three versions of the royal charter as well. If so, either B was taken from another source than A, or A is a later effort to produce a convincing ecclesiastical confirmation of the early endowments by combining an authentic letter of protection with an early version of the royal charter, or perhaps with a draft for its forging. Archbp William's more general charter, below 70, refers to an anathema of Ralph on those who harm the priory, though not to a detailed confirmation. For another spurious charter in the name of Herbert of Norwich see *EEA* vi no. 4. There seems no convincing reason for supposing that Abingdon had ever had genuine charters for Colne in the names of either the archbp or Herbert of Norwich.

44. Edwardstone church

Letter to bishop Herbert of Norwich on behalf of the monks of Abingdon in his diocese. [26 April 1114 × 23 Feb. 1117]

B = BL Cotton Claudius C ix fo. 148ra. s. xii ex. C = BL Cotton Claudius B vi fo. 135rb. s. xiii.
Pd *Hist. Abingdon* ed. Stevenson ii 63, ed. Hudson ii 94 from B and C.

Frater Radulfus indignus Cantuariensis ęcclesię minister venerabili domino et confratri Herberto Norwicensi Dei gratia episcopo, salutem et amicitiam et fideles orationes pro posse. Quia notum[a] sanctę prudentie vestrę non ignoramus reverentiam et religiositatem domni abbatis Abbendonensis[b] Faritii et totius congregationis illi a Deo commisse, non est opus vobis eam intimare. Pro his igitur oratam esse volumus caritatis vestre bonitatem quatinus gratia Dei cuius sunt et nostri qui vester sum et ipsorum etiam qui amici vestri et filii esse profitentur, quosdam fratres ęcclesię in quadam ęcclesia a quodam parrochiano vestro illis in elemosinam concessa paterna suscipiatis benignitate et consilium et auxilium prout potestis et scitis amicabiliter prebeatis. Quod faciendo Deus omnipotens diu conservet incolumem[c] sanctam paternitatem vestram nostri memorem. Valete.

[a] notam C   [b] -si BC   [c] -umen B (C *abbrev.*)

The text is remarkably vague about the site of the church, though assigning it at least to the diocese of Norwich, but the abbey chronicle inserts it in its account of the cell of Edwardstone. Edwardstone church was given to Abingdon by Hubert de Montchesni in 1114 × 5, and his grant was confirmed by kg Henry I in a charter also dated in 1115 in a note attached to it in the Abingdon cartulary. Abbot Faricius established two monks there, but they were transferred to Earls Colne priory under abbot Walkelin (1159–1164) during the rule of bp William of Norwich (d.1174): *Hist. Abingdon* ed. Hudson ii 92–4, and ed. Stevenson ii 288; *Reg. regum* ii no. 1089; *Cart. Colne* no. 65. Compare this text with the opening to 43 above.

*45. Glastonbury abbey

Grant of an indulgence of fifteen days. [26 April 1114 × 20 Oct. 1122]

Mentioned only, from a charter already lost in the thirteenth century, in Cambridge, Trinity College ms R 5.33 (James no. 764) fo. 78 (for which see *4 above). Printed in *Johannis . . . Glastoniensis chronica siue historia de rebus Glastoniensibus* ed. T. Hearne ii 378: 'De Radulfo archiepiscopo Cant' xv dies.'

46.   Lewes priory

Grant of the church of Burstow on the entry into the priory of R. the priest, to whom Anselm and Ralph after him had given it, as R.'s parents had intended.

[26 April 1114 × 20 Oct. 1122]

A = PRO Ancient Deeds E 40/ 15416. Endorsed, s. xii: Rad' archiepiscopi Cant'. De Burstoue; s. xv: vii. 168 × 65 mm, with the foot slit for a seal tag, and the remains of a wrapping tie 3 mm deep. Below the slit the face of the document is noticeably paler, but the step for a tie makes it most unlikely that there was ever a plica.

Pd J. Blair, 'The Surrey endowments of Lewes priory before 1200' *Surrey Archaeol. Coll.* lxxii (1980) 119 no. 5, with facs. at 102 fig. 3.

R. Dei gratia Cantuariensis archiepiscopus Wal' de Burestou, salutem. Scias quia venerabilis predecessor noster domnus Anselmus archiepiscopus et ego postea ecclesiam de Burestou secundum petitionem patris tui cum omnibus ad eam pertinentibus R. fratri tuo concessimus. Nunc itaque, quia idem frater tuus Deo inspirante apud sanctum Pancratium monacus factus est, eandem ecclesiam eisdem monacis sancti. Pancratii liberam et quietam concedimus, secundum devotionem patris tui et matris, qui eundem filium suum cum predicta ecclesia apud eundem locum Sancti Pancratii quondam devotissime Deo voluerunt offerre, sicut ipse bene nosti. Quapropter volumus ut eandem ecclesiam predictis monacis in presenti deliberes, et si quid de rebus ad eam pertinentibus accepisti, ex integro eis restituas.

For the endorsements of this and the following Lewes charters see Galbraith in *Sussex Archaeol. Coll.* lxv (1924) 196–205. The formulae and content present no evident anachronisms, for such a mixture of plural and singular forms is found widely elsewhere. Burstow is listed among the priory's holdings in 48 of 1121 below. A confirmation 'ex donacione antecessorum nostrorum' is Saltman, *Theobald* no. 153 of 1154 × 8, and it was also confirmed by bp Henry of Winchester by *EEA* viii no. 63 of 1153 × 1167. For Burstow, an outlier of Wimbledon, see Du Boulay, *Lordship* 383–4. Blair, 'The Surrey endowments of Lewes priory' 100 notes that eventually the church reverted to Canterbury, citing *VCH Surrey* iii 182. For evidence of friendly contact between Christ Church and Lewes around this time see Leclercq, 'Écrits spirituels' 75–87 ep. v, a letter of Elmer to Robert, monk of Lewes.

47.   Lewes priory

Grant to Lewes priory of the land at Caresleia formerly held by Alwin the priest and his son for a silver mark of rent, two pennies for works and six shillings of gable.

Charing, 1121

A = PRO Ancient Deeds E 40/ 6689. Endorsed, s. xii: R. Cant' arch' de Carisle; s. xiii/xiv: De rap de Peuenese; s. xv: vii. 112 × 96 + 14 mm. The foot folded over and slit, with a doubled tag but no trace of a seal. Written in a small neat book hand with long ascenders. (Plate IIb)

Pd *Ancient charters royal and private prior to AD 1200*, 10 no. 7

R. Dei gratia Cantuar' archiepiscopus tam futuris quam presentibus in perpetuum. Terram in Caresleia quam tenent Alwinus presbiter et filius eius dedi Deo et sancto Pancratio Latisaquensi ita liberam et absolutam cum redditibus et consuetudine sicut ego unquam eam melius tenui. Solvit autem terra illa unam marcam argenti et duos denarios de opere vero et gablo sex solidos. Hoc autem dedi pro animabus tam mea quam antecessorum meorum archiepiscoporum et pro salute post nos instituendorum.

Data Cerringis anno verbi incarnati M°C°XX°I° in manu filii nostri domni H. Latisaquensis prioris.

> In the same hand as the next charter, which confirms the gift of the 'mansio' at 'Caresleia'. Both have unusual diplomatic forms, and were probably drafted and written by the beneficiary. An Ailwin, son of the priest of Pulborough, appears in *Cart. Lewes* i 144–5, 175 c. 1150. Ailwin the priest and his son are said to have held the land of 'Karesle' in the time of archbps Ralph and William in Saltman, *Theobald* no.153 of 1154 × 8, suggesting that the payments specified in the charter were to be made to the priory, not the archbp. 'Caresleia' or 'Carisle', in the Rape of Pevensey according to the endorsement, was not identified by Round.

48. Lewes priory

General confirmation at the request of prior Hugh of a long list of (specified) benefactions of lands and churches, particularly by kings William I, William II and Henry I, and William I and II, earls of Surrey, the founders, in the dioceses of Chichester, London, Winchester, Salisbury, Exeter, Lincoln, Norwich and York.   Malling, 1121

> A = PRO E 41/ 464. Endorsed, s. xii/xiii: Rad' Cant' arch' generalis; s. xiii: Rad' Cant' arc'; Confirmatio archiepiscopi; s. xv: vii; s. xiv/xvi: Rcs (?) Middelton'; s. xvi/xvii pro omnibus rectoriis pertinentibus priori Lewes [in provincia Cant' *added*]. 282 × 368 mm, with no surviving trace of sealing. However an irregular 'bite' has been lost from the centre of the foot, 76 mm long and 20 mm deep. Along its upper edge a 20 mm horizontal stretch is straight, possibly for one side of the slit for a seal tag, while the rest is much more ragged. Written in a very formal hand, with elongated ascenders and elaborate tittles.
>
> Pd in *Ancient charters royal and private* 11–14 no. 8. Text and facsimile in C. Johnson and H. Jenkinson, *English court hand AD 1066 to 1500* i 90–4 ii pl. 3. Partial text in *Early Yorkshire charters* viii 68–69 no. 10.

Radulfus Dei gratia Cantuariensis archiepiscopus et totius Britannię primas omnibus in Cristo filiis presentibus et futuris in perpetuum. Pię sollicitudinis est et Domino placitum ęcclesiis pacem providere et religiosorum quietem protegendo servare. Pro nostra igitur pastoralis cura officii Latisaquense monasterium in honore beati Pancratii martiris consecratum, quod est Cluniacensis cenobii proprium, et paterno affectu diligimus et religionis gratiam quę in eo a tempore predecessorum et dominorum meorum Lanfranci et Anselmi archiepiscoporum ad nostra usque tempora profecit plurimum amplexamur. Quapropter tam ipsum monasterium in episcopatu Cicestrensi situm quam et ea quę possidet episcopali benedictione firmamus, et pia petitione filii nostri Hugonis ipsius loci prioris nostri auctoritate privilegii roboramus. Habet enim prefatum monasterium in episcopatu Cicestrensi terram que dicitur Suthovre cum burgo et duobus stagnis et tribus molendinis, cum insula que proxima est ipsi monasterio cum pratis, et in castro iuxta se posito habet ęcclesias et capellas, videlicet sancti Iohannis et sancti Petri et sancte Trinitatis et sancti Nicholai et sancti Andreę et beatę Marię et sancti Martini et sanctę Marię de Westota, quarum illam que dicitur sancti Iohannis cum capella in cimiterio sancti Pancratii sita, ex dono venerabilis fratris nostri Radulfi Cicestrensis episcopi libere et quiete possidet, et terram quę dicitur Swanberga cum capella et duo molendina apud Mechingas cum ęcclesia, et Falemeram cum ęcclesia, et Burgameram cum capella, et Molescumbam et possessionem in Wistendena et terram que dicitur Piceleswia, et terram in Aldrinchtona, et in Bristelmestuna cum ęcclesia, et terram in Chingestona, et in Blacinctona cum capella, et terram in Alinctona et in Dicelingis cum ęcclesia et duabus capellis, terram quoque de Bradeherst et de Vlfeole et de Belvidere cum capellis, et terram in Orsteda cum capella, et Langaniam et Achinctonam cum galeto et capella, et terram in Dodinctona et in Thornh, et decimam de Prestetona, et terram apud Herbertingas, x et viii acras cum pastura centum ovium in Orthlaveswica, et ęcclesiam de Ifordo et capellas de Redmella et de Northesa, et ęcclesiam de Rotingesdena, et de Claetona, et de Chimela, et de Cucufelda, et de Balecumba, et de Herdingheleia, et de Grenesteda, et de Hangeltona, et de Hadlega, et de Pellincis, et Niwicha, et de Bercham, et de Waldrena, et de Bergham[a], et de Gretheam, et de Helingeam, et de Suthona, et de Loventona, et de Stoctona, et de Meretona, et de Tangamera, et apud Grafam decimam terrę Rogeri de Caisneto, et virgatam terrę cum uno rustico, apud Brembram salinas iv quas dedit Philippus de Braiosa, et ibidem unam salinam quam dedit Radulfus de Grenesteda, et ęcclesiam de Cunctona cum his quę Rogerius de sancto Iohanne ibidem dedit; apud Lundoniam dimidium capellę sancti Botulfi et domos et terras cum ea libertate quam dominus noster rex Henricus ibidem sancto Pancratio dedit; apud Essedunam[b] Gaufredi Bainardi xliiii acras terrę et tres pratorum et decem silvę et unum quercum et pastionem x porcorum; apud Estunam carrucatam terrę et unum rusticum; apud Strathford unam mansionem ex dono reverendi fratris nostri Ricardi Lundoniensis episcopi; apud Princiduelam monasterium sancte Marię et quicquid ibidem dedit monacis Cluniacensibus sub sancto Pancratio Robertus Sweni filius; apud Stanagatam monasterium sancte Marię Magdalene cum omnibus quę ibi dedit sancti Pancratio per manum domini nostri regis Anglorum Henrici Radulfus Brieni filius; apud utranque Canefeldam et apud Essendonam ęcclesias cum terris. In episcopatu Wintoniensi habet ęcclesiam de Gatetuna et quę ibidem dedit Herfredus, et in eodem loco dimidiam virgatam terrę quam dedit Oddo de Donmartini, et ęcclesiam de Suthwerca. In episcopatu Saresberiensi habet ęcclesiam de Winterburna, et de Bissoppestreu, apud Mapeldream unam hidam de manu R. cancellarii, et in Melesberia hidam et dimidiam. In episcopatu Exoniensi habet ęcclesias de Hertesberie, de Brai, de Betesdenna, de Brugia. In episcopatu Lincoliensi habet ęcclesias de Fachestuna et de Meltuna cum terris. In Eliensi, Carlentonam et Wilingeam cum ęcclesiis. In Wella xl sol'. In Norwicensi monasterium sancte Marię de Accara, et quicquid ibidem Willelmus de Warenna et cęteri fideles monacis Cluniac' dederunt, apud Tethfordum duas capellas, et terram in Santona et ęcclesiam sancte Helenę cum terra, et terram de Resinges cum ęcclesia, et dimidium Waltonę cum dimidia ęcclesia, et dimidium de Animera cum dimidia ęcclesia, et terram in Terintona, et terram de Cungheam de qua solvit^c Azor tres marcas, et Herceam cum ęcclesia et quę ad eam et ad manerium pertinent [et apud]^d Gemengheam^e xl solidatas terrę, et terram in Catestuna, et in Mertuna lx acras terre, in Miseburna xii solidatas terrę, et in Dodilenctuna x solidatas et dimidium Walpole cum dimidia ęcclesia et medietate^f molendinorum eiusdem soce, ęcclesias quoque de Mertuna et de Bruneam et de Herpelai, et^g unam in Nicheburna, et dimidiam in Falwella, et unam et dimidiam in Ristuna, et unam in Luna, ęcclesias quoque de Wiltona et Gemingheam. In episcopatu Eboracensi ęcclesias de Wachefelda et de Cuningesburch et quę ad eas pertinent. Ego ipse do eidem monasterio mansionem in Caresleia cum terra liberam et quietam, et ęcclesiam de Burestou. Confirmo etiam et laudo quęcunque eidem monasterio donata sunt et concessa a dominis nostris regibus Willelmo primo et Willelmo secundo et Henrico, et a comitibus Suthregie Willelmo primo et Willelmo secundo devotis ipsius monasterii fundatoribus, qui omnia quę sancto Pancratio dederunt ita libere et absolute dederunt sicut melius ea ipsi tenuerunt. Hęc et quęcunque a ceteris benefactoribus eidem monasterio collata sunt et nos confirmando donamus, et ne ulla potestas quęlibetve persona auferre vel minuere praesumat, ex parte summi iudicis interdicimus. Qui autem presumpserit nisi emendando satisfecerit, corripiat eum vindicta Domini. Pax benefactoribus, Gratia conservatoribus, Benedictio Deo servientibus.

+ Ego Radulfus Cantuar' archiepiscopus dedi et subscripsi. +^{h}

Dat' Melling' per manum Iohannis cancellarii et archidiaconi. Anno verbi incarnati Mº.Cº.XXº.I. Papa Romanorum Calixto ii. Rege Anglorum Henrico.

^a *a very short tailed* g, *possibly a later correction*   ^b *corr. from* -onam   ^c *partially obscured*
^d *lacuna*   ^e *corr. to* -ingheam   ^f *corr. fr.* medit-   ^g et *repeated*
^h *The two crosses are quite distinct, but neither appears to be in the hand of the main text.*

This remarkable imitation of a papal privilege has been much discussed, not least as a critical witness to the growth of the endowments of Lewes. See in particular Cheney, *EBC* 28, *Acta of. . .Chichester* ed. Mayr-Harting, 62n, 70n. Strictly, there can be no confidence that it was ever approved by the archbp, since the evidence for any authentication beyond the crosses at the foot is not decisive. No other charter of Ralph employs this primatial title, though it became standard under Theobald (above p. lxx). Similarly no charter in the name of an archbp before Theobald has a dating clause of this elaboration, though the lost 95 below may have done; all these features might be explained if our text was drafted by the Cluniac beneficiaries, and Cluny was among the earliest houses to introduce this way of listing possessions by bishopric—D. Lohrmann, *Archiv für Diplomatik* xxvi (1980) 302. The script of this text is in a version of the curial minuscule, which was abandoned by the papacy in the 1120s; its last true representative is JL 7075a (*Italia Pontificia* i 184 no. 4); such palaeographical indications tend to support the authenticity of the text, uncertain though the issue must remain. The brief and unusual *arenga* is very close to that employed in two Lewes fabrications of charters in the name of bp Ralph of Chichester (*Acta of . . . Chichester*, no. 10, PRO E 40/14176, no. 11, PRO E 40/ 15427), and may have inspired them. Rather later Lewes secured general confirmations, which have not excited suspicion, from bp Gilbert Foliot of London (*EEA* xv no. 132 from Foliot, *Letters* no. 394), bp Henry of Blois of Winchester (*EEA* viii no. 63) and bp William Turbe of Norwich (*EEA* vi no. 111). These help to identify some of the places, but they also differ from archbp Ralph's grant by omission and addition in a way which also tends to support its authenticity.

49. Lewes priory

Grant of thirty-six loads of beans as the churchscot of Pagham.

[26 April 1114 × 20 Oct. 1122]

A = PRO Ancient Deeds E 40/ 15415. Endorsed, s. xii: Rad' Cant' arc' de fab' xxxvi summas donat; s. xv: vii. 233 × 76 (lhs), 66 (rhs) with only a rough 5 mm step for tongue or wrapping tie.
Pd in *Ancient charters royal and private* 16 no. 9. Cal. by G.F. Duckett, *Sussex Archaeol. Coll.* xxxv (1887) 118.

Radulfus Cant' archiepiscopus Rad' Cicestrensi episcopo atque omnibus fidelibus suis, salutem. Sciatis me dedisse fratribus nostris monachis videlicet sancti Pancratii de Lauuis semper in posterum deinceps habendum illum redditum fabarum quem retinui et habeo in dominio nostro apud villam nostram Pagheham, et vocatur circeset, et habebunt inde singulis annis xxxvi^a sumas de fabis. Test' Theoder' priore Cantuar', Hug' monacho, Felice monacho, Anfr' dap', Roberto de Ceresio, Rog' de sancto Albano, Hunfr' clerico, Rollando medico, Roberto filio Riculfi.

^a xvi *written over an erasure.*

Conrad appears to have been conventual prior at Canterbury throughout Ralph's pontificate; a monk Theoderic was of some importance at Christ Church at this time, but there is no other reason to suppose that he was styled prior: Greatrex, *Biographical register* 302. However, since the text does not otherwise excite suspicion, it is possible that he was second or third prior—compare 97 below. The hand, though unidentified elsewhere, has features reminiscent of Christ Church script (above p. lxiv), and is quite unlike that of the preceding three acts. Since this gift is not listed in the preceding text of 1121, possibly to be dated 1121 × 1122. For other references to churchscot in the period see Brett, *English church* 224–5. In Domesday the archiepiscopal manor of Pagham answered for thirty-four hides, and had a church, with another dependent church in Chichester owing 64d—presumably annually to the archbp.

50. Llandaff cathedral

Indulgence to all those who assist in the building of the new cathedral of one quarter of the penance imposed by their confessors.

[26 April 1114 × 20 Oct. 1122, ? April 1120]

B = Aberystwyth, NLW 17110E (Book of Llandaff) fo. 53v col. 100. s. xii.
Pd *Book of Llan Dâv* 87, *Cartae Glam.* i 46 no.xlii. Cal. J. Conway Davies, *Episcopal acts* ii 618 no. L35.

Radulfus Dei gratia Cantuariensis archiepiscopus omnibus ecclesię filiis Francis et Anglis atque Gualensibus et cuiuscunque sint nationis hominibus, salutem et benedictionem Dei et suam. Rogamus karitatem vestram ut oculis misericordię respicere velitis indigentiam Landavensis ecclesię. Confisi etenim de vestrarum elemosinarum auxilio eandem ecclesiam edificare disposuimus, ut ibidem populus Dei convenire possit ad audiendum verbum Domini. Quicunque igitur ad edificationem predictę ecclesię aliquid de suo impertiri pro karitate Dei voluerit, sciat se nostrarum orationum atque benefactorum esse participem. Sed et de onere penitentię suę quod sibi a suis confessoribus impositum est quartam partem ei de misericordia Dei et potestate nostri ministerii confisi relaxamus.

According to *Book of Llan Dâv*, 86 bp Urban determined on the building of a new cathedral church at Llandaff on 14 April 1120, and began the work as he received this indulgence. The passage occurs in the main hand of the manuscript of s. xii med. (Huws, 'The making' 143–4). Cardinal John of Crema in 1125 (*Book of Llan Dâv* 48) confirmed the indulgences granted by 'Cantuarienses archiepiscopi', which presumably included this and possibly another by archbp William, adding fourteen days more on behalf of the apostolic see. It is notable that the archbp speaks of the decision to build at Landaff as his own.

51. Malling abbey

Confirmation of the vill of Little Malling as granted by Anselm.

[26 April 1114 × 20 Oct. 1122]

B = PRO C53/134 (Charter Roll 21 Edward III, confirming numerous charters for the abbey, dated 8 May 1347) m. 11.
Pd *Cal. Ch. Rolls* v 61.

+ Ego Radulfus Dei gratia Cantuariorum archiepiscopus notum facere curavi presentibus et post futuris Francis et Anglis quod ego concedo atque confirmo castimonialibus que in territorio Rofensi apud Mellingas Domino Cristo famulantur donationem quam fecit eis predecessor meus beate memorie Anselmus de villa que vocatur Mellinges et prope illas sita. Et ut hoc ipsum prosit animabus tam successorum quam predecessorum meorum precor et postulo firmum illibatumque imposterum custodiri.

Compare Anselm's charter, above 22, of which there are verbal echoes here, and below *83. The charter appears to be one of those cited in the suspicious Saltman, *Theobald* no. 173, though there are no evident inconsistencies in the text here. 'Castimonialis' is a rare word, but its scattered appearances do not point to any particular source.

52. Malling abbey

Grant to Adeliza of two mills which he has bought from Calvellus for £15, to be held for an annual rent of 12 pence.   [1120 × 20 Oct. 1122]

B = PRO C53/ 134 (Charter roll for 21 Edward III, dated 8 May 1347) m. 11.
Pd *Cal. Ch. Rolls* v 62.

Radulfus archiepiscopus Cant' Ern' episcopo Roff' et omnibus hominibus Francis et Anglis de hundredo de Westgate, salutem. Sciatis me concessisse et dedisse sorori nostre Azeliz duo molendina que emi a Calvello*a* quindecim libris, unde ipse solebat reddere xx solidos, amodo pro duodecim denariis ad recognoscendum curie nostre de Westgat', et hoc hereditarie sibi et heredibus suis. Testibus Seifredo abbate Glestra*b* et Iohanne archidiacono Cant' et Giffard et Anfrido dapifero.

a add pro?   *b* apparently for Glastonie.

Also mentioned in the suspect Saltman, *Theobald* no. 173 (see 22 above), but the text seems consistent with its apparent date. For the family of William Calvellus see above 15. S. Thompson, *Women religious* 246 identified Azeliz with the abbess Alice appointed in 1108 (*Heads* i 215, 294). A nun Avitia is addressed in Leclercq, 'Écrits spirituels' 101–4 ep. xii. However, since it would be unusual to grant a nun and her heirs land in inheritance, it is at least as possible that the beneficiary was the archbp's sister by blood, and that the land passed to Malling by some later transaction.

53. Rochester cathedral

Confirmation of the gift by Anselm to the cathedral priory of the church of Northfleet, grant of an acre in Ifield, of tithes in Dunne, and remission of 5 shillings rent from New Weir.

[27 June 1115 × Sept. 1116, Jan. 1120 × 20 Oct. 1122]

B = Strood MALSC DRc/ R 1 (Textus Roffensis) fo. 179v no. 94, s. xii (a replacement leaf). C = BL Cotton Domitian x (Rochester cartulary) fos 120v-121, s. xiii in. D = Strood MALSC DRc/ T 57, suspicious inspeximus by bps Walter of Exeter and Hugh of Ely, dated May 1260.
Pd from B in *Text. Roff*. 155. Cal. Flight, *Bishops and monks* 264 no. 214.

Radulfus archiepiscopus Cantuar' omnibus Cristi fidelibus salutem. Notum sit omnibus tam presentibus quam futuris[a] quod ego concedo et confirmo donationem venerabilis patris Anselmi quam fecit monachis sancti Andree de Rovecestra de ecclesia de Nortdflitae[b] et omnibus ad eam pertinentibus in terris, in decimis, in oblationibus et in omnibus aliis rebus. Et de[c] meo dominico do eis unam acram terrę in mea propria cultura in campo qui dicitur Gudlesfeld ad edificandas domos sibi[d] et suo capellano ad opus supradictę ecclesię et totam decimam de meo dominico, et omnes decimas omnium villanorum qui habent terram in Dunne, necnon et aliorum omnium quorum decimę meo tempore adquisitę sunt, vel quocunque temporę adquirentur. Concessi ętiam eis inperpetuum v solidos qui mihi debebantur singulis annis pro piscatoria quę vocatur Niwewere quę est in territorio de Grean. Test'[e] domno Aernulfo Rofensi episcopo, Iohanne Cantuar' archidiacono,[f] Herviso archidiacono Rofensi, Ioseph, Edmero monacho Cant', Rodberto monacho Sagiensi, Silvestro, Hugo monacho Roff', Ansfrido capellano, Ansfrido dapifero, Rodberto filio Bad' clerico[gf] et multis aliis de familia nostra et domni Aernulfi[h] episcopi.

[a] futris B   [b] Norfliete C; Northflete D   [c] *superscr*. B   [d] sibi domos C   [e] Teste C
[f-f] *om*. C   [g] Radl' clerici D   [h] Rof. *add*. C

Compare above, 25-6 and below +88 for doubts over this group of Northfleet charters. For rights in Ifield and 'la Dune' see *EEA* ii +194-5, and the list of tithes received by Rochester priory early in s. xiii in *Cust. Roff*. 33. For the appointment of archdn John see above, 35; Ralph was out of England continuously from Sept. 1116 to the end of 1119, but the witness list suggests very powerfully an English setting for the grant. Eadmer was in Scotland from 27 June until after 25 Nov. 1120 (Eadmer, *Historia* 225, 236-7, 282, 288).

+54. Rochester cathedral

Confirmation to the bishop and priory of the grants of his predecessors, especially the right to exercise all episcopal functions on Canterbury estates in the diocese, rights in Freckenham and Isleham, the church of Northfleet, and grant of an acre at Ifield and the tithes of the villeins of Doune.

[24 Sept. 1114 × 20 Oct. 1122]

B = BL Cotton Faustina B v (Historia Roffensis) fo. 69v. s. xv. copy of an inspeximus by prior Richard and the chapter of Christ Church, Canterbury dated 5 Feb. 1333, in turn inspecting a charter of Hubert Walter, *EEA* iii no. +592, including this.
Pd from B in *Reg. Roff.* 442–3. Cal. Flight, *Bishops and monks* 264 no. 215.

Radulphus *Dei gratia* archiepiscopus Cant' omnibus Cristi fidelibus, salutem. Notum sit omnibus tam presentibus quam futuris quod ego concedo, *ratifico* et confirmo *omnes donationes, concessiones et assignaciones omnium maneriorum, terrarum, ecclesiarum, decimarum, pensionum, libertatum, consuetudinum, iurium et rectitudinum quas* venerabiles *predecessores nostri Lamfrancus et* Anselmus ecclesie sancti Andree de Rovecestr' *et Gundulpho episcopo et monachis per ipsum introductis fecerunt, imposuerunt et disposuerunt pro perpetua elemosina habenda. Volo etiam et concedo quod episcopi Roffens' omni tempore teneant et habeant omnia iura episcopalia que habui et tenui toto tempore^a quo eram episcopus Roffn' in maneriis ecclesie Cant' in episcopatu Rovecestr' situatis in manerio de Frekenham et Iselham quos predictus Lamfrancus ecclesie Roffen' et prefato Gundulpho episcopo reddidit et cum omni iure episcopali restituit ita plene et bene sicuti ego habui et usus fui in eisdem, et* ecclesiam de Northfflete quam Anselmus dedit monachis in Roffa *Deo famulantibus, cum* omnibus ad eam pertinentibus in terris, in decimis, in oblationibus et in omnibus aliis rebus *eternaliter possidend' auctoritate pontificali concedo et confirmo* et de meo dominico do eis unam acram terre in mea propria cultura in campo que dicitur Gudlesfelde, ad edificandum domos sibi et suo capellano, ad opus predicte ecclesie et totam decimam de meo dominico et omnes decimas villanorum qui habent terram in Doune, necnon et aliorum omnium quorum decime meo tempore adquisite sunt, vel quocunque tempore adquirentur. Concessi etiam eis imperpetuum quinque solidos qui mihi debebantur singulis annis pro piscatoria que vocatur Newewer' que est in territorio de Grean. *Quicunque ausu temerario contra donaciones et confirmaciones antedictas facere presumpserint maledictionem Dei quam beatus Anselmus in presumptores tulit et nostram sciant se incursuros.* Testibus domino Arnulpho Roffen' episcopo et aliis.

^a *con. fr.* tempore toto

Distinguished from the preceding charter chiefly by its wider terms and the addition of a reference to Freckenham and Isleham; the additions are broadly indicated by italic type. There is no decisive objection to the text as it stands, but it is found in deplorable company. Every other text in the inspeximus of Hubert (*EEA* iii no. +592) is a forgery concerned with the Suffolk property, and the whole inspeximus is itself spurious. Compare +5, +7, +8, +28, +29 above. It is by no means improbable that the charter was based on a genuine text of Ralph, comparable to 25 above or 87 below, confirming the gift of Canterbury's episcopal rights in the lands and churches of the diocese of Rochester.

55. Rochester cathedral

Confirmation of the grant of the church of Norton with its appurtenances and half the tithes of the demesne as given by Hugh and Fulk of Newnham in his presence.   [27 June 1115 × 20 Oct. 1122]

B = BL Cotton Domitian x (Rochester cartulary) fo. 184v no.[1]78. s. xiii in.
Pd from B in *Reg. Roff.* 507. Cal. Flight, *Bishops and monks* 263 no. 213.

Radulfus gratia Dei Cant' archiepiscopus omnibus fidelibus Cristi salutem et Dei benedictionem. Notum sit omnibus vobis me concessisse et presenti scripto confirmasse monachis ęcclesię sancti Andree apostoli de Rovecestria ecclesiam de Nortuna cum tota terra que ad eam pertinet et dimidiam decimam de dominico curie eiusdem ville et omnibus aliis pertinentiis suis sicut Hugo de Niweham assensu Fulconis filii sui in perpetuam elemosinam in nostra presentia eis concessit. Testes Iohannes archidiaconus Cant', Herveus archidiaconus Roffen' et cet'.

The church had been granted by Hugh of Newnham with the consent of his wife and Fulk his son (Textus Roffensis fo. 190v no. 156).

56. Priory of St Osyth

Confirmation of the gifts of bishop Richard of London with the consent of king Henry and the canons of St Pauls, including the manor of Chich, the churches of Southminster and Clacton with their tithes and customs, a sheepfold at Southminster, the tithes of the wild animals of the park at Clacton and a hind on the feast of St Osyth.   [26 April 1114 × 20 Oct. 1122]

B = London, Guildhall Library ms 9531/4 (Register of Richard Clifford, bp of London) fo. 176 (olim 81). s. xv in.
Pd in D. Bethell, 'Richard' 320 no. VIII.

Rad[ulf]us Dei gratia Cantuarien' archiepiscopus omnibus Cristi fidelibus episcopis et clericis, abbatibus et monachis, reliquisque cuiuscumque condicionis sunt ecclesie filiis, salutem Deique benedictionem et suam. Sciatis quod ego concedo et auctoritate Dei et nostra confirmo ea que Ricardus London' episcopus consensu regis Henrici et assensu capituli sancti Pauli dedit canonicis sancte Osithe servituris. Videlicet totum manerium de Chich et omnia que ad ipsum pertinent, et ecclesias de Southmenstre et de Clacton', cum rectis decimis omnium que decimari solent proprie possessionis ipsius episcopi et aliorum, et cum terris ad ecclesias easdem pertinentibus, et cum consuetudinibus quas habuerunt predicte ecclesie temporibus predecessorum eiusdem episcopi, et unam bercarium in Southmenstre pro decima ovium, et decimam ferarum parci de Clacton', et unam damam in unoquoque festo sancte Osithe. Hec predicte ecclesie auctoritate Dei et nostra confirmo, et omnia alia que fideles ecclesie eidem dederunt, et qui hec firmiter custodierint benedictionem Dei et nostram consequantur. Si quis vero quod absit hec violare presumpserit Deus inde vindicet. Valete.

The fullest account of bp Richard of London's gifts to the priory of St Osyth at Chich and to the canons 'Deo famulaturis' there is given in *EEA* xv no. 27 (? 1119 × Jan. 1121). The first element in this is the exchange of episcopal land for the manor of Chich, which allowed the foundation on land formerly assigned to St Pauls, as confirmed by the kg and archbp Ralph. The kg's confirmation, *Reg. regum* ii no. 1209, dated at Rouen (Bethell 'Richard' 318 no. V) and attested by archbp Ralph, is suspicious in form; if the longer version of the royal text is even approximately trustworthy it may be dated Sept./Oct. 1116 or late 1117 × late 1119, given the archbp's itinerary. The second element is the grant of the churches of Clacton and Southminster, associated with tithes, sheepwalks and the hind on the feast of St Osyth, as here. The third was a further hide at Chich bought by the bp for the canons' use, but not confirmed by the archbp. The archbp's confirmation does not require that bp Richard's surviving charter, as opposed to his gifts, had already been granted. The archbp's confirmation, like the bp's, is to those canons who will serve in the church, as is 57, but 58 below is addressed to a community apparently in place. Cambridge. Corpus Christi Coll. ms 329 fo. 217 (105) a fifteenth-century list of dates of monastic foundations, apparently from Ixworth priory, assigns the 'Introductio' of the canons to St Osyth to 1119. A rather different list apparently compiled at Leiston abbey, which survives in sixteenth-century copies in Cambridge, Trinity College Coll. ms 724 fo. 20v, Oxford Bodl. Gough Essex 1, fo. 14 and Cambridge, Corpus Christi Coll. ms 111 fo. 335v, places this 'Introductio' in 1121. Uncertain though these assertions must be, they combine to suggest a date of 1120 × 1121 for 56–7, with 58 a little later. See further, Bethell, 'St Osyth' 120.

57. Priory of St Osyth

Grant of the church of Petham with all its tithes and a field for an annual rent of 8 pence as Gunter the priest held it. [26 April 1114 × 20 Oct. 1122]

Lambeth Palace, Reg. Warham 1 fo. 158. s. xvi in.
Pd. Bethell, 'Richard' 320 no. IX.

Radulphus Dei gratia Cant' archiepiscopus Ernulpho Roffen' episcopo et omnibus clericis et laicis Francis et Anglicis de Kent, salutem et Dei benedictionem et suam. Sciatis me concessisse in elemosinam pro remedio anime mee et predecessorum et successorum meorum ecclesie sancte Osithe et canonicis ibidem Deo servituris ecclesiam de Petham cum omnibus rectis decimis manerii et nostre proprie possessionis, et omnium aliorum ad eandem ecclesiam pertinen[tium] tam segetum quam pecorum et unum campum pro viii denariis de gabulo singulis annis ad nativitatem beate Marie sicut Gunterus sacerdos tenuit et reddidit.

> Probably the charter cited by archbp Theobald in *Letters of John of Salisbury* i no. 76. Petham was on the archbp's demesne in *Domesday monachorum* 83, with two churches. Petham vicarage is listed at *Taxatio* 5, but not the church; in *Valor* i 39 it appears as an appropriated church of St Osyth.

58. Priory of St Osyth

Grant of Petham church, and exhortation to the parishioners to pay their due tithes. [26 April 1114 × 20 Oct. 1122]

> Lambeth Palace, Reg, Warham 1 fo.158. s. xvi in.
> Pd by Bethell, 'Richard' 321 no. X.

R. Dei gratia Cant' archiepiscopus hominibus suis de Petham salutem et Dei benedictionem et suam. Sciatis me concessisse in elemosinam ecclesie et canonicis sancte Osithe ecclesiam de Petham cum omnibus decimis que ad eam pertinent. Precor itaque ut qui rectas decimas ecclesie concesserunt amodo libentius dent, et si qui non dederunt amodo concedant pro remedio animarum suarum, et qui concesserunt Dei benedictionem et meam habent. Valete.

> For other exhortations to the better payment of tithes see Brett, *English church* 224. If the text may be taken at face value, it is worth note that tithe-paying was still not universal, even on an archiepiscopal estate.

59. Theulf, bishop of Worcester

Letter relating that the bishop's men have come before him to answer on the bishop's behalf concerning a law suit, but since no action has taken place he has sent them back, suspending the case indefinitely.

[26 April 1114 × 20 Oct. 1122]

> B = BL Cotton Vespasian E iv (fragment of a book from Worcester) fo. 207 s. xiii. At one point this leaf seems to have been used as a wrapper, and the text is badly rubbed, occasionally to the point of illegibility even under ultra-violet light.

Frater R. sancte Cant' ecclesie debilis minister venerabili amico suo T. Wig' episcopo et clero ac populo a Deo sibi commisso, salutem et Dei benedictionem et suam. Venerunt ad nos termino a nobis secundum iudicium vobis constituto venerabiles viri a fraternitate vestra nobis transmissi, qui parati fuerunt ad reddendas rationes, si forte opus esset, de iis unde causa vestra apud nos tractari debebat. Sed quia hac vice ex his nichil actum est remittimus eo[s] ad vos cum pace et dilectione nostra, o[mn]i hac causa ex parte nostra sine certo termino in tranquillitate remanente quousque aliud audiamus. Si vero ulterius ex hoc ortum aliquid fuerit unde nos rati[on]abiliter oporteat in causam intrare, nostrum erit vos convenienter et canonice summonere ut [v]enientes [ra]tiones vestras secundum . . ... [habitas] sermones sive querelas [ante] . . ..discutiatis. Val[ete].

> Nothing seems to be known of the occasion for this letter, though Malmesbury, *GP* 290n refers to several disputes between the bp and his monks, said to be reaching a peak near the bp's death on 20 Oct. 1123. The text is discussed briefly in Brett, *English church* 94. In the manuscript it follows immediately on *EEA* viii no. 138 of 1139 × 1143.

WILLIAM OF CORBEIL 1123–1136

*60. Barnwell priory

Grant of forty days indulgence to benefactors of the priory.

[18 Feb. 1123 × 30 August 1131]

A charter in the name of bp Hervey of Ely (*Liber memorandorum ecclesie de Bernewelle* ed. J.W. Clark 44–5 from BL Harley 3601 fo. 14) confirms several gifts, continuing: 'relaxantes eis qui iamdictis canonicis et ecclesie sue aliquid boni fecerint xl dies de iniuncta sibi penitentia secundum quod carta venerabilis patris nostri W. Cantuar' archiepiscopi testatur'.

The scale of the indulgence is unexpected, and the charter of Hervey, like most of the early muniments of Barnwell, is extremely suspicious.

61. Ralph Basset

Grant to Ralph Basset his clerk of all the churches of the demesne of Ralph Basset his father, as he gave them to him in the archbishop's presence, and protection for him, his churches and his clerks.   [Mid 1126 × 29 March 1130]

B = BL Cotton Vitellius E xv (cartulary of Osney abbey) fo. 33. s. xii/xiii. The text was significantly damaged in the Cottonian fire.
Pd *Cart. Oseney* vi 130 no. 1046.

Willelmus Dei gratia Cantuariensis archiepiscopus sedis [apost]olice legatus omnibus episcopis in quorum [parochiis] Radulfus Basset ecclesias habuit in do[minatu suo], salutem. Sciatis quod Radulfus Basset in presentia [nostra] dedit et concessit Radulfo clerico nostro, [filio suo], quicquid iuris et potestatis habuit [in] ecclesiis et capellis que sunt de cunctis dominiis suis. Quapropter rogatu prefati Radulfi patris illas ecclesias et capellas cum omnibus ad eas pertinen[tibus] terris et decimis et omnibus aliis rebus eidem Radulfo clerico nostro concedimus et scripto nostro confirmamus. Mandamus igitur atque precipimus quatinus eum et res suas et clericos suos quibus ipse prefatas ecclesias canonice dare voluerit manuteneatis, nec eis aliquam iniuriam irrogari permittatis. Valete.

Salter used Oxford, Bodl. Dodsworth 39 fo. 93, Dodsworth's copy of Agarde's notes from B before its damage, to restore 'filio suo' and 'in' above. His other restorations have no manuscript authority but are accepted here in their entirety. Ralph Basset the elder, one of the most successful of those who rose in the service of Henry I, died before 29 March 1130 (*Basset charters* pp. xxviii–xxx); Round suggested 1127 in *DNB* iii (1885) 385, but the editors of *Reg. regum* in their notes to ii no. 1576 suggest late in 1129. Saltman, *Theobald* no. 191 cites this grant when confirming twelve churches and their chapels to Osney as granted by his father to Ralph Basset, and by the son to Osney. The manors are identified and discussed in W.T. Reedy in *Northamptonshire Past and Present* iv(4) 1969–70, 241–5, though Salter noticed that few of the churches remained under Osney's control later. The scribe of B usually includes at least part of the witness list in his transcripts, so this text probably never had one.

62. Bexley church

Grant to Jordan his clerk and the church of Bexley of pasture for ten beasts and the right to feed ten pigs without pannage and the tithes of his pannage.

Canterbury [April 1125 × 1136]

A = London PRO Ancient Deeds E 40/ 7915. Endorsed, s. xii: Will' archiepiscopus de x animalibus in dominico herbagio, et de x porcis sine pannagio, et de decima pannagii in Bixle que ipse contulit ecclesie et Iordano clerico; s. xii/xiii: Bixle. 200 × 64 mm (rhs), 55 mm (lhs), with 12 mm tongue and 3 mm tie below. The 'shadow' of the lost seal on the tongue is some 50 mm across.

Will' Dei gratia Cant' archiepiscopus Iohanni episcopo Roff' et Anfr' dap' et omnibus hominibus de Bix, salutem et Dei benedictionem. Sciatis me concessisse Iord' clerico meo et ecclesie sancte Marie de Bix decem animalia in dominico herbagio nostro, et decem porcos in bosco nostro sine patnagio, et totam decimam de patnagio nostro de porcis et de denariis. T' Iohanne episcopo et Giffard' capell' et Simone canon' et capell' et Godefrido et Alano et Iord' de Dover&*a* Rodberto filio Riculfi et Rad' Picot et Will' de sancto Albano et Rad' camer' apud Cantorobiriam.

a The scribe otherwise uses a tironian et *and this ampersand is emphatic.*

Compare 35 above; this grant must be earlier than 80–81, granted after Elmer became prior of Christ Church, Canterbury. The grant is noticed by Du Boulay, 'Bexley' 42. For canon Simon see 64 below. If the absence of the legatine style is significant, then April–Sept. 1125. Jordan was a canon of Dover and cousin of Roger Folet, of the Kentish knightly family, according to Saltman, *Theobald* no. 58; cf *Domesday monachorum* 48n.

63. Calke priory

Record of the surrender by abbot William of Chester of all claims on the church of Calke to the prior and canons in a council, held at London in his presence and that of the archbishops of York and Rouen in the time of king Henry, restoring all, including the charter of the earl, that had been taken from them.

[24 April 1132 × 21 Nov. 1136]

A = BL Add. charter 7214. Endorsed, s. xii: De restitutione de Kalc facta coram W. archiepiscopo Roberto priori L'. 120 × 133 mm, sealed on a tongue on the left-hand side, with fragment of an elliptical seal in reddish-brown wax; 6 mm wrapping tie at foot.

Pd I.H. Jeayes, *Descriptive catalogue of Derbyshire charters* 66–7; Cheney, *EBC* 150, with facs. as pl.1; *Councils* i(2) 760–1.

Will' Dei gratia Cantuar' archiepiscopus et sedis apostolice legatus Rog' eadem gratia Cestrensi episcopo et Rannulfo comiti et omnibus sancte Dei ecclesie fidelibus per Angliam, salutem et Dei benedictionem. Notum omnium devotioni sit quoniam Will's abbas Cestrensis, in presentia nostra [et arc]hiepiscoporum Eboracensis et Rotomagensis et aliorum episcoporum [qui co]ncilio Lundonie interfuerunt, quod celebravimus in dominica quando cantatur Ego sum pastor bonus tempore Henr' regis, canonicis de Calc reddidit ecclesiam suam de Calc, et quietam clamavit, et omnia sua que per illum vel per suos illis ablata fuerunt reddere vel restaurare de suo promisit, et quod etiam cartam comitis de eadem re quam habuerant quamque per ipsum perdiderant restitueret. Unde volo et firmiter precipio ut eadem ecclesia amodo ad opus predictorum canonicorum ad serviendum Deo libera et quieta permaneat. Rogo etiam vos omnes ut pro amore Dei*a* et nostro eandem ecclesiam consilio vestro et auxilio muniatis. Val'.

a superscript

The council was held on 24 April 1132 (*Councils* i(2) 757–61); the reference to the time of kg Henry suggests the charter may be later than Dec. 1135. The canons of Calke moved by stages to Repton later in the century. The act is written in a script reminiscent of other Canterbury work, and is sealed in the same curious Christ Church fashion as e.g. 16, 38 above, but the colouring of the seal is unique among archiepiscopal seals on genuine acts before 1139. Practice was very different later; see Saltman, *Theobald* 226.

64. Canterbury: lands of the see

Grant to Edward of Cornhill and Godelif his wife of the land at Addington for the same service and rent as rendered to archbishop Ralph.

[18 Feb. 1123 × 21 Nov. 1136]

A = London, PRO Duchy of Lancaster DL 25/ 105. Endorsed, s. xii: Carta Willelmi archiepiscopi de Adint'; s. xii: Edinton' (on the tongue); s. xiii: fact' Edwardo de Cornhulle. 174 × 88 (lhs), 66 (rhs), with a 13 mm tongue, on which only a 50 mm 'shadow' of the seal remains. The document has undergone at least two repairs. The first strengthened the junction of the tongue and document with red-brown silk. The second followed a break in the tongue; the broken section was laid onto the surviving length, and a small vertical slip was inserted behind both, and the whole was stitched together. This leaves a misleading impression of a step for a tie, but there is no trace of one.

Ego Will's archiepiscopus concedo Ædwardo de Cornehelle et uxori eius Godelif et heredibus suis terram de Eadintune que fuit Wlsini pro viginti solidis denariorum, quos inde dabit in thesaurum meum singulis annis. Et faciet mihi servitium inde quod fecit Ra[d]ulfo antecessori meo, unde est Æ. noster homo et mihi et successoribus meis in placitis nostris serviet, et nulli preposito nisi ipsi archiepiscopo inde respondeat. T' Roberto monacho et Rogero canonico et Siwardo canonico et Anfr' dap' et Rannulfo fratre archiepiscopi et Henr' clerico.

> Compare 36 above, which this follows closely; the significance of the absence of legatine style is therefore uncertain. This and the following charter are discussed in Round, *Geoffrey de Mandeville* 304–12. For Siward, the canon of Aldgate whom prior Norman sent with William the later archbp to St Osyth, and the archbp subsequently called Simon, see *Cart. Aldgate* 228.

65. Canterbury: lands of the see

Grant to Gervase and Agnes his wife, daughter of Godelif, of the land at Addington as Godelif held it, for 20 shillings a year and the same service as paid to Ralph his predecessor. Gervase is to answer for it to none but the archbishop.

Lambeth [April 1125 × 21 Nov. 1136]

> A = London PRO Duchy of Lancaster DL 25/ 106. Endorsed, s. xii: Willelmi Cant' archiepiscopi de Adintun' concess' et c'. 192 × 75 (lhs), 50 (rhs), with 13 mm wide tongue, 6 mm wide tie; the 50 mm 'shadow' of a seal in natural wax. (Plate IIIc)

Ego Will'mus Dei gratia Cantuariensis archiepiscopus concedo Gervasio et Agneti uxori sue filie Godeleve et heredibus eorum terram de Eadintuna que fuit eiusdem Godeleve, pro viginti solidis denariorum quos inde dabit in thesaurum*a* meum singulis annis. Et faciet inde mihi servicium quod fecit Radulfo archiepiscopo*b* antecessori meo. Unde est idem Gervasius noster homo, et mihi et successoribus meis in placitis nostris serviet. Et nulli preposito nisi ipsi archiepiscopo inde respondeat. T' Helewis archid', Rad' de Cadomo, Iord' de Dovera, Rad' pic', Helg' fratre archiepiscopi, Gaufr' pic', Heltone filio Ric' filii Malgeri, Alano filio Huberti, Willelmo filio Ewardi, Roberto Bel, Willelmo filio Ricelde, Serlone clerico apud Lamhed'.

a teshaurum A   *b* achiepiscopo A

> Compare above 36, 64. This is clearly later than the last, which presents a problem. If Edward did the service for the land to archbp Ralph and to archbp William by virtue of Godelif's inheritance, Gervase could scarcely have done the same service for the same land to archbp Ralph by virtue of his marriage to Godelif's daughter. Moreover, Gervase, who lived until at least 1183, was, or had recently been, in wardship in the Pipe Roll of 1130 after the departure of his father to Jerusalem, which makes it even more improbable that he could have done any service before 1122; Agnes's father Edward was still alive in 1125, which also suggests that

this grant belongs after William's legateship (Round, *Geoffrey de Mandeville* 305–9). In principle the archbp's charter could have been granted between the death of Honorius II and the renewal of his legation in 1131 × 2, explaining the absence of the legatine title. Alternatively both the lack of title and the false reference to Gervase's service to Ralph could be derived from the mindless use of 64 as an exemplar for the text of an authentic 65. However, the apparent lateness of some of the letter forms in this very awkward piece of penmanship (above p. lxvi) arouses the suspicion that this is not authentic. The oddness of its aspect is increased by the steady change in the size of script, from a relatively compact first line to a large and rough last. The possible complexities are if anything increased by Bishop, *Scriptores regis* no. 427*, a purported charter of Henry II for Gervase of 1164–5 written in the hand of a royal scribe, Bishop's no. xlvii, who does not otherwise appear until the last years of the kg (Bishop, *Scriptores* 35, nos 206, 757, S 21)—this Bishop interpreted as a 'renovation'; the problems presented by 65 are no simpler, however, if it was a 'renovation'.

66.   Canterbury: Christ Church

Letter to the men of London, commanding them to give a true verdict on the land disputed between Christ Church and the abbey of Barking, after the abbess had at first agreed at Lambeth to a judgement, then withdrawn, and again agreed to a settlement.   [18 Feb. 1123 × 21 Nov. 1136]

A = Canterbury D. & C. C.A. L 70. Endorsed, s. xii/xiii: Breve Willelmi archiepiscopi pro placito quod fuit inter nos et abbat' de Berkinges de quadam terra in Lundonia; s. xiii/xiv: Non. l. Lond'. 177 × 112 mm. Seal at foot in white wax on a very narrow (5 mm) tongue which is probably shorter than it once was; the seal became detached during the moving of the archives during the 1939–45 war but was subsequently re-attached. The edge of the impression with the legend is much damaged, and only ..SIGIL.. can be recovered. (Plate IV)
B = Canterbury D. & C. Register B fo. 243r-v (248) no. l. s. xiv in.
Pd from B as van Caenegem, *Lawsuits* i no. 289.

Will' Dei gratia Cant' archiepiscopus clericis et laicis baronibus et probis hominibus Lund', salutem Deique benedictionem et suam. Novit et bene novit multorum vestrorum dilectio quoniam hec causa inter ecclesiam nostram matrem vestram et monasterium de Berchinges diu deducta est, et multis de causis demorata. Tandem venit abatissa in presentia nostra apud Lamhedam, et concessit nobis ut die statuto et termino, si legales haberemus testes de civitate Lund' qui hoc inveritare*a* vellent quod ecclesia nostra*b* umquam foret investita de terra illa unde querimonia fuit, post probationem illorum abatissa ecclesiam nostram inde investiret, ut sic quandoque*c* huius infiniti laboris finis*d* foret. Ad terminum illum venerunt nostri muniti testibus, qui parati erant probare sicut ego et abatissa paravimus. Optulerunt nostri testes, noluit abatissa recipere, non preter solitum vertit se ad alia, dicens quod ita non sed aliter intellexerat. Noluerunt nostri aliud facere quam statutum fuit, et sic recedentes nichil profecerunt. Tandem venit abatissa ad nos iterum*e* dicens sicut predixerat, quod aliter intellexit, sed tamen in fine ita esse recognovit. Ecce dies et terminus iste statutus est ut iustum iudicium fiat, sicut res ista acta est et sicut eam vobis scribo. Precamur itaque vos ut fideles sancte ecclesie in caritate que Deus est ut cum Deo sitis in hoc negotio, et nec mihi nec abatisse parcatis quin iustum[f] iudicium secundum conscientiam vestram faciatis. Hoc precor, hoc moneo, et vos in fide Cristi coniuro ut rectum facientes, non que vestra sint sed que Iesu Cristi in hac causa queratis, et finem debitum illi imponatis, secundum quod abatissa probationem nobis concessit et die statuto recipere noluit, sed aliter esse confirmavit, et iterum[e] coram nobis ita esse recognovit. Val'

[a] inveritare A; in veritate B   [b] erasure in A   [c] q' B
[d] A rather obscured; fines after corr. B   [e] t'cum A; certum B   [f] lacuna follows A

The absence of the legatine title may be significant; if it is, then 1123–Sept. 1125, or early 1130–late 1131 × early 1132. The scribe of B, who reproduces the first endorsement as a rubric, was equally uncertain where the land in question lay. The dispute may have concerned lands associated with All Hallows, Barking, where the abbey, Christ Church and even Rochester seem to have had interests—B.W. Kissan, *Trans. London and Middlesex Archaeological Society* ns viii (1938) 58, 65–6. The text is not, as a first reading might suggest, a summons to the hearing, since it specifies neither place nor day; the exasperation of 'non preter solitum' seems to reflect this informality.

*67. Canterbury: Christ Church

Grant of eight pounds of rent from Reculver, given at the dedication of the cathedral.   [*c.* 4 May 1130]

W. Somner, *Antiquities* (1640) 210–23, (1703 Appx 36–41 no. xxxvi) printed a list of benefactions to Christ Church running up to the reign of Henry IV from an unspecified source. *Mon. Angl.* (1655) i 18 prints the same list, possibly from Somner, though *Mon. Angl.* (1817) i 95 attributes it to 'Chronicis Gervasii Dorobernensis ms. in bibliotheca Cottoniana', possibly a mistaken reference to Lambeth 303, noted below. This chronological series is distinguished from such earlier lists of benefactions as that for 1052–1130 in BL Cotton Galba E iii fos 31–4 or that lying behind BL Arundel 68, which are in calendar form (Fleming, 'Lists' 118–9). Somner's version appears to be an enlargement of one compiled about 1400, perhaps by Stephen of Birchington, which survives in six copies: three rolls of benefactors, Canterbury D. & C. C.A. C 156 and 157 s. xv, C 158 s. xvi, and three manuscripts, Oxford, Corpus Christi Coll. ms 256 fo. 84v s. xv (Salter in *Arch. Cant.* xxix (1911) lxxxv-vi, wrongly giving it as from Christ Church), Lambeth Palace ms 303 (Birchington's enlargement of Gervase) fos 112–9v s. xv in., and Cambridge, Corpus Christi College ms 298.ii (Christ Church collectanea) fos 61–79 s. xvi in. See E. G. Box in *Arch. Cant.* xlv (1932) 103–19. All these include the text below.

Anno supradicto [sc. 1130] Willelmus archiepiscopus dedit octo libras annui redditus de manerio suo de Reculvere monachis ecclesie Cristi Cant' in dotem ipsius ecclesie Cantuar' in perpetuum, et hoc tempore regis Henrici primi [a]quod donum sanctus Edmundus archiepiscopus postea confirmavit[a].

a-a For 'quod donum—confirmavit' *Lambeth 303 and Oxford, Corpus 256 have*: Et postea sanctus Edmundus archiepiscopus inspiciens munimenta et evidencias [evid. et mun. *Corpus*] ipsorum prioris et conventus illam donacionem octo librarum annui redditus per sigillum suum confirmavit.

Gervase i 96 reports the archbp's gift of a ten-pound rent at the dedication, without specifying its source. A charter of archbp Edmund, printed from Canterbury D. & C. Reg. A by W. Wallace, *The Life of St Edmund of Canterbury* 487, confirms the gift of an annual rent from Reculver as due 'iure antique consuetudinis', without mentioning William.

68. Canterbury: priory of St Gregory

Grant of the church of St Nicholas, Thanington, as William of Malling surren-dered it into his hand in the presence of bishop John of Rochester and many others, and consented to the gift.   [Mid 1126 × 21 Nov.1136]

B = Cambridge UL Ll. 2. 15 (cartulary of St Gregory) fo. 2r-v s. xiii.
Pd *St Gregory's cartulary* 3 no. 3.

Willelmus Dei gratia Cant' archiepiscopus et sancte Romane ecclesie legatus omnibus ecclesie catholice filiis, salutem Deique benedictionem et suam. Notum sit omnium dilectioni quia Willelmus de Meallinges in presentia nostra et Iohannis episcopi Roffen' multis coram astantibus concessit et in manu nostra reddidit quantum in ipso erat et ipsi pertinebat [fo. 2v] ecclesiam sancti Nicholai de Tanintuna. Ego vero ipso Willelmo annuente et rogante dedi eam iure perpetuo possidendam ecclesie sancti Gregorii Cant' et canonicis ibidem Deo servientibus et illis qui in posterum servituri sunt. Test' sancta sinodo Cant'.

The corporate attestation is most unusual, and 'Cant.' might be the place of granting rather than an adjective. In two charters of abbot Hugh II of St Augustine's the witness list begins 'Teste conventu eiusdem loci et hiis testibus' (BL ms Cotton Claudius D x, fos 98v, 273). Conceivably the text here was a truncated version of something similar. Otherwise the diplomatic of this charter arouses none of the suspicions provoked by +1, +20 above. The family of William of Malling apparently descend from the Godfrey who appears sometimes as of Malling, sometimes of Thanington and sometimes as *dapifer* (above, p. xxxii n). It was this William presumably who quitclaimed any right in Patching to prior Walter Durdent (prior *c.* 1143–1149) according to Saltman, *Theobald* 535. Thanington church was appropriated to the priory later in the century (*St Gregory's cartulary* nos 22–3), having been confirmed to the priory in bulls of 1146, 1159–81 and 1185 (*PUE* iii nos 59, 282, 373). It is likely that this grant was made at or after the reconstitution of the house as a community of regular canons, and if so it should probably be placed in 1131 or later (above, pp. liv–v).

*69.   Dover priory

Grant of the prebend of Deal and the quarry of St Martin at Caen.

[29 April 1132 × 21 Nov. 1136]

The grant of the prebend is mentioned in general confirmations by pope Lucius III of 11
May 1182 (*PUE* ii 414–16), archbp Richard (*EEA* ii no. 125, *Literae Cantuarienses* (RS)
iii 372–4), and later texts. A passage in the chronicle of Dover in London BL Cotton
Vespasian B xi fo. 77, s. xv, printed in *Mon.* iv 535, enters into more detail. After
recording the original gift by kg Henry I, it continues:

Cuius auctoritate donationis, dictus archiepiscopus, impetrato prenotato*[a]*
lapicidinio seu quarrera apud Cadomum in Normannia quod hodietenus
vocatur La Quarrere Sanct Martyn, ecclesiam novi operis Dovorr' sive
monasterium a fundamento construxit, et in idem monasterium canonicos
regulares de monasterio sancte Osithe in Estsexia introduxit, et eidem
monasterio dictum lapicidinium cum prebenda de Dale dedit et carta sua
confirmavit.

  [a] ms: premittunt; premonito *would do as well.*

Dated on the assumption that the archbp's gift was later than the issue of the kg's formal
grant of Dover to the archbp, which was made in 1131 but not apparently committed to
writing until 1132, to judge by the surviving text (*Reg. regum* ii no. 1736).

70.   Earls Colne priory

*Confirmation of all the gifts in land, churches, tithes, liberties and all other
things made by Aubrey de Vere, Beatrice his wife, their descendants and others,
and of the excommunication placed on all who harm them, imposed by
archbishop Ralph.*

[Mid 1126 × 21 Nov. 1136]

B = Colne Priory estate archives, deposited at Chelmsford, Essex Record Office D/D Pr 149
   (cartulary of Colne) fo. 6. s. xii ex.
   Pd *Cart. Colne* 7–8.

Willelmus Dei gratia Cant' archiepiscopus et sancte Romane ecclesie legatus
omnibus sancte ecclesie fidelibus atque filiis per Angliam constitutis, salutem
et benedictionem Dei et suam. Universitati vestre notum fieri volumus nos
confirmasse et munimento presenti roborasse omnia bona et possessiones et
elemosinas in terris et ecclesiis, decimis, libertatibus aliisque rebus quecunque
donatione Alberici de Ver vel uxoris eius Beatricis eorumque posteritatis, vel
aliorum fidelium seu aliis piis modis, monachi de Abendonia apud Colun in
Essexa Deo famulantes possederunt vel possessuri sunt. Deinde sententiam
quam antecessor noster domnus Radulfus archiepiscopus malefactoribus

eorum inposuit Dei et domini pape et nostra auctoritate corroboramus. Eorum vero benefactoribus fraternitatis tam Cantuarie quam Abendonie participium concedimus atque donamus. Valete.

Compare above +43.

71. Hereford: diocese

Notification to Roger de Chandos, Ralph de Tornai, Robert of Bacton, 'Oregga' and her men of Poston, and the parishioners of Bacton, Peterchurch and St Weonards (Herefs) that the dispute between bishop Robert of Hereford and bishop Urban of Llandaff has been determined by the common counsel of the bishops at the command of pope Innocent II and with the consent of king Henry. Henceforward they are to obey bishop Robert as their diocesan.

[24 April 1132 × late 1134]

B = Bodl. Rawlinson B 329 (cartulary of Hereford) fo. 153 (formerly 165) s. xiii/xiv. C = Harley 6203 (transcript of B) fo. 31. s. xviii.

Pd from B in M.G. Cheney, 'The compromise of Avranches of 1172 and the spread of canon law in England' *EHR* lvi (1941) 179n. Cal. from C by Bannister, 'Cartulary' 274, and from Bannister in Conway Davies, *Episcopal acts* ii 633 no. L82.

Will's Dei gratia Cant' archiepiscopus et sedis apostolice legatus Rogero de Chandos et Radulfo de Tornai et Rodberto de Bachintona et Oregge et hominibus suis de Possintone et omnibus parochianis ecclesie de Bachintona et ecclesie sancti Petri et sancti Leonardi, salutem. Notum sit omnium vestrum devotioni quoniam, ex precepto domini nostri apostolici Innocentii et regis Angl' Henrici consensu et communi nostro et fratrum nostrorum episcoporum iudicio, cause vestre et ecclesiarum vestrarum inter Robertum episcopum Hereforden[sem] et Urbanum Landavensem episcopum debitum finem imposuimus, unde ex auctoritate domini pape et nostra mandamus omnibus vobis et quoniam iustum est et iudiciario ordine iudicatum precipimus ut amodo domino Roberto Hereforden' sicut episcopo vestro intendatis et ad salutem animarum vestrarum diligenter obediatis. Dominus sit vobiscum.

The charter appears to refer to a judgement delivered by the archbps of Canterbury, York and Rouen at the council of 24 April 1132 (*Councils* i(2) 757–61, Conway Davies, *Episcopal acts* ii nos L80–L87, above 63), according to the terms of Innocent II's letters of 21 Nov. 1131 and 13 Feb. 1132 (*Book of Llan Dâv* 62, 66–7). If so, it was presumably drawn up then or shortly afterwards. Urban of Llandaff appealed against the judgement to the pope, and seems to have died shortly before 9 Oct. in 1134. Bacton, Poston and Peterchurch lie along the Golden Valley, which bp Urban had claimed for his see.

72. Abbey of St Benet of Holme

Confirmation of the gift of the church of St Michael, Norwich, as granted by Stigand and Thuruert his son, with the consent of bishop Everard of Norwich.

[Mid 1126 × 21 Nov. 1136]

> B = BL Cotton Galba E ii (cartulary of Holme) fo. 44. s. xiii ex.; C = Ibid., a second version added at the foot of the leaf without explanation.
> Pd *St Benet of Holme* i 45 no. 76.

Willelmus*[a]* Dei gratia Cantuar' archiepiscopus et sancte Romane ecclesie legatus clero et populo de Northfolch', salutem et benediccionem. Confirmamus ecclesiam sancti Michaelis de Norwico*[b]* sancto Benedicto de Hulma et monachis eiusdem ecclesie in perpetuum possidendam, quam Stigandus et Thuruert filius eius predicte ecclesie dederunt cum omnibus pertinentiis suis, hoc idem etiam concedente Ebrardo Norwyc' episcopo. Et prohibemus ex auctoritate Dei et nostra ne quis imminuere vel inquietare hanc donationem presumat, sed in pace et quiete predictam ecclesiam illam sicut sua cetera possideat, salvo iure episcopali.

[a] W. C   *[b]* Norwich' C

The charter of bp Everard confirming the same gift (*St Benet of Holme* i 49 no. 83, *EEA* vi no. 33) is addressed to abbot Conrad (d. 16 × 18 Feb. 1127, after 18 weeks in office), but William's charter need not be of the same date. For the family of Stigand and Thurbert the priest (and elsewhere also dean) see *St Benet of Holme* esp. i nos 86–7, 110, 183, 249, ii no. 240. They retained control of St Michael 'ad placita' through the century, while paying a modest pension to the monks.

73. Abbey of St Benet of Holme

Grant of an indulgence to all those who come to the abbey with a pious intention on the feast of the translation of St Benedict or within the octave, given on the occasion of his visit to the abbey with bishop Everard.

[Mid 1126 × 21 Nov. 1136]

> B = Norwich, Norfolk RO DCN 40/ 8 (cartulary of Holme) fo. 40 (54). s. xiv ex.

Willelmus gratia Dei archiepiscopus Cantuariensis et sancte Romane ecclesie legatus universis fidelibus Cristi, benedictionem Dei et suam. Quoniam tranquillitati serviencium Deo religiosorum cura sollicita caritate debet intendere, nos apud sanctum Benedictum de Holm cum venerando episcopo Norwycensi ecclesie Ebrardo constituti hanc concessionem sancte caritatis intuitu eidem loco ad honorem Dei et beati Benedicti concessimus, ut quicumque ad eandem ecclesiam in translatione eiusdem patris mense Iulio

[11 July] et infra octabas eiusdem solempnitatis devota mente convenerit, si in penitentia quinque vel septem vel amplius annorum fuerit, et vere confessus extiterit, et in penitentia permanserit a Pascha usque ad festum sancti Martini, et a natale Domini usque ad capud ieiunii, eodem anno omni septimana unus ei dies relaxetur. Qui uero in iniuncta penitentia fuerit, triginta dies illi relaxentur per annum, et si penitentiam extra ecclesiam egerint, eisdem diebus intrent ecclesiam. Deus pacis et dilectionis sit semper vobiscum.

> It is possible that this visit was the occasion for the grant by Everard, confirmed by the previous charter. If so, it may be dated 1126 × 1127. The *arenga* is only found here among William's acts, and the provisions for different indulgences according to the status of the penitent are unusual and problematic. Firstly the formulation of 'five or seven years' is surprisingly vague. The use of penitentials in England between the Norman conquest and the later twelfth century has not been subjected to detailed scrutiny, but none which might have been used is known to have used a five-year penance as a standard for grave crimes. The *Corrector* of Burchard does give some prominence to a seven-year term, as did many of its predecessors. Even if one were to read this as referring to the age of the penitents the uncertainty is still disconcerting. It is tempting to suppose either that the scribe could not read his exemplar clearly, or that the exemplar already offered alternative readings. Secondly the distinction between penitents serving long penances and those who are in 'iniuncta' penance is far from clear. If a passage has been lost, perhaps before 'triginta dies', then the second problem might be more easily resolved.

74. Leeds priory

Grant of all the churches of his lands which Robert de Crevecoeur has surrendered to the archbishop in the presence of bishop John of Rochester, and both bishops have confirmed to the priory.   [Mid 1126 × 21 Nov. 1136]

> B = Strood MALSC DRc/ T 380 (formerly B 2087), Inspeximus by bp Gilbert de Glanville (*EEA Rochester*, no. 89, of 1185 × 1214), slightly damaged. C = Maidstone CKS U 120/ Q 13 (cartulary of Leeds priory) fo. 3v s. xiv in. in inspeximus by archbp Kilwardby of 28 May 1278, which inspects this with many other charters of Leeds. D = Inspeximus by Hubert Walter (*EEA* iii no. 520) also inspected by Kilwardby (as in C), ibid. fos 3v-4. E = Maidstone CKS DRb/Ar1/1 (Reg. Hethe, formerly DRc/R4) fo. 9. s. xiv in. in inspeximus by bp Gilbert. F = Cambridge UL Ee. 5. 31 (Register of prior Henry de Eastry of Canterbury) fo.151. s. xiv in., Inspeximus by prior Henry and the chapter of Canterbury, dated 3 Sept. 1314, including Hubert Walter's inspeximus. G = Maidstone CKS DRb/Ar1/13 (Reg. Fisher) fos 72v-3r (formerly DRc/ R7 fos 6/ 89v-90r). s. xvi in., a copy of an inspeximus by prior Hamo and the chapter of Rochester dated 13 Nov. 1314, including the charter of Gilbert de Glanville. H = Lambeth Palace, Reg. Warham 1 97v. s. xvi copy of Kilwardby's inspeximus. J = ibid. 103v copy of Henry of Eastry's inspeximus. K = ibid fo. 97v (from *EEA* iii no. 520). Noted in Lambeth Palace, Carte Misc. V/111 (list of charters of Leeds priory). s. xiii.
> Pd in *Reg. Roff.* 213, citing G, and 353-4. Cal. from C in Sherwood, 'Leeds' 27, from E in *Reg. Hethe* i 12, from CFHJ in Hubert Walter's inspeximus as *EEA* iii no. 520.

Willelmus*a* Dei gracia Cantuar' archiepiscopus et sancte Romane ecclesie legatus omnibus ecclesie catholice filiis, salutem Deique*b* benedictionem et suam*c*. Notum sit omnium dilectioni quia*d* Robertus de Crepito Corde in presentia nostra et Iohannis episcopi Rofen' multis coram astantibus concessit et in*e* manu nostra reddidit quantum in ipso erat et ipsi pertinebat ecclesias de tota terra sua. Ego vero, ipso Roberto*f* annuente et rogante, concedente episcopo*g*, dedi eas iure perpetuo possidendas, et episcopus ex*h* sua parte, ecclesie de Ledes et canonicis ibidem Deo*i* servientibus et in posterum servituris*j*. Testibus*k* Ansfrido*l* dapifero, Hamone*m* Vitalis filio et Elya de Crepito Corde.

Hubert Walter's confirmation adds: Quia igitur sigillum huic scripto appensum per vetustatem vidimus omnino*n* fere consumptum, ne eiusdem instrumenti fides per vetustatem sic periret, ad eius fidem perpetuendam continentiam ipsius in scriptum presens reduximus.

a W. CDEFHJK   *b* Dei et G   *c* et suam *om.* E   *d* quod CHK   *e om.* J   *f om.* CH
g Roff' *add.* F   *h* pro J   *i interlined* D   *j* futuris BG ; BEG *end here.*   *k*Teste DK
l Humfrido K   *m* Hantone C   *n interlined* D

The churches were granted by Robert de Crevecoeur for the soul of his uncle, Haimo dapifer (C fo. 3v); this is Haimo II, who ceased to be sheriff of Kent in 1114 × 1116 apparently, and probably in 1114 (Green, *Sheriffs* 50). He was still in office in *Reg. regum* ii 1162 of April 1114 × Sept. 1116, but had been replaced by William of Eynsford by *Reg. regum* ii 1093, dateable within the same limits. Before then he appears constantly in royal acts, but the only charters in which he occurs dated later are all suspect at best—*Reg. regum* ii 1404 (a Battle charter granting a cornucopia of liberties), 1535 and 1585 (a forgery, for which see Chaplais, 'Seals' 275). This suggests that he died or suffered some disabling incapacity around the date he left office. His lands were divided between Robert de Crevecoeur and Robert of Gloucester, who had married his brother's daughter; the entries in the Pipe Roll for 1129–30 concerning these transactions have been interpreted as meaning he had died recently, but the only entry under the new pleas is a danegeld exemption from a small portion of his extensive estate, 7s 7d 'de dominicis carrucis terre Hamonis dapiferi' (*Pipe Roll* 67), which is consistent with his having died much longer ago. For the background see Du Boulay, *Lordship* 86–7, Colvin, 'List' 9.

75. Leeds priory

Grant of the church of Chart Sutton at the presentation and request of king Henry.   [Mid 1126–Dec. 1135]

B = Maidstone CKS U 120/ Q 13 (cartulary of Leeds), fo. 6 s. xiv in., in another inspeximus of archbp Kilwardby, also dated 28 May 1278. C = Lambeth Palace, Reg. Warham 1 fo. 98v from Kilwardby's inspeximus s. xvi in.
Cal. Sherwood, 'Leeds' 28.

Will's Dei gratia Cantuarien' archiepiscopus Anglorum primas et apostolice sedis legatus omnibus ecclesie catholice filiis, salutem Deique*a* benedictionem et suam. Notum sit omnibus nos amore Dei et ad presentationem et petitionem domini H. illustris regis Anglie dedisse canonicis de Ledes ecclesiam sancti Michaelis de Chert cum pertinentiis perpetuo possidendam. Testibus domino Iohanni Roffen' episcopo, Ansfrido dapifero, Roberto de Crepito Corde, Elya fratre suo, Hamone Vitalis filio et aliis.

a salutemque Dei C

If genuine, probably of the same date as the preceding charter, and before the news of kg Henry's death could reach England. This is the only charter in the name of William with any claim to contemporary drafting to employ the primatial style, which became standard under Theobald after 1145 (above pp. lxxii–iii). The reference to presentation is troublingly early, and some confusion attended the subsequent status of the church. By *EEA* ii no. 145 archbp Richard appears to create a perpetual vicarage there, but by *EEA* ii no. 146, a year or two later, he confirmed the church to a rector paying the canons a pension, and it was still a rectory in the patronage of Leeds in the *Taxatio*.

+76. Leeds priory

Grant of the church of Woodnesborough for the clothing of the canons, as surrendered into his hand by Ascelina the patron of the church.

[18 Feb. 1123 × 21 Nov. 1136]

A = Lambeth Palace, Carte Misc. V/ 110, supposed original. Badly faded. Endorsed, s. xiii: Ecclesia de Wodnesberghe; there is a second undeciphered endorsement. 210 × 87 + 18 mm, with some slight damage. Written in a cursive hand of s. xiii, with the foot folded, with green hemp cords for sealing, but only the faintest traces of wax on them.
B = Maidstone CKS U 120/ Q 13 (cartulary of Leeds) fo. 4, s. xiv in. in inspeximus of archbp Kilwardby, dated 28 May 1278. C = Cambridge UL Ee. 5. 31 (Register of Henry de Eastry) fo. 151. s. xiv in. in inspeximus by prior Henry and the chapter of Canterbury dated 3 Sept. 1314. D = Lambeth Palace, Reg. Warham 1 fo. 97v, s. xvi in. copy of Kilwardby's inspeximus. E = ibid. fo. 104 from prior Henry's inspeximus.
Cal. from B by Sherwood, 'Leeds' 27.

Omnibus sancte matris ecclesie*a* fidelibus Willelmus Dei gratia Cantuar' archiepiscopus, totius Anglie primas, eternam in Domino salutem. [A]d notitiam vestram volumus pervenire quod Acelina patrona ecclesie de Wodnesberghe*b* in presentia nostra constituta con[cessit]*c* et in manus nostras reddidit quantum in ipsa erat et ei pertinebat ecclesiam beate Marie de Wodnesberghe cum omnibus [pertin]entiis suis*d*. Nos autem ad instantiam et petitionem dicte A. predictam ecclesiam priori et conventui de Ledes dedimus et concessimus in proprios usus perpetuo possidendam, specialiter ad inveniendum canonicis ibidem Deo in perpetuum ministrantibus necessaria indumenta. Unde ut*e* hec nostra donatio*f* et concessio firma et stabilis in eternum^g permaneat hoc scriptum^h sigilli nostri appositione dignum duximus roborare. Hiis testibus: Magistro Andrea^j Coventrensi, officiali nostro, ^{k}Ricardo Ebor', domino R. Haket, Willelmo de Ho, domino H. capellano.

^{a} sancte matris ecclesie] Cristi B
^{b} Wodnesberghe AE; Wednesbergh' B; Wodnesbergh' C; Wodenesbergh' D
^{c} conc. const. B ^{d} suis pert. D ^{e} *om.* C ^{f} ordinatio C ^{g} perpetuum BD
^{h}scripum A ^{j} Audoeno C ^{k} magistro *add.* E

Clearly a forgery; the script belongs to s. xiii, as do many of the forms and the style of the 'official'. The status of 75 is uncertain, but it has less obviously anachronistic forms, and this charter may have drawn some elements, including the primatial title, from it. The church was appropriated to Leeds in the *Taxatio*.

77. Leominster priory

Mandate to Peter, archdeacon of Hereford, and his ministers to ensure that the priory receives the tithes of Broadward, Wharton, Newton, Gattertop, Achis, Eaton, Hamnish, Hatfield [Magna] and Hatfield [Parva], Hampton, Risbury and Broadfield, on pain of ecclesiastical sanction.   [15 August 1127 × 1130]

B = BL Egerton 3031 (cartulary of Reading) fo. 93v. s. xii ex. C = BL Cotton Vespasian E xxv (cartulary of Reading) fo. 120v. s. xiv in.
Pd *Reading cart.* i no. 355.

W. Dei gratia Cant' archiepiscopus et sancte Romane ecclesie legatus P. Hereford'^{a} archidiacono et ministris suis salutem. Mando vobis ut^b ecclesie Leomenist'^{c} viriliter reddi faciatis decimas de omnibus terris que in parochia supradicte ecclesie sunt^d, et nominatim de Bradeford et de Wauretun' et de Niwetun' et Gatredeopa et Achis et Etona et Hameschis^e et Hetfeld' et alia Hetfeld' et Heamton' et Riseberia et Bradefeld'. Quod si reddere noluerint ecclesiastice non dormiat severitas iustitie. Val'^{f}

^{a} Herford' C ^{b} et C ^{c} Leomen' C ^{d} sint C ^{e} Hameness' C ^{f} *om.* B

Apparently issued during the vacancy after the death of bp Richard de Capella on 15 or 16 August 1127 (*Fasti* viii 3). If of the same date as the next charter, then before the election of abbot Hugh of Reading to Rouen in 1130. This is the earliest known occurrence of archdn Peter of Hereford, who seems to have survived until *c.* 1179 (*Fasti* viii 23–4). Kemp proposed the identifications, though offering Eaton and Hampton (Mappenore) with caution.

78. Leominster priory

Mandate to Peter, archdeacon of Hereford, and his ministers to remove the clerks installed in the chapelries of Ford and Hampton [Mappenore], belonging to the church of Leominster, whom abbot Hugh of Reading complains have been installed without his knowledge or consent, until the abbot has done what is needed, on pain of the ecclesiastical penalties for the negligent.

[August 1127 × 1130]

B = BL Cotton Vespasian E xxv (cartulary of Reading) fo. 121. s. xiv in.
Pd *Reading cart.* i no. 340.

Will's Dei gratia Cant' archiepiscopus et sedis apostolice legatus P. Herford' archidiacono et ministris suis salutem. Dominus Hug' Radyng' abbas conqueritur quod in capellis Forde et Hamtun' ad ecclesiam Leom' pertinentibus, ipso abbate nesciente nec concedente nec assenciente, clericos intromisistis quod nequaquam sic facere debueratis. Mandamus itaque super hoc vobis quatinus hoc cicius emendetur clericos inde removendo donec per abbatem fiat quicquid inde fiet. Quod nisi feceritis et clamorem inde audiam, quod ad me pertinuerit*ᵃ* faciam sicut de negligentibus et obedire refugientibus ad ea que per auctoritatis apostolice manum firmata cognovimus. Val'.

ᵃ -uerint B

Abbot Hugh was elected archbp of Rouen in 1130. This, like the preceding charter, seems to be a vacancy document. Reading claimed to have two general privileges from Calixtus II and Honorius II, *PUE* iii nos 9, 12, the second and fuller of which is dated 13 April 1125. Neither includes an explicit control over appointments to churches, though the second, which may have been improved, or worse, by the beneficiaries, could certainly be read as including it.

79. Bishop Urban of Llandaff

Summons to the bishop with the archdeacons, abbots and priors of his diocese to attend the council to be held by the cardinal legate John [of Crema] at London on 8 September 1125. [March × August 1125]

B = Aberystwyth NLW 17110E (Book of Llandaff) fo. 43 col. 58. s. xii.
Pd *Book of Llan Dâv* 49; *Cartae Glam.* i 53 no. xlix; *Councils* i(2) 736 citing earlier conciliar editions. Cal. Conway Davies, *Episcopal acts* ii 619 no. L42.

Willelmus Cantuariensis archiepiscopus Urbano Landavensi episcopo, salutem. Litteris istis tibi notum facere volumus quod Iohannes ęcclesię Romanę presbiter cardinalis atque legatus legis ordinatione nostraque coniventia*ᵃ* concilium celebrare disposuit Lundonię in nativitate beatę semper virginis Marię. Propterea precipimus ut in prefato termino in eodem loco nobis occurras cum archidiaconibus et abbatibus et prioribus tuę dyocesios, ad definiendum super negotiis ęcclesiasticis et ad informandum seu corrigendum que informanda vel docenda seu corrigenda docuerit sententia convocationis nostrę.

a -corr. fr. conv- B

This text occurs in a complex quire which did not form part of the first stage in the formation of the book (D.Huws 'The making' 138–41, 154–5). This is the only surviving summons to the council, and the reference to the abbots of the diocese, where there were apparently no abbeys in 1125, suggests that it represents a form used for all. The legate arrived in England in Lent (*ASC* i 255).

80.   London: priory of Holy Trinity, Aldgate

Grant of the church of Bexley.   Aldington [1128 × 21 Nov. 1136]

A = London PRO Ancient Deeds E 40/ 4985. 134 × 129 + 25 mm, sealed on a tag with fragmentary impression of seal in natural wax (heavily varnished), with . . .MI D'I GR'A CANTVARIEN.. legible. Endorsed, s. xii: Carta Will'i archiepiscopi de ecclesia de Bix [nobis data added in another hand]; s. xii/xiii: Bixle (repeated in the tag).

B = PRO E 41/437, the first of nine charters on Bexley in a transcript of 1258 × 60, since one of the five seals attached is that of bp Fulk Basset of London, and the last text is a letter to the canons from Hugh Mortimer, official of the archbp. C = Lambeth Palace, Reg. W. Warham i fo. 147. s. xvi in.

Pd Du Boulay, 'Bexley' 50 (no. 2) and pl. 2.

Will'*a* Dei gratia Cant' archiepiscopus et sedis apostolice legatus Iohanni eadem gratia Roff' episcopo et omnibus hominibus et amicis suis tam clericis quam laicis totius archiepiscopatus, salutem et Dei benedictionem. Sciatis me concessisse et dedisse in elemosina ecclesiam sancte Marie de Bix*b* monasterio sancte Trinitatis Lundonie et canonicis ibidem Deo famulantibus tam presentibus quam futuris inperpetuum. Teste eodem episcopo Iohanne Roff' et Helewis arch', Giffardo capell', Willelmo et Alano monachis, Simone et Alveredo canonicis, Godefr' et Lupello, Wulfrico, Iord', Alano, Henrico, Moise, Gildewino, Godzelino clericis, Willelmo de Einesford patre et Willelmo filio eius et Anfr' dapiferis, Osberto, Willelmo de Albano et Rodb' filio Rad', Willelmo de Pagaham et Giff' filio eius, Rodb' filio Ric', Rad' camer' et Wlmaro, cum multis aliis apud Aldintuna.

a Willeminus B   *b* Bixle C

According to the narrative printed from the s. xv cartulary in *Cart. Aldgate* 229 (where the editor identifies the church as Bexhill) archbp William's brother became a canon at Aldgate, perhaps the occasion of this grant. A charter of Elmer, prior of Canterbury 1128 × 4 May 1130–11 May 1137, printed by Du Boulay, 'Bexley' 51–2 no. 4 pl. III, records his presence at the gift. Compare above 35, 62, and the similar charter by bp John of Rochester (*EEA*

Rochester no. 22, forthcoming). A thirteenth-century rental of Christ Church Canterbury attributes the institution of a vicarage to the time of archbp William, and the patronage of this vicarage was disputed between Aldgate and the archbp for much of the thirteenth century (Du Boulay, 'Bexley' 43–8, esp. 43 n. 4). Alured the canon may be the later prior of St Gregory's. For William of Eynsford, sheriff of Kent before 1129 and later monk of Christ Church, see particularly 88n below, *Domesday Monachorum* 46, 109 (*EEA* ii no. 85), and S.E. Rigold, 'Eynsford castle and its excavation', *Arch. Cant.* lxxxvi (1971) 109–71, esp. 111–3.

81. London: priory of Holy Trinity, Aldgate

Grant of the church of Bexley with all its tithes, including the tithes of pannage in pigs and coin, and pasture for ten beasts and the right to keep ten pigs without pannage.   Aldington [1128 × 21 Nov. 1136]

A = London PRO Ancient Deeds E40/ 15739. 166 × 106 mm. Endorsed s. xii: Will' archiepiscopus de ecclesia de Bixle, et de x animalibus in dominico herbagio, et de x porcis sine pannagio et decima pannagii; s. xii/xiii: Bixle; there is one further inidentified mark. Slit for a tag, now lost. The slit is immediately below the last full line of text, but above the final four words on the line below, which makes it unlikely a *plica* has been lost.

B = PRO E 41/437, the second charter of the transcript of 1258 × 1260 (see the preceding text). C = BL Lansdowne 448 (cartulary of Holy Trinity, London) fo. 11v. s. xv in. D = Lambeth Palace, Reg. W. Warham i fo. 147. s. xvi in.

Pd *Cust. Roff.* 86 (from C), Du Boulay, 'Bexley' 51 no.3 (from A).

Will'mus Dei gratia Cant' archiepiscopus, sedis apostolice legatus, Iohanni eadem gratia Roff' episcopo et omnibus hominibus et amicis suis clericis et laicis totius archiepiscopatus, salutem et Dei benedictionem. Sciatis me concessisse et dedisse in elemosina ęcclesiam sancte Marie de Bix*ᵃ* monasterio sancte Trinitatis Lund' et canonicis ibidem Deo famulantibus tam presentibus quam futuris inperpetuum, cum omnibus decimis omnium rerum que decimari debent et nominatim de patnagio de porcis et de denariis. Et decem animalia in dominico herbagio nostro et decem porcos in bosco nostro sine patnagio, et cum omnibus rectis consuetudinibus eidem ecclesie pertinentibus. Teste Iohanne episcopo Roff' et Helewis arch' Cant', *ᵇ*Willelmo et Alano monachis, Simone et Alveredo canonicis, Godefrido, Lupello, Wlfrico, Alano capellanis, Henrico, Moise, Gildewino clericis*ᶜ*, Willelmo de Einesford et Willelmo filio eius et Anfr' dap', Osberto, Willelmo de sancto Albano, Rodberto filio Rad', Willelmo de Pagah' et Giffard' filio eius, Rad' camerario et Wlmaro cum multis aliis*ᵇ* apud Aldint'.*ᵈ*

ᵃ Bixle D   *ᵇ⁻ᵇ* Willelmo et Alano—aliis ABD; et pluribus qui sunt in carta C   *ᶜ* -ico BD
ᵈ pax benefactoribus suis *add.* BCD

An enlargement of 80 above, with added provisions taken (partly *verbatim*) from 62. The added phrase in BCD might suggest that they were taken from a second original, or from an intermediate copy.

82.   London: priory of Holy Trinity, Aldgate

Mandate commanding dean William and the archdeacon and chapter of St Paul's to invest prior Norman with the church of St Botolph [Aldgate] as it was adjudged to him by the archbishop's chapter in his presence.

[Mid 1126 × 21 Nov. 1136; probably after Jan. 1128]

B = Glasgow UL Hunterian U. 2. 6 (cartulary of Holy Trinity) fo. 172. s. xv in.
Pd Brett, *English church* 95; cal. *Cart. Aldgate* no. 965.

Will's Dei gratia Cant' archiepiscopus et Romane ecclesie legatus W. decano et archid' et capitulo sancti Pauli, salutem. Mandamus vobis atque precipimus ut domino Normanno investituram parochie sancti Bothulfi quam ei capitulum nostrum in presentia nostra iuste adiudicavit restituatis, prohibentes ne ab aliis ecclesiis parrochiani illi suscipiantur. Val'.

The church of St Botolph was granted to Holy Trinity by the 'cnihtengild' of London in 1125, and confirmed to the priory by kg Henry I in 1126 (*Cart. Aldgate* 168–9, *Reg.* ii no. 1467). In the cartulary the text is preceded by the narrative of a dispute over parochial rights between St Botolph and St Peter le Bailey before archdn William in 1157, and this act is introduced as evidence of an earlier dispute between Robert as priest of St Botolph and Derman of St Peter's. A letter of bp Gilbert of London (*EEA* xv no. 38, 1128 × 34) orders archdn William and Haco the dean to do full justice to the canons over the church, since Derman the priest has detained it from them (*Cart. Aldgate* no. 966). The archbp's act is presumably but not certainly later.

*83.   Malling abbey

Confirmation to the nuns of their lands and possessions.

[18 Feb. 1123 × 21 Nov. 1136]

Mention only in the suspect Saltman, *Theobald* no. 173. According to *Cal. Ch. Rolls* v 55–63 of 1347, the nuns still had this and charters of Anselm, Ralph (above, 22, 50) and Theobald after a serious fire, possibly that of 27 July 1190 recorded in Gervase i 485, which destroyed all their early charters of bishops of Rochester.

84. Minster-in-Sheppey priory

Grant of Gillingham church with all its chapels and appurtenances.

[Mid 1126 × 21 Nov. 1136]

B = Lambeth Palace, Reg. W. Warham 1 fos 135v-6, s. xvi in., incorporated in an inspeximus of this charter, the next and a charter of Theobald (*EEA Canterbury 1139–61*, forthcoming) of 1243–4, addressed to pope Innocent IV by abbot R[obert] of St Augustine, Canterbury, R[oger] prior of Christ Church, Canterbury, and N[icholas] prior of St Gregory, Canterbury.

Willelmus Dei gratia Cant' archiepiscopus et apostolice sedis legatus universis sancte matris ecclesie filiis, salutem et Dei benedictionem. Tam presentibus quam post futuris innotescat nos dedisse et in elemosinam concessisse ecclesiam de Gillingeham cum capellis et omnibus redditibus et proventiis suis tam in marisco quam in terris ecclesie beate Dei genitricis et virginis Marie et sancte Sexburge in Scapeya, tam victus quam vestitus ancillis Dei ibidem commorantibus in tantum conferens solacia. Et quoniam imperpetuum quod super hoc actum est observari decrevimus, de cetero ex auctoritate Dei et beati apostolorum principis et nostra penitus inhibemus ne aliquis predictis Dei ancillis super hoc iniuriam faciat seu aliquid auferat vel minuat quod prefate ecclesie de Gillingeham pertinere debeat. Si quis igitur huius nostre donationis elemosinam quam usibus ancillarum Dei caritative erogavimus temere surripiendo violare presumpserit iram Dei incurrat quoadusque famulabus Dei ingratus [fo.136] existat et in nostram maledictionem incidat, nisi tua citatione commonitus peniteat. Quod si in temeritate sua perseverando diabolo obligari magis quam Deo Deique ancillis satisfaciendo reconciliari elegerit, perpetuo innodetur anathemate. Teste Iohanne episcopo Rofens'.

As it survives, the text is very oddly drafted. While 'tua citatione commonitus' in the anathema makes little sense in a text with a general address, replacing 'tua' with 'sua' or 'nostra' would only make a modest improvement. For the archbp as founder of the priory see above p. liv.

85. Minster-in-Sheppey priory

General confirmation of all gifts to the priory, with grant of free election, freedom from archidiaconal exactions and right of burial for the whole isle.

[1128 × 21 Nov. 1136]

B = Lambeth Palace, Reg. W. Warham 1 fo. 136 in the inspeximus cited above under 84. s. xvi in.

Willelmus Dei gratia Cant' archiepiscopus apostolice sedis legatus omnibus sancte matris ecclesie filiis, salutem et Dei benedictionem. Sciant tam presentes quam posteri quod nos suscepimus ecclesiam sancte Marie et sancte Sexburge de Scapeya et moniales ibidem Deo famulantes earumque possessiones in Dei et Cant' ecclesie et nostram protectionem, et omnes donationes tam a nobis quam ceteris fidelibus eidem ecclesie factas pietatis intuitu, et quecunque bona memorate iuste et canonice a quocumque adipisci poterunt presentis scripti patrocinio confirmamus. In quibus dignum duximus propriis hec exprimenda vocabulis: predictam scilicet ecclesiam sancte Sexburge de Scapeya cum capellis, scilicet cum capella de Eastcherche cum omnibus decimis et appenditiis suis, et cum capella de Leysdone cum decimis et omnibus appenditiis suis, et cum capella de Wardone cum decimis et omnibus appenditiis suis; et ecclesiam de Gillingeham cum capellis et decimis et omnibus appenditiis suis; et terras in insula sitas et terras de Gryen' quas ex nostra emptione predicte ecclesie contulimus cum mariscis et pertinentiis suis. Statuimus autem ut prefata ecclesia liberam et canonicam de conventu suo habeat electionem, et tam in hiis que prelibavimus quam in ceteris iam habitis vel postmodum habendis secundum canonicam conferentium dispositionem plenariam optineat dignitatem, scilicet in decimis, in terris, mariscis, in pratis et pascuis et bosco et plano. Preterea ab omnibus exactionibus quas archidiaconus suique ministri*a* a subiectis parrochiis extorquere solent, quemadmodum conventualem decet ecclesiam et ut antiquitus constat fuisse, liberam et quietam fore decernimus. Presertim quemadmodum sanctorum predecessorum nostrorum tempore unicam et totius insule sepulturam optinuit, ut ita in perpetuum optineant*b* nostra auctoritate precepimus et ne aliter fiat inhibemus. Rogamus itaque et obsecramus in Domino omnes successores nostros huius vie viros inveniri*c* quatinus predictam ecclesiam pro Dei amore et nostro in animarum suarum salutem*d* in eundem statum libertatis et eandem reverentiam religionis quam nos statuimus post decessum nostrum illis commissam tenere et manutenere studeant, ut mercedem quam nos speravimus pro institutione eandem et ipsi ab omnium bonorum remuneratore consequantur*e* pro tuitione. Si quis vero contra huius nostre institutionis sententiam venire temptaverit anathemate innodetur quousque de ingratitudine sua satisfaciendo peniteat. Quod si contumax et impenitens decesserit, et temeritatem suam ad heredes perpetuandam transmiserit, nostre maledictionis divineque ultionis sententiam incurrat. Teste Iohanne Rofensi episcopo, Eylmero priore Cant' ecclesie et Fulcone priore de sancta Osyda et Fulcone priore de Ledes.

Prior Elmer's predecessor became abbot of Dunfermline in 1128, and was a frequent witness to the charters of King David thereafter (*John of Worcs.* iii 184, *Charters of King David I*, esp. no. 22). Like the last, this text as it stands is apparently partially corrupt. The first recorded prior of Leeds is Alexander, whose profession to Theobald is printed as Saltman, *Theobald* 549. Since Leeds had been founded at least twenty years earlier, the names of one or more early priors have been lost. If this Fulk was one, Leeds may have had three early priors of the same name, for the prior Fulk who occurs in Leland's notes from William de Vere's lost Miracles of St Osyth (Leland, *Itinerary* v 171) is mentioned in the context of the early years of Henry II, though these notes at least are not in rigorous chronological sequence, and it may be a reference to an earlier officeholder, but at least two other priors held office before another Fulk who occurs as prior from 1207 onwards (here expanding on *Heads* i 170, 281–2). It is remarkable that Theobald's general confirmation on the same leaf (*EEA Canterbury* 1139–61, forthcoming) contains more detail on archbp William's benefactions than is recorded here, adding as it does:

> dimidium sulingum terre de feodo Richardi de Lucy de Newenton' ex adquisicione Willelmi archiepiscopi per Avelinam matrem eiusdem Ricardi et terram de Ripaneia in insula de Scapeya. In insula de Gryen' redditus sex librarum quas predictus Willelmus archiepiscopus emercatus est de ipsis heredibus, salvis consuetudinibus curie de Gillingham, terram de Readefeld' quam sepedictus archiepiscopus emercatus est ab Aeldiva et Ordiva et heredibus suis.

These may, of course, have been later gifts. The general confirmation by kg John of 3 May 1205 in *Rot. chart.* 148b echoes a phrase or two of William's text, rather than Theobald's, to which it is otherwise closer. The charter also appears to have been known to kg Henry III in his confirmation of 7 April 1234 (*Mon. Angl.* ii 50) recited by Edward III in 1329 (*Cal. Ch. Rolls* iv 112–3), and to archbp Stratford, in texts recited in letters patent of archbp William Courtenay dated 5 Jan. 1396 (*Cal. Pat. Rolls* 1399–1401, 340).

86. Reading abbey

Confirmation at the request of king Henry of the foundation, and of the king's gifts, including Reading and Leominster with all their churches and chapels, Thatcham and Cholsey, with the churches of Cholsey and Wargrave which the king has exchanged with the abbey of Mont St Michel before giving them to Reading, as Reading, Leominster and Cholsey were formerly abbeys.

[11 June 1123 × 1130]

B = BL Egerton 3031 (cartulary of Reading) fos 49v-50. s. xii/xiii. C = BL Harley 1708 (cartulary of Reading) fo. 188. s. xiii. D = BL Cotton Vespasian E xxv (cartulary of Reading) fo. 108v. s. xiv.
Pd Saltman, *Theobald* 438–9n, cal. *Reading cart.* i no.174.

Ego Dei gratia Cant' ecclesie archiepiscopus Willelmus concedo ecclesie Radingensi et eius abbati primo domno Hugoni et monachis in eadem ecclesia Deo et beate Dei genitrici virgini Marie, in cuius honore ipsa ecclesia constructa est, servientibus omnia illa que dominus noster Henricus rex Anglorum eidem dedit ecclesie. Hec sunt et Radingia in qua ipsa ecclesia*ᵃ* constructa est, cum ecclesiis et*ᵃ* capellis et ceteris omnibus ad eam pertinentibus, et Leoministria cum ecclesiis et*a* capellis et omnibus ad eam perti[fo. 50]nentibus, et Thacheham et Chealseia cum ecclesia sua, quam scilicet ecclesiam*b* et ecclesiam de Weregrave dominus noster H. rex ab abbate et monachis de Periculo Maris escambiavit et ecclesie Rading' concessit. Hec predicta sicut dominus noster rex monasterio Rading' libere et quiete dedit ego concedo, et quia Rading' et Leoministria et Chelseia antiquitus abbatie fuerunt et nostris temporibus pio studio domini nostri H. regis ad abbatiam Radingensem per Cristi gratiam redacte sunt, nos concedimus et presenti carta confirmamus, et Dei benedictione et*a* nostra prosequimur. Amen*c*

a om. D   *b* et de escambio ecclesiarum de Chaus' et Weregrave *add.* D
c Amen CD; *om.* B

This act, if secure, was presumably issued after the exchange with Mont St Michel, recorded in *Reading cart.* i no. 3 (cf ii no. 771), which was given at Les Andelys; the king crossed to Normandy in 1123 on June 11, about the time that the archbp reached Normandy from Rome. If Kemp is right in seeing the absence of Cholsey from the bull of Calixtus II of 19 June 1123 (*Reading cart.* i no. 139, cf ii no. 770) as evidence for its having been acquired later, this confirms the rather later upper limit. Kemp accepts the likelihood that *Reg.* ii no. 1427, *Cart.* i no. 1, contains the elements of a royal confirmation of mid-1125. William appears among the witnesses, and it would be easy to interpret the archbp's confirmation as its companion piece. The text is rather curious, with the changes between singular and plural even more abrupt than usual and the unexpected reference to Hugh as first abbot before he had a successor, but compare the charter of bp Richard of Hereford of about this date *Reading cart.* i no. 354, *EEA* vii no. 11. Several of the earliest charters of Henry I for the house (*Reg. regum* ii nos 1427, 1448, 1474, Kemp, *Cartularies* i nos 1–2, 5) have clearly been substantially altered at least, and it is possible that the earliest papal privilege of Honorius II confirming the abbey rights in detail (*PUE* iii no. 12) has also undergone some 'revision'. The archbp's charter therefore cannot be regarded with complete confidence, but the nature of the gifts themselves is not in serious doubt and our text, or something very similar, is cited directly in Saltman, *Theobald* no. 215, which agrees with BC against D in their major divergence. For the king's interest in the conversion of ancient minsters see C.N.L. Brooke, *Churches and churchmen in medieval Europe* (London/Rio Grande 1999) 153–4.

87. Rochester cathedral

Confirmation to bishop John and the church of episcopal rights over all Canterbury men and estates in the diocese of Rochester, as bishops Gundulf and Ernulf enjoyed them.   Canterbury [Mid 1126 × 21 Nov. 1136]

B = Strood MALSC DRc/ R 1 (Textus Roffensis), fo. 203 (a replacement leaf) no. 195. s. xii.
Pd *Text. Roff.* 203; cal. Flight, *Bishops and monks* 264 no. 216.

Will' Dei gratia Cant' archiepiscopus, sedis apostolice legatus omnibus hominibus et amicis suis tam praelatis quam subditis cuiuscunque conditionis sunt ęcclesię filiis, salutem Deique benedictionem et suam. Noscant presentes et postfuturi me reddidisse et firmiter concessisse et ex parte Dei et beati Petri et nostra iure inconcusso hoc presenti scripto meo confirmasse consilio et assensu clericorum et laicorum nostrorum ecclesie sancti Andree Roff' et dilecto filio nostro Iohanni episcopo omnem potestatem et iura episcopalia illi pertinentia in maneriis nostris et clericis et laicis sui episcopatus sicut unquam melius vel honorabilius tenuerunt antecessores sui Gundulfus vel Arnulfus episcopi. Test' Helewis arch' Cant' et Fulc' priore sancte Oside et Abel canonico, Alveredo priore sancti Gregorii, Rad' Cad' cum multis aliis clericis et laicis apud Cantoroberiam.

> Compare 25, 53, +54 above and +88 below, for the uncertain status of the charters on the replacement leaves of the Textus. This is the first recorded occurrence of Alured as prior of the reformed community at St Gregory's, which suggests a date in or after 1131 (above pp liv–v).

+88.   Rochester cathedral

Confirmation of the gift of Northfleet church with its appurtenances, as granted by archbishops Anselm and Ralph, and of Boxley church with all its rights and customs, as granted by king Henry at the dedication of the cathedral and assigned by bishop John to the monks.   [?8 May 1130 × 1135]

> B = Strood MALSC DRc/ R 1 (Textus Roffensis), fos 179v-180 (replacement leaves) no. 95. s. xii med. C = BL Cotton Domitian x (Rochester cartulary), fo. 121r-v no. 32. s. xiii in. D = Strood MALSC DRc/ T 57 no. 3 (suspicious inspeximus by bps Walter of Exeter and Hugh of Ely) dated May 1260.
> Pd from B in *Text. Roff.* 156–7; cal. Flight, *Bishops and monks* 264 no. 217.

Willelmus gratia Dei Cantuariensis archiepiscopus et sedis apostolice legatus omnibus Cristi fideli[fo.180]bus, salutem. Sciatis me concessisse et confirmasse monachis ecclesię sancti Andrę de Rovecestra in perpetuum ecclesiam de Northfliete et quicquid ad eam pertinet, sicut venerabilis pater Anselmus*a* dedit eis et carta sua confirmavit, et successor eius Radulfus predecessor noster. Ęcclesiam quoque de Boxle cum omnibus beneficiis ad eam pertinentibus quam Henricus rex in dedicatione praedicte Rofensis ecclesie in dotem dedit et Iohannes eiusdem ecclesię episcopus eisdem monachis concessit et dedit cum omnibus possessionibus et beneficiis et consuetudinibus et libertatibus illis hactenus rationabiliter indultis autoritate offitii quo fungimur ipsis confirmamus et praesentis scripti testimonio communimus. Si quis igitur contra donationes et confirmationes tantorum patrum et nostram aliquando venire temptaverit, sit separatus in praesenti a communione sancte ecclesię Cristi et in futuro a societate sanctorum omnium

nisi ad satisfactionem venerit.[b] Testimonio Herewisi archidiaconi Cantuar',
Gaufridi prioris, Eadmeri monac' Cant', [c]Fulconis prioris de Cic, Ricardi
archidiaconi de Norwic', Willelmi vicecomitis, Ansfridi dapiferi, Haimone
filio Vitalis[c] et aliorum multorum.

[a] Ans. pat. *before corr.* C   [b] Valete *add.* D   [c-c] *om.* C

Rochester was dedicated on 8 May 1130 (John of Worcs. iii 194). Richard, archdn of Suffolk,
was consecrated bp of Avranches in 1135 though elected in 1134 (*Fasti* ii 67, cf 35 above). If
the charter were genuine, and Eadmer is the historian, this would be by far the latest reference to him. However, prior Geoffrey became abbot of Dunfermline in 1128, and his attestation here presents a serious difficulty (*Heads Scot.* 67, cf 85 above). While the Northfleet
section is predominantly in the singular, the whole Boxley section is in the plural. It is possible that this is an early Rochester forgery, in which a genuine confirmation of rights in
Northfleet (compare 25, 53, and their notes above), has been interpolated with a confirmation of Boxley church to the monks, rather than the bp. The ownership of the church was
disputed between the monks and archdn Robert only a few years later (*PUE* ii no. 33). If so,
and if the Northfleet section may be accepted, the original form was granted *c.* May 1126 ×
1128. William was sheriff of Kent from around 1116, but was not in office in 1129–30
(Green, *Government* 247, *Sheriffs* 50–1, above 74). The only evidence for his holding office
again after 1130 is the very dubious *Reg. regum* ii no. 1867. Bishop, *Scriptores* no. 659 noted
it as a local hand, and Flight, *Bishops and monks* 287 no. 524 had no hesitation in dismissing
it as a forgery.

+89. Rochester cathedral

*Confirmation to the bishop and monks of all the grants of Lanfranc, Anselm
and Ralph, particularly Canterbury episcopal rights in the diocese and in
Freckenham and Isleham, restored by the testimony of the abbot of St Osyth,
and confirmation of Northfleet church as given by Anselm and confirmed by
Ralph, and of Boxley church as given by king Henry and assigned by bishop
John to the monks.*   [Mid 1126 × 21 Nov. 1136]

> B = BL Cotton Faustina B v (Historia Roffensis), fos 69v-70. s. xv, copy of inspeximus by
> prior Richard and the chapter of Christ Church, Canterbury dated 5 Feb. 1333, which
> includes the charter of Hubert Walter (*EEA* iii no. +592), in turn reciting this and other
> texts.
> Pd *Reg. Roff.* 443; cal. Flight, *Bishops and monks* 264 no. 218.

Willelmus Dei gratia Cant' archiepiscopus et sedis apostolice legatus
omnibus Cristi fidelibus, salutem. Sciatis me concessisse et confirmasse
ecclesie sancti Andree de Rovecestr' *omnes donaciones, concessiones et
confirmaciones et restituciones predecessorum nostrorum Lamfranci, Anselmi
et Radulfi* [fo.70] *quas fecerunt et cartis suis confirmaverunt.* Concedo insuper
et restituo predicte ecclesie et episcopo Iohanni *omnia iura episcopalia in
maneriis ecclesie Cant' que sunt in suo episcopatu, et in manerio de Frekenham
et Iselham, quod est in decanatu de Bockyng', ad habendum et tenendum adeo*

bene sicuti Lamfrancus ea reddidit et Gundulphus episcopus ab eo recepit, et sicut episcopi Roffen' usque ad tempora nostra continuarunt, ut testimonio F. abbatis sancte Osithe est testificatum et probatum. Preterea concedo monachis ecclesie sancti Andree de Rouchestr' imperpetuum ecclesiam de Northfflete et quicquid ad eam pertinet sicut venerabilis pater Anselmus dedit eis et carta sua confirmavit et successor eius Radulphus predecessor noster, ecclesiam quoque de Boxle cum omnibus ad eam pertinentibus beneficiis quam H. rex in dedicatione predicte Roffn' ecclesie in dotem dedit, et Iohannes eiusdem ecclesie episcopus eisdem monachis concessit et dedit et cum omnibus possessionibus, consuetudinibus et libertatibus ecclesie Roffen' hactenus rationabiliter indultis auctoritate officii qua*ᵃ* fungimur ipsis confirmamus et presentis scripti testimonio communimus. Si quis igitur contra donaciones et confirmaciones tantorum patrum et nostram aliquando venire temptaverit, sit separatus in presenti a communione sancte ecclesie Cristi et in futuro a societate sanctorum omnium nisi ad satisfactionem venerit. *Valete. Testibus F. abbate sancte Osithe et aliis.*

ᵃ quo B

This is a conflation of 87 and +88 above, interpolated with reference to Freckenham and Isleham, and may be compared with the texts of Anselm and Ralph which were treated in the same way, above +27, +54; the inserted material is in italics. Like them this charter is found only in the forged inspeximus of Hubert Walter, and the reference to an abbot of St Osyth is clearly an error, since it remained a priory until at least 1139 × 1140 (Saltman, *Theobald* no. 161).

+90. Rochester cathedral

Record of a judgement of the archbishop's court. On the evidence of a charter of Gundulf and the testimony of bishop John and the verdict of the men of Mottingham he has adjudged the tithes of Mottingham in the parishes of Eltham and Chiselhurst, as granted by Ansgot the chamberlain, to the monks against the claims of the rector of Eltham. He has also inspected the ordinance of bishop Gundulf on the establishment of monks in his cathedral, the appointment of sergeants and the annual render to the bishop on the feast of St Andrew, which he confirms. '1131'

A = Rochester mun. Supposed original, now lost.

B = Rochester mun. Lost inspeximus by the notary William de Dene, dated 30 Sept. 1316, of this and a charter of archbp Richard (*EEA* ii no. +193). C = Maidstone CKS DRb/ Ar 1/17 (Registrum Spiritualium), fo. 21v. s. xvi/xvii (from A). D = Ibid. fo. 23 (from B).

Pd from A in *Reg. Roff.* 346, and from B, ibid. 349 ; cal. Flight, *Bishops and monks* 264–5 no. 219.

Willelmus Dei gratia[a] Cantuariensis archiepiscopus et sedis apostolice legatus omnibus Cristi fidelibus, salutem. Sciat universitas vestra quod per auctentica scripta pie memorie Gundulphi episcopi de Roucestr' ac testimonio Iohannis episcopi successoris eius[b], per inquisitionem proborum virorum, monachi de Rovecestr' coram nobis legitime docuerunt eos pacifice possedisse et quadraginta annis et amplius ante tempora nostra decimas de Modyngham in parochiis de Eltham et Chisilherste de dono Ansgoti camerarii de quibus per rectorem de Eltham coram nobis fuerunt impetiti. Propterea de consilio et assensu iuris peritorum nobis assidentium predictas decimas eisdem monachis adiudicamus iure perpetuo possidendas. Preterea inspeximus diligenter ordinationem[c] Gundulphi episcopi de introductione monachorum et institutione seriantorum et exennio faciendo die sancti Andree apostoli episcopo presenti in ecclesia Rovecestr' quam ordinationem rite et proinde factam auctoritate officii quo fungimur ipsis confirmamus et presentis scripti testimonio communimus[d]. Si quis igitur contra adiudicationem nostram et confirmationem aliquando venire temptaverit, sit separatus in presenti a communione sancte ecclesie Cristi et in futuro a societate sanctorum omnium nisi ad satisfactionem venerit. Valete. Testimonio Heremusi archidiaconi Cantuariensis, Gaufridi prioris, Eadmeri monachi Cantuariensis, Fulconis prioris de Cic, Ricardi archidiaconi de Norvic', Willelmi vicecomitis, Ansfridi dapiferi, Hamonis filii Vitalis et aliorum multorum. Actum anno incarnationis domini nostri Iesu Cristi MCXXX primo.

[a] gratia Dei D   [b] et add. D   [c] predicti add. D   [d] communivimus D

The phrasing of the Mottingham section is wholly anachronistic; the witness list is taken from +88 above, which also provided the elements of the sanction. Archbp Richard's charter is also probably spurious, as is *Reg. Roff.* 346, a grant of the tithes of Mottingham in the name of Ansgot the king's chamberlain, apparently based on Textus Roffensis fo. 188 no. 132. The mention of an 'ordinatio' of Gundulf on the establishment of the priory sergeants places this with or after Gundulf's forged charter (*EEA Rochester* forthcoming no. +12) which survives in a twelfth/thirteenth-century 'original'.

*91. Priory of St Osyth

Confirmation of the church of Petham.   [18 Feb.1123 × 21 Nov. 1136]

Mentioned only, in confirmation by archbp Hubert Walter (*EEA* iii no. 600). Compare 57 above.

92. Sées: abbey of St Martin

Record, addressed to bishop Bernard of St Davids and the faithful, that he had heard king Henry say in a council at Westminster that earl Arnulf had granted all the churches of his lands in Wales with tithes and twenty carucates of land, and ten pounds from churches and tithes in England, and that the king had granted all these gifts to the monks of the abbey at Pembroke. The archbishop too confirms these gifts as they were recorded in the king's charter.

[*c.* Feb. 1126 × 25 Jan. 1129]

B = Sées, Archives episcopales, Liber Albus of Sées (composite cartulary of St Martin, s. xii/xiii) fo. 108 (128). s. xiii. C = Alençon, Bibl. Mun. 190 (copy of B made in 1747) fo. 89. D = Alençon, Archives de l'Orne H 938. ii, pp. 45–6 no. cclxvi s. xix. Round in *CDF* 232n notes that D gives fo. 89 in the margin, suggesting that it is taken from C. E = London PRO Transcripts 31/8/140b/3 p.186 (transcript of copy made by Léchaudé d'Anisy) s. xix. The variants of C, D and E are insufficient to suggest an ultimate source other than B, and are not recorded in the apparatus.

Paris BN fr. 18953 contains s. xvii extracts from the lost 'Livre rouge' of Sées, for which see J-M. Bouvris in *Annales de Normandie* xliii (1993) 255–7. On pp. 45–6 and 216 there are versions of this with no substantial variants.

Pd from E in *Reg. regum* ii no. 1484, Appx 357 no. cxc. Cal. from C, D and E in Round, *CDF* 239 no. 670, Conway Davies, *Episcopal acts* i 247 no. D72.

Guillermus Dei*ª* gratia Cantuarien' archiepiscopus et apostolice sedis legatus B. episcopo de sancto David et omnibus sancte ecclesie filiis, salutem Deique benedictionem et suam. Testificor sicut a domino rege audivi tempore concilii habiti apud Westmonast' ecclesias fuisse datas ab Arnulfo comite [fo. 108v] monachis sancti*ᵇ* Martini Sagii tocius terre sue quam habebat in Walis et decimas et xx carrucatas terre cum aliis pluribus et x libratas ecclesiarum et decimarum quas habebat in Anglia, et hec eadem regem dedisse et concessisse fratribus supradictis quorum quidam morabantur et morantur apud Penbroc. Ego vero illud idem ex nostra parte concedo et confirmo sicut ipse rex confirmat et in carta sua confirmatum habetur. Teste episcopo Winton' Will', Seifrido Cicest' et Ioanne Rost'.

ª repeated and canc. B   *ᵇ corr. from* sancte B

The council mentioned here cannot be identified, since it is unclear whether it was secular or ecclesiastical, or whether William was already archbp when he heard the king's testimony. Dated on the assumption that the archbp might have issued this document as legate while in Normandy on his way back from Rome early in 1126, rather than in England, and certainly before the death of bp William of Winchester on 25 Jan. 1129. The kg's charter is *Reg. regum* ii no. 1611, of 1126 × 1135. Arnulf's grant is dated Sept. 1 1098 in the chapter of Sées, and survives in two versions (Round, *CDF* 666, 668); in 668 (B fo. 108) the witnesses are followed by the signa of a king (unspecified), archbp Anselm, bp Wilfrid [of St Davids], Arnulf and Robert fitz Hamo. Since Anselm was out of the realm altogether from late 1097 to *c.* August 1100, and if the text is genuine, Anselm's signum must have been added after the grant, presumably at Sées. If so, this was probably in the early autumn of 1100, as Anselm travelled through Normandy back to England, where he remained from late Sept. 1100 until mid-1103. Arnulf appears to have forfeited his lands, at least temporarily, in 1102 (Orderic, iv 302, vi 30–2, but cf Eadmer, *Vita Ans.* 146–7). Farrer in *Early Yorkshire charters* iii 28 provides some background and notices archbp William's charter briefly.

93. Shrewsbury abbey

Record that Philip de Belmeis had failed in his suit in the king's court at Woodstock in the presence of the king and archbishop, and that the land at Betton Abbots had been judged to the monks. [16 Jan. 1127 × 21 Nov. 1136]

> B = Aberystwyth NLW 7851 (cartulary of Shrewsbury) p. 54. s. xiii ex. Eyton's transcript of B is now Bodl. Top. Salop d 2 fo. 16 (s. xix).
> Pd in R.W. Eyton, *Antiquities of Shropshire* vi 183, *Cart. Shrewsbury* i 59–60 no. 56b, Bethell, 'Richard' 322 no. XIII, van Caenegem, *Lawsuits* i no. 273.

Willelmus Dei gratia Cantuariensis archiepiscopus sedis apostolice legatus omnibus sancte Dei ecclesie fidelibus per Angliam salutem. Noscant presentes et postfuturi quoniam monachis de Salopesbiria iudicata est quieta et libera terra sua de Beitona, quia Philippus de Belmesio in curia regis Henrici apud Wodestoke defecit a iustitia in presentia regis et nostra. Valete.

> The case arose after the death of bp Richard of London on *c.* 16 Jan. 1127 (see 94 below). In *EEA* xv nos 31–2, provisionally dated near the bp's death, Richard restored two other estates to Shrewsbury.

94. Shrewsbury abbey

Record, addressed to Pain fitzJohn and all the barons of Shropshire, that prior Fulk of St Osyth had testified that bishop Richard of London had confessed to him that he had held the manor of Betton for life, and not by hereditary right, and had quit-claimed the land to them in his life-time.

[16 Jan. 1127 × 21 Nov. 1136]

> B = Aberystwyth NLW 7851 (cartulary of Shrewsbury) p. 20 no. xxiii. s. xiii ex. C = ibid. p. 55 no. lvii.
> Pd Eyton, *Antiquities* vi 182–3, *Cart. Shrewsbury* i 23–4 no. 23, Bethell, 'Richard' 322 no. XII.

Will's Dei gratia Cantuar' archiepiscopus Pagano filio Iohannis et omnibus baronibus de Salopessir'[a] salutem. Sciatis quoniam Fulco prior sancte Oside mihi testificatus est quod Ricardus episcopus London'[b] in confessione sua sibi recognovit quod[c] manerium de Bertona[d] non erat suum hereditarie nisi in vita sua, et liberum et quietum clamavit illum monachis de Salop'[e] in vita sua quorum erat manerium illud et a quibus ipse tenuit eum. Valete.

a Salop' C *b* Lund' C *c* in *add.* B *d* Beitona C *e* Salopesb' C

Apparently a reference to bp Richard's deathbed confession. See 93 above. Although manifestly after the first grant of the archbp's legation, the style does not appear here, though the copyist of the cartulary did include it in 93. See above p. lxxi for the possibility that this places the act between spring 1130 and late 1131.

*95. Thetford priory
Confirmation. [18 Feb.1123 × 21 Nov. 1136]

Mention only. The dorse of PRO E40/ 14810 has a 'Kalendarium rotuli munimentorum lib(erati) Magistro Hugoni de Musele'. Hugh of Mursley was a notary in the service of archbp Winchelsey, and attended him during his visitation of the diocese of Norwich in 1304 (C.R. Cheney, *Notaries public,* 35–6n). Many of the texts are identified by their first or last words, as here. The calendar includes a section beginning with a confirmation by bp John II of Norwich, probably *EEA* vi Norwich no. *419, the entry below, and then an otherwise lost confirmation by archbp Theobald (*EEA Canterbury* 1139–61 forthcoming).

Confirmatio Willelmi Cant' archiepiscopi fi. Amen. Amen

To judge by the conclusion, this may have been another privilege modelled on the use of the papal chancery, and if so it invites comparison with 48, also for a Cluniac beneficiary. However, it may simply have ended with an anathema similar to 24.

96. Thorney abbey

Confirmation of whatever indulgence bishop Hervey of Ely and his fellow bishops may decide to offer to visitors to the house at the impending dedication feast or its anniversary. [Mid 1126 × 1128]

B = Cambridge UL Add. 3020 (Red Book of Thorney) fo. 166. s. xiv in.

Will's Dei gratia Cantuar' archiepiscopus et apostolice sedis legatus Herveo eadem gratia Elyensi episcopo, salutem Deique benedictionem et suam. Super dedicatione sancte Marie Thornensis ecclesie quam ad presens facere disponitis congratulamur et laudamus inceptum et ad bonum finem pervenire*a* exoptamus. Et quia huiusmodi conventus fiunt pro animarum salute et redemptione peccatorum, ubi etiam homines penitentiarum relaxationem magis expetunt, quicquid huiusmodi rationabiliter tam in die dedicationis quam in annua ipsius diei revolutione vestra et fratrum nostrorum coepiscoporum prudentia relaxandum*b* decreverit et nos ex Dei parte et nostra et auctoritate nobis a Deo commissa firmamus. Val'.

a provenire B *b* concedimus *added in mg in another hand*

Thorney was dedicated in 1128 according to notes in B fos 166, 167v, and to the annals at the beginning of the ms (fo. 7), and also in the annals in London BL Cotton Nero C vii fo. 80. s. xii. A much later hand added there 5 Nov., which was a Monday in 1128.

97. Thorney abbey

Confirmation of the grant by bishop Hervey of Ely to the abbey at its dedication of all customs and secular causes which Ely had in the hundreds of Witchford from Thorney's land and men at Whittlesey, saving only the royal dues. Lambeth [1128 × 21 Nov. 1136]

B = Cambridge UL Add. 3020 (Red Book of Thorney) fos 166v-7. s. xiv in.

Will's Dei gratia Cantuar' archiepiscopus et sedis apostolice legatus tam presentibus quam futuris salutem. Notum sit omnium devotioni me concessisse et confirmasse donationem illam quam concessit et donavit Herveus Elyens' episcopus Thornensi ecclesie in dedicatione eiusdem ecclesie quando ipse eam dedicavit, scilicet omnes illas consuetudines et causas seculares quas habebat Eliensis ecclesia in hundredis suis de Wicheford' de terra et hominibus Thornensis ecclesie de Witles' exceptis regalibus consuetudinibus que [fo. 167r] super terram illam evenerint que nec ad episcopum nec ad ecclesiam suam pertinent. Teste Iohanne episcopo Roff', Thom' priore et Helewis arch' Cant' ecclesie cum multis aliis apud Lamhedam.

After the dedication in 1128 (above 96). The grant by bp Hervey (d. 30 August 1131), and a confirmation by bp John of Rochester, are printed in E. Miller, *Abbey and bishopric of Ely* Appx nos vi, xiv. Another confirmation by bp Gilbert of London, in terms indistinguishable from those of John of Rochester, occurs in B fo. 167r–v (*EEA* xv no. 40). The reference to bp Hervey suggests, without proving, that he was still living. A royal confirmation is in *Reg. regum* ii no. 1798 Appx no. cclxxvii, given at Ditton, apparently between the death of Hervey and the kg's last crossing the sea in late July 1133. There is no other record of Thomas as prior of Rochester, if that is the house in question, and he does not appear to have been commemorated at Rochester. There is however ample space between the last occurrence of prior Orduin and the first of prior Brien for his term of office (*Fasti* ii 78). A Thomas, third prior of Christ Church, occurs in Saltman, *Theobald* no. 40n, some twenty years later. It is unlikely that he is the same man; alternatively he may be from elsewhere.

APPENDIX I

PURPORTED JUDGEMENT ON THE PRIMACY OF CANTERBURY

A = BL Add. MS 57946, no. 1. 122 × 150 mm. No endorsements. A piece of shiny and discoloured parchment, said to have been found under the floor of a house in Mercery Lane, Canterbury, which first came to light about 1930. It has been prepared for sealing sur double queue at the bottom left hand side, though it cannot be determined whether any seal was ever applied to the very narrow tag which passes through two slits in the face, and is knotted below. There is no plica. As it stands it appears to be a barely decipherable but crude forgery, written in the sixteenth century or later, though some effort has been made to produce the effect of late Anglo-Saxon minuscule script in the text, and Lanfranc's subscription uses forms unlike those of the others who sign.

Sin.... iura(?) Dunelm(?)................
Lanfrancus dep......[Dorobernen]sis archiepiscopus ex [antiqua] antecessorum consuetudine ostendit sed ob amorem .... Eboracensi archiepiscopo sacr[amentum] relaxavit, scriptamque [tantum] professionem recepit, non preiudicans successoribus suis qui sacramentum cum professione a successoribus Thoma voluerint. Si archiepiscopus Cantuariensis vitam finierit Eboracensis archiepiscopus Doroberniam [v]enerit et eum qui electus fuerit cea *[sic]* ceteris praefate aecclesie .... [primati] proprii iure consecrabit. Quod si Eboracensis archiepiscopus obierit[a] is qui est successurus eligitur accepto a rege archiepiscopatus dono Cantuariam vel ubi Cantuariensi archiepiscopo placuerit accedet ordinat. . . canonico. Huic constitutioni consenserunt prefatus rex et archiepiscopi Lanfrancus Cantuariensis et Thomas Eboracensis et ceteri qui intererunt episcopi.

Signum + Guill' regis   + Ego Remigius Dorcacestrensis
    Signum + ...
                    + Ego Erfastus subscripsi
+ Ego Lanfrancus Dorobernensis archiepiscopus subscripsi[b]
+ Ego Walchelinus [Winton'] episcopus subscripsi

[a] oberit A   [b] *Lanfranc's subscription in red*

The illegibility of the first line makes it unclear whether this was intended as a royal grant or one by Lanfranc; the first is more probable. It is clearly based on Canterbury, Dean and

Chapter Chartae Antiquae A 2 (*Letters of Lanfranc* no. 3 (iv), the version of the primacy settlement of 1072), from which the signa have been imitated, and this has been used for some conjectural readings above. C.A. A 2 was once sealed *en placard*, but the method used in this forgery is wholly different. It is difficult, if not impossible, to identify the illegible subscription as that of archbp Thomas.

APPENDIX II

POSSIBLE FURTHER LOST ACTS

The records of Tywardreath priory, formerly owned by the Arundells of Wardour, have now passed to Truro, Cornwall Record Office. Among these is ART 6/7, a single leaf formerly folded as a narrow bifolium, s. xv/xvi, containing an inventory of charters in a (lost) cartulary, which are cited by folio and line in summary fashion. The first section of the cartulary seems to have dealt with the manor and church of Downinney in Treneglos, given by Robert fitz William, with related confirmations i.a. by bps Robert of Exeter in 1145, Henry of Exeter in 1155 *(sic)*, William (Brewer) in 1225, and a kg Henry in the nineteenth year of his reign. The list includes 'Confirmacio Cant' archiepiscopi fo. <viiio> ixo; Nota de ecclesia S. Marie de Valle linea iia et decima totius corod'' and 'Confirmacio Willelmi archipresule *(sic)* Cant'. Nota de Duncenif' fo. ixo linea xvia in dorc''. A now lost charter, probably of archbp Theobald, was printed by G. Oliver, *Monasticon dioecesis Exoniensis* (Exeter, 1846–54) 41 no. xiv, with the name Thomas in the title, which could be the first of these. Of the Exeter charters only *EEA* xi no 73 seems to survive. As no text listed in the inventory is manifestly later than archbp Pecham, the second archiepiscopal act could have been of archbp William of Corbeil.

A. Duchesne, *Histoire genealogique des maisons de Guines, d'Ardres, de Gand et de Coucy* (Paris 1631), Preuves 39 printed from an original charter in the archives of St Leonard, Guines, a grant by Count Manasseh and Emma his wife, a daughter of William of Arques, of the church of Newington with its dependent chapels of 'Alschot' and 'Celpham', and tithes at 'Herst' and 'Bliseinghes' 'per manum domini Guillelmi Cantuariensis archiepiscopi et Henrici archidiaconi sui'. 'Nos quoque ut hoc donum ratum et inconvulsum perpetuo permaneret, et ne ab aliquo malivolo infringi in posterum posset, sigillorum nostrorum impressionibus munivimus, et ut idem Guillelmus archiepiscopus auctoritate sua et privilegio roboraret impetravimus'. The document is dated 1120, and drawings of the seals of the count and his wife are added. This presents numerous difficulties, discussed at length by Stapleton in *Archaeologia* xxxi (1846) 216–37. The date cannot be right, if the text is genuine, and presumably Henry is an error for Helewise, but even if one attributes these mistakes to Duchesne, some other sources for the foundation of the nunnery of Guines suggest that the foundation was only carried forward after the count's death in 1129 × 1132, though in the fourteenth century there seems to have been a foundation charter dated 1129[1]. I have not been able to find any evidence that the exemplar transcribed by Duchesne, which was then at another family foundation at Bourbourg, has survived.

---

[1] Lambert of Ardres in *MGH Scriptores* xxiv 580, 586; *Willelmi chronica Andrensis* ib. 699–700; Iohannes Longus, *Chronica S. Bertini* in *MGH Scriptores* xxv 797. Certainly no impression of the seal of Count Mannasseh is recorded in any of the standard repertories, including Demay's detailed scrutiny of the archives of Picardy and Flanders

APPENDIX III

CANTERBURY ITINERARIES[1]

LANFRANC

1070

15 August	Nominated	John of Worcs. iii 14; *Memorials of St Dunstan* 232 gives as date of reception at Canterbury.
29 August	Canterbury, consecrated	Orderic ii 254; *Memorials Dunstan* 232; *Councils* i(2) 588.[2]

1071

October	Rome	Lanfranc, *Letters* p. 43; JL 4692

1072

7 April	Winchester (Council)	*Councils* i(2) 591
	London	*Acta Lanfranci* ed. Bately 85
	Canterbury	do.
27 May	Windsor (Council)	*Councils* i(2) 603

1075

[prob. April–May]	London (Council)	*Councils* i(2) 607–8

1076

1 April	Winchester (Council)	*Councils* i(2) 616

1077

21 March	Canterbury	*Life of Gundulf* 39; *Acta Lanfranci* 86

---

[1] Since the narrative sources for parts of the careers of the archbishops, and particularly for Anselm, are relatively full, it is often possible to establish a sequence of stopping points, even though absolute dating is impossible.

[2] Orderic gives this as the date of his enthronement after election and consecration, but enthronement is an integral part of consecration for an archbishop (more or less always consecrated at Canterbury) in contemporary pontificals. See above p. xlii n.

9 April	Canterbury consecration of cathedral	*UGQ* 4, amended in Gibson, *Lanfranc* 172, 218[3]
14 July	Bayeux	Orderic iii 11–12 and n.[4]
13 September	Caen	L. Musset, *Les actes de Guillaume le Conquérant . . . pour les abbayes caennaises* (Mémoires de la Société des Antiquaires de Normandie xxxvii (1967) 14–5.
?27 September	Caen	E. Deville, *Revue catholique de Normandie* xiv (1904–5), repr. as *Notices sur quelques manuscrits normands conservés à la Bibliothèque St Geneviève* iv (1905) 20–21.[5]
23 October	Bec	*Vita Herluini* 106; Orderic iii 11n.
1078		
?May	London (Council)	*Councils* i(2) 624–5
1079		
29 December	Canterbury	John of Worcs. iii 32
1080		
July 14	Bonneville-sur-Touques	Bates, *Acta* no. 175
Christmas	Gloucester (Council)	*Councils* i(2) 629–30
1081		
February	Salisbury	Bates, *Acta* no.154
May 31	Winchester	Bates, *Acta* no. 39[6]
1082		
	Caen	Bates, *Acta* no. 59[7]

---

[3] See too *The monastic constitutions of Lanfranc*, ed D. Knowles. 2 ed rev. C.N.L. Brooke (OMT 2002) 89 n. 263.

[4] Bates, *Acta* no. 83, citing J.-M. Bouvris, 'La dedicace de l'église cathédrale Notre Dame de Bayeux (14 juillet 1077)', *Soc. des Sciences , Arts et Belles-Lettres de Bayeux* xxviii (1982) 3–16.

[5] Notes from a transcript of the then lost but now rediscovered cartulary of St Etienne: 'post quam dedicationem, 27 die eiusdem mensis, placitavit Osbernus Gifardus, cum uxore sua Adeguisa contra abbatem Willelmum, in praesentia Lanfranci archiepiscopi, de domo que fuit Roberti Abrincensis'.

[6] The status of this document in its various forms is a perpetual conundrum; the witnesses are some of the least controversial elements—see the discussion by Bates.

[7] Dated 1082, 16 William I, in the fifth indiction; if these figures may be trusted, since William was crowned on Christmas Day, the indiction used is either the Greek or Bedan one, which would place it before 24 September.

1085

	Canterbury	Colker, 'Polemic' 108; *UGQ* 4
Christmas	Gloucester (Council)	*Councils* i(2) 632–4; *Annales*
		monastici ii 34

1086

24 May	Westminster	*ASC* i 216–17, Malmesbury,
		GR i 542, 710; Orderic iv
		120–1

1087

c. 9 September	Canterbury, St Augustine	*PL* clv 46
26 September	Westminster	*ASC* i 222; John of Worcs.
		iii 46[8]

1088

2– 3 November Salisbury	*De iniusta vexatione* 81–95

1089

28 May.	Canterbury. Died	Above p. xxxi

Other places where Lanfranc is reported as staying, if at uncertain dates, include:
Aldington, 'villa sua', apparently after the Pennenden Heath pleas, perhaps 1072 ×
1073: *Memorials Dunstan* 239 (cf Bates, *Acta* no. 69).
Bury St Edmunds, where he held a plea before nine shires over the claims of bp
Herfast on the abbey some time before 1081. The report comes from the *De
miraculis* of Herman *archidiaconus*: *UGQ* 254, also in *Memorials of St Edmund's
abbey* i 65–7. For further discussion see Gibson, *Lanfranc* 148–9, 157.
Canterbury: no. 9
Freckenham: Lanfranc, *Letters* no. 44.

ANSELM[9]

1093

6 March	Elected at Gloucester	Eadmer, *Historia* 37, *Vita*
		Ans. 65, *UGQ* 75; *Fasti* ii 3
17 April	Winchester	Eadmer, *Vita Ans.* 65

[8] *ASC* gives three days before Michaelmas, meaning either 26 or 27 September, depending how
the annalist counted. John of Worcs. iii 46 understood his (probable) *ASC* source as meaning 26,
adding, rightly, that it was a Sunday. *De iniusta vexatione* 74 gives 27 September explicitly, as
does William of Malmesbury *GR* i 542–4. Orderic iv 110 gives Michaelmas itself. F. Barlow,
William Rufus 57 preferred 26 September.

[9] There are two valuable printed itineraries of Anselm by Fröhlich in *Letters* i 335–43 and by I.
Biffi in *Anselmo d'Aosta* iii 509–21. These differ from the one that follows in providing something
nearer a continuous narrative, and in making certain assumptions about the archbishop's presence at royal courts which may well be right, but cannot be proved. Similarly the dating of some
Regesta texts is treated more sceptically here.

Summer	Rochester	Eadmer, *Historia* 39
	Windsor	ibid. 40
	Winchester	ibid. 41
25 September	Enthroned at Canterbury	ibid. 41, 218
4–5 December	Consecrated at Canterbury	ibid. 42, John of Worcs. iii 68; *UGQ* 4, 75; Hugh the Chanter 12
25–7 December	Gloucester	Eadmer, *Historia* 43, *Vita Ans.* 67; *ASC* i 228; *Reg. regum* i no. 338

1094

	Harrow	Eadmer, *Historia* 45–6, *Vita Ans.* 67
11 February	Battle	Eadmer, *Vita Ans.* 69n; cf *Chron. Battle* 96, John of Worcs. iii 70
12 February	Hastings	Eadmer, *Historia* 47, *Fasti* iii 1
[22 February]	Hastings	ibid. 48

1095

Jan. × Feb.	Gillingham (Wilts)	*ASC* i 230; Eadmer, *Historia* 52
25–7 February	Rockingham	Eadmer, *Historia* 53–67, corr. ibid. lxii, *Vita Ans.* 85–7; Malmesbury, *GP* 89 follows error of Eadmer, *Historia*
13 May	Mortlake	Eadmer, *Historia* 70
c.20 May	Hayes	ibid. 70
23 May	Windsor	ibid. 71
27 May	Assumed pallium at Canterbury	ibid. lxii, 72–3; 13 May *ASC* i 232; John of Worcs. iii 74–6, Malmesbury, *GP* 91 follow Eadmer, *Historia*'s error of 10 June
25 × 31 December	Windsor	*De iniusta vexatione* ed. Offler 100

1096

20 April	Winchester	Eadmer, *Historia* 74
7 June	Lambeth	ibid. 74
8 June	London, St Pauls	ibid. 74; 15 June John of Worcs. iii 86; Diceto i 221
28 December	Canterbury	Eadmer, *Historia* 77

1097

24 May	Windsor	ibid. 79, *Vita Ans.* 88
	Hayes	Eadmer, *Vita Ans.* 89

15 October	Winchester	Eadmer, *Historia* 80, 87
24–5 October	Canterbury	ibid. 87–8
25 Oct. – 8 Nov.	Dover	ibid. 88, *Vita Ans.* 97–8 and nn.; *ASC* i 233 ; *UGQ* 4 and n.
8 November	Wissant	Eadmer, *Historia* 88
c. 10–16 November	St Bertin	ibid. 89, *Vita Ans.* 101n
	St Omer	Eadmer, *Historia* 89
22 December	Cluny	ibid. 90

1098

January– 16 March	Lyon	ibid. 91, 94
20 March	Aspres-sur-Buech	ibid. 95; Eadmer, *Vita Ans.* 103n
	Susa	Eadmer, *Vita Ans.* 103
26–28 March	Chiusa	ibid. 104
April × June	Rome	Eadmer, *Historia* 95–6, *Vita Ans.* 105n
	Schiavi(Liberi)	ibid. 97; Eadmer, *Vita Ans.* 106
June?	Capua	Eadmer, *Historia* 97, *Vita Ans.* 109; Geoffrey of Malaterra in L.A. Muratori, *Rerum italicarum scriptores* (new ed.) v (1927) 106–7; Orderic v 206, 252
	Aversa	Eadmer, *Historia* 98–9
	Schiavi	ibid. 104
3 October	Bari	*Councils* i(2) 650
10 October	Benevento	JL p. 694, Eadmer, *Historia* 110
10 October	Sinuessa	do.
3 November	Ceperani	do.
bef. November 24	Rome	JL 5714, Eadmer, *Historia* 110
25 December	Rome	Eadmer, *Historia* 111

1099

c. 24 April	Rome	*Councils* i(2) 651, Eadmer, *Historia* 112–4
before 29 July (for a year and five months)	Lyon	Eadmer, *Historia* 114–5
22 September	Vienne	Eadmer, *Vita Ans.* 117

1100

	Cluny	ibid. 120
	Anse, Council	Hugh of Flavigny *MGH SS* viii 487
	Macon	Eadmer, *Vita Ans.* 121
	Lyon	ibid. 121–2
30 July	Marcigny	ibid.123
31 July– 5 August	Lyon	ibid.124
August	La Chaise-Dieu	Eadmer, *Historia* 118, *Vita Ans.* 125
	Lyon	Eadmer, *Historia* 118
	Cluny	ibid. 118
	Sées (?)	above no. 92 n
23 September	Dover	Eadmer, *Historia* 119; cf *ASC* i 235
c. 29 September	Salisbury	Eadmer, *Historia* 119, *Vita Ans.* 127; *Reg. regum* ii no. 494
Oct. × 11 Nov.	Lambeth	*Councils* i(2) 661
11 November	Westminster	*ASC* i 236; John of Worcs. iii 96

1101

21 April	[Winchester	*ASC* i 236; Eadmer, *Historia* 126; *Annales monastici* ii 41]
9 June	?St Albans	*Reg. regum* ii no. 1124, Eadmer, *Historia* 126[10]
June × July	Winchester	*Reg. regum* ii no. 531 (*Reg. ant.* i no.73, which supplies the place)
3 September	Windsor	*Councils* i(2) 656; Eadmer, *Historia* 131; *Reg. regum* ii 544, *EEA* vi no.12, above no. 23
	Winchester	Eadmer, *Historia* 132

---

[10] The identification of the Whitsun court at St Albans in *Reg. regum* ii no. 1124 (also found, and rather more fully, in *Registrum palatinum Dunelmense* ed. T.D. Hardy (RS 62) iii 52) as that of 1101 is based on an inference by W. Farrer, *An outline itinerary of king Henry the first* (Oxford n.d., reprinted from *EHR* xxxiv, 1919) 8. Though followed by *Reg. regum*, Fröhlich, Biffi and most recently Hollister, *Henry I* 114 it is in principle thoroughly insecure, depending as it does on the notion that the kg could not have deprived Flambard of estates at any time after 1101. That Flambard was also in disfavour later is shown by *Reg. regum* ii no. 1181, and that the king moved from Winchester to St Albans at Whitsun, as Duke Robert's invasion loomed ever larger, seems improbable. Anselm was certainly at the Whitsun court, but it is unlikely to have been held at St Albans.

1102

| | London | ibid. 137 |
| c. 29 September | Westminster (Council) | Councils i(2) 668; Annales monastici i 7[11] |

1103

?February 18–21	Mortlake	Eadmer, Historia 145–6; Councils i(2) 657n
8–10 March	Canterbury	Eadmer, Historia 146; Reg. regum ii no. 636[12]
29 March	Winchester	Eadmer, Historia 148; ASC i 238
	Canterbury	Eadmer, Historia 149
27 April	Wissant	ibid. 149; ASC i 238
	Boulogne-sur-Mer	Eadmer, Historia 149
	Bec	ibid. 149
17 May	Chartres	ibid. 151
until mid-August	Bec	ibid. 151
	Chartres	ibid.
bef. 10 Nov. – after 16 Nov.	Rome	Chronique de Saint-Pierre-le-Vif de Sens, ed. R.-H. Bautier and M. Gilles, 1979, 144, 261–3; JL 5955 = EA 303
	Florence	Eadmer, Vita Ans. 129
after 23 November	Piacenza	JL 5956= EA 305; Eadmer, Historia 157–8
Christmas till mid-1105	Lyon	Eadmer, Historia 159,163; JL 6028 = EA 353

1104

| | Lyon | v. sup. |

1105

after 1 April	Cluny	Eadmer, Historia 163–4
	La Charité	ibid. 164
	Blois	ibid.
25 June	Chartres	ibid. 165; PL clxii 290
21 × 22 July	L'Aigle	Councils i(2) 661
	Bec	Eadmer, Historia 167
	Reims	ibid. 168–9

---

[11] The Annals of Margam, which appear to have had an otherwise lost list of councils, place the meeting on 27–8 Sept.

[12] See above no. 24 for the date 6 March.

1106

After 28 March	Rouen	ibid. 177–80; cf Orderic vi 68–70[13]
	Bec	Eadmer, *Historia* 180; cf. Porée, *Histoire du Bec* i 334
Before 15 July	Jumièges	Eadmer, *Historia* 182
15 August	Bec	ibid.; cf *Vita Bosonis* in *Lanfranci opera,* Appendix 47
Before 28 September	Dover	Eadmer, *Historia* 183; cf *EA* 401, *Reg. regum* ii no. 788

1107

April 17	Windsor	Eadmer, *Historia* 184–5;[14] *ASC* i 241
until *c.* 9 June	Bury St Edmunds	Eadmer, *Historia* 185[15]
1–*c.* 4 August	Westminster	*Councils* i(2) 691; cf. *Reg. regum* ii no. 832
11–15 August	Canterbury	Eadmer, *Historia* 187–8
18–21 September	Canterbury	ibid. 188
18–21 December	Canterbury	ibid. 188

1108

27 February	Lambeth	ibid. 190
c. 10 March	Rochester	ibid.192, *Fasti* ii 75
c. 28 May	London (Council)	*Councils* i(2) 695; cf *Reg. regum* ii no. 570
5–8 June	Mortlake	Eadmer, *Historia* 196
29 June	Canterbury	ibid.196
26 July	Pagham	ibid.198
9 August	Canterbury	ibid.
8 November	[Canterbury	Eadmer, *Historia* 203–4[16]]

1109

22 March	Died at Canterbury	above, p. xxxvi

[13] Anselm was at Rouen when he received the letters written by Paschal II to archbp William of Rouen on 28 March (JL 6074, transcribed by Eadmer).

[14] Eadmer, *Vita Ans.* 139 has London.

[15] cf *Consuetudines Burienses* 117.

[16] This was the day set by Anselm for the consecration of archbp Thomas, though he did not come.

RALPH

1114

26 April	Windsor. Postulated	*UGQ* 5; Eadmer, *Historia* 223; John of Worcs. iii 134; *ASC* i 245 (H) (apparently miscopying *vi kl Mar.* for *vi kl Maii*); Diceto i 240; 'Rogation tide' [early May] Hugh the Chanter 54; *Fasti* ii 3; 31 May Annals of Southwark in BL Cotton Faustina A viii fo. 133
16 May	Canterbury. Enthroned	Eadmer, *Historia* 223
September	Westbourne	*Reg. regum* ii no.1070
28 September	Canterbury	Eadmer, *Historia* 225
10 October	Rochester	ibid. 225
1 November	Canterbury	ibid. 226

1115

27 June	Canterbury. Assumed pallium	ibid. 229–30; John of Worcs. iii 136
16–19 September	Westminster	*Councils* i(2) 709; Eadmer, *Historia* 231–6; *Reg. regum* ii no.1091; John of Worcs. iii 138; Hugh the Chanter 62
26 December	Canterbury	Eadmer, *Historia* 236–7; John of Worcs. iii 138

1116

19–21 March	Salisbury	Hugh the Chanter 68; Eadmer, *Historia* 237; John of Worcs. iii 138
c. August	London	Eadmer, *Historia* 239
c. 9 September	Normandy	John of Worcs. iii 138–40; Eadmer, *Historia* 239
	La Ferté	Eadmer, *Historia* 239
December	Lyon	ibid. 240

1117

for four weeks	Piacenza	ibid. 241
before 12 March – after 24 March	Rome	Gervase ii 378; Eadmer, *Historia* 242–3, JL 6547
	Sutri	Eadmer, *Historia* 243
	Rome	ibid.
	Sutri	ibid.
before c.December	Rouen	ibid. 243–5; Hugh the Chanter 94

1118

All year	Normandy	Eadmer, *Historia* 243–9; Hugh the Chanter 84–100
c. 5 June	?Préaux	above, no. 42
7 October	Rouen	Orderic vi 202; cf C.H. Haskins, *Norman institutions* (Cambridge, Mass. 1918, repr. 1960) 294

1119

All year	Normandy	Eadmer, *Historia* 249–59; Hugh the Chanter 100–40
June	[Rouen	*Reg. regum* ii no.1204]
11 July	[?Rouen	Orderic vi 318 and n.; cf Hugh the Chanter 100–01n.][17]

1120

	Dover	Eadmer, *Historia* 259
4 January	Canterbury	ibid. 259
4 April	Westminster	ibid. 260; John of Worcs. iii 146

1121

6 January	London	Eadmer, *Historia* 290, John of Worcs. iii 148; Hugh the Chanter 164
c. 7 January	Westminster	*Reg. regum* ii no.1243
16 January	Lambeth	Eadmer, *Historia* 291; John of Worcs. iii 148
29–30 January	Windsor	Eadmer, *Historia* 292, Simeon ii 259; John of Worcs. iii 148–50, Malmesbury, *GP* 132n; Hugh the Chanter 164; *Reg. regum* ii no. 1247
13 March	Abingdon	Eadmer, *Historia* 293, John of Worcs. iii 150
12 June	Canterbury	Eadmer, *Historia* 294, John of Worcs. iii 150
c. June/July	Canterbury (?)	Eadmer, *Historia* 296; *ASC* i 250
2 October	Lambeth	Eadmer, *Historia* 298

1122

20 October	Canterbury. Dies	see above p. xlv and n.

---

[17] Eadmer and Hugh agree on the day of the archbp's stroke, but it is unclear whether they intended 1118 or 1119. *Anglia sacra* i 7 and the archbishop's known illness in the autumn of 1119 rather suggest 1119; the date of *Reg. regum* ii no. 1204 is insecure.

Ralph is also attested at:

Abingdon: *Hist. Abingdon* ii 66, 334–6 (April 1114 × August 1116, since in the time of abbot Faricius, who d. before Ralph's return to England in late 1120)

Caen: Deville noted from the cartulary of St Stephen (above p. 95 n) an act of William d'Albini *pincerna* for Vitalis of Savigny 'in castello Cadomi in praesentia Regis Henrici et baronum . . . quando abbas et monachi obedientiam de Moritonio reddiderunt domno Vitali heremitiae, quam ab eodem Vitale habuerant, nulla tamen necessitate coacti immo eius inopiae et paupertati compassi', in the presence also of archbp Ralph, bp Ranulf of Durham etc. (*Reg. regum* ii no. 1215, suggesting 1118). Ranulf Flambard was in Normandy in late 1116, and again in the autumn of 1119 (Hugh the Chanter 80, 122). Either is possible, but neither excludes an intermediate date.

Canterbury: no. 62; *Life of Christina* 84.

Charing: above, no. 47 (1121)

[South] Malling: above, no. 48 (1121)

Pagham: above, no. 37 (1115–22)

WILLIAM

1123

2–4 February	Gloucester. Elected	*ASC* i 251–2; *Councils* i(2) 726; John of Worcs. iii 152; Symeon ii 268–9; Hugh the Chanter 184; Gervase ii 379–80; *UGQ* 94
18 or 25 February	Canterbury. Consecrated.	Sunday 18 February *UGQ* 5, 78; 16 February John of Worcs. iii 152; 19 February Gervase ii 380; Sunday 25 February Symeon ii 269; *Fasti* ii 4
4 March	Woodstock	Hugh the Chanter 186; *Councils* i(2) 726
13 March	Leaves for Rome	*UGQ* 5; *ASC* i 252; John of Worcs. iii 152–4
	Sutri	Hugh the Chanter 188
Before 15 May	Rome	ibid. 191; *PUE* ii no. 5; JL 7071
After 4 June	Normandy	Symeon ii 273; Hugh the Chanter 200
22 July	Canterbury	John of Worcs. iii 154; Diceto i 244; Gervase ii 380
26 August	London, St Pauls	John of Worcs. iii 154; Diceto i 244

1124

| | Normandy | John of Worcs. iii 156; cf ibid. iii 157 n. 6 |

1125

8–14 March	Normandy	*Chron. Battle* 134, cf *ASC* i 255, *Reg. regum* ii 1425
29 March	Canterbury	*ASC* i 255
12 April	Lambeth	John of Worcs. iii 158
23–4 May	Canterbury	ibid.; Diceto i 245 n.[18]
8–*c.*11 September	Westminster (Council)	*Councils* i(2) 733
soon after 29 Sept.	Normandy	*ASC* i 255, John of Worcs. iii 164, Hugh the Chanter 204

1126

before 4 – after 30 Jan.	Rome	*Councils* i(2) 741–3; Hugh the Chanter 208; JL 7241, *PUE* iii no.13
	Normandy	Hugh the Chanter 216
before 29 June	Canterbury	ibid.
25 December	Windsor	John of Worcs. iii 166; Gervase ii 382; Hugh the Chanter 216

1127

1 January	London	John of Worcs. iii 166; Symeon ii 281–2; Malmesbury, *HN* 8
29 April	Westminster	Malmesbury, *HN* 6–8; John of Worcs. iii 176[19]
13–16 May	Westminster (Council)	*Councils* i(2) 743
12 June	Chichester	John of Worcs. iii 172
after 12 June	Sandwich	below p. 107

1128

| 22 January | Canterbury | John of Worcs. iii 176 |
| After 24 March | Lewes | John of Worcs. iii 184–6 |

1129

30 Sept.–	London (Council)	*Councils* i(2) 751
4 October	Winchester	Symeon ii 283
17 November	Canterbury	*ASC* i 260, John of Worcs. iii 188

---

[18] John of Worcs is in great confusion here, but his ed. and Stubbs agree in suggesting that the dates 23–4 May are probably right. It is possible that bp Simon was formally received at Worcester on 21 June, if Stubbs is right in suggesting that John had misread June for July in his notes.

[19] Following Hollister, *Henry I* 317–8 and John of Worcs. iii 182–3 n in assuming that John's text is here a year out.

22 December	Canterbury	John of Worcs. iii 188[20]

1130

4 May	Canterbury	*ASC* i 260; *UGQ* 5; Gervase i 96, ii 382–3; John of Worcs. iii 192
8 May	Rochester	John of Worcs. iii 194; *ASC* i 260[21]

1131

28 June	Oxford	John of Worcs. iii 196[22]
?August	Waltham	*Reg. regum* ii no. 1711
?8 September	Northampton	*Reg. regum* ii no. 1715[23]

1132

24 April	London (Council)	*Councils* i(2) 757–9

1133

8 February	London	*Councils* i(2) 760
30 April	Winchester	Huntingdon 488[24]
c. 2 August	Westbourne	*Reg. regum* ii no.1782, cf John of Worcs. iii 210
1 October	Lambeth	*Liber Eliensis* 284; 'Winchcombe annals' 127

1134

	Normandy	Huntingdon 490

1135

22–6 December	Westminster	*Reg. regum* iii nos 270n, 45; Malmesbury, *HN* 28–9 and n.; John of Worcs. iii 214–15 and n.1; *Chron. Battle* 140

[20] Simeon ii 283 has this on 17 November, with the cons. of bp Henry.

[21] 5 May, Gervase ii 383.

[22] A Sunday, so here correcting John's 29 (a Monday), as Wharton had in *Anglia sacra* ii 307n. At Rochester, but no date: Gervase ii 381.

[23] The witness list indicates a grand council; since it is attested by bp Robert of Hereford, who was consecrated on 28 June 1131, it must be after 1 August, shortly after which kg Henry returned to England (*ASC* i 261), but before the nominations of Geoffrey to Durham and Nigel to Ely in May 1133. The suggestion of the editors of *Regesta regum* that the occasion was the council at Northampton on 8 September described by Huntingdon 486–8 is therefore very probable.

[24] Huntingdon does not explicitly mention the archbp's presence, but the context seems to require it.

1136

January 5	Reading	*Reg. regum* iii no. 386; Huntingdon 704; *UGQ* 11
c. 22 March	Westminster	*Reg. regum* iii nos 46, 944–9, John of Hexham in Symeon ii 287–8
April	Oxford	*Reg. regum* iii no. 271
c. November	Mortlake	Gervase i 97
21 November	Died at Canterbury.	above p. liii n

William is also attested at:

Aldington: nos 80–1 (1126–36)

Bury St Edmunds: Consecrated the infirmary chapel of St Michael temp. ab. Anselm[25]

Canterbury: no. 62 (1125–8), no. 87 (1126–36)

Hulme: no. 73 (1126–36)

Lambeth: no. 65 (1125–36), no. 66 (1123–36), no. 97 (1128–36)

Sandwich (1127): A rather convincing account of a plea there, dated 1127 in the presence of the archbp (as legate and primate), abbot Hugh of St Augustine's, sheriff William and many others, was printed from a version of the Custumal of Sandwich which was written in the reign of Edward IV, amplifying an earlier account of *c.* 1375, in turn based on a form attributed to Adam Champeneys of 1301, by W. Boys, *Collections for a history of Sandwich* (Canterbury 1792) 551–3, and thence in D.M. Stenton, *English justice between the Norman Conquest and the Great Charter* (Memoirs of the American Philosophical Soc. lx, 1964) 116–23.[26] This is significantly fuller than *Reg. regum* ii no. 1511 Appendix no. cxcvii – a version which is found in a number of copies among the Christ Church archives.[27] Both versions agree on the conjunction of abbot Hugh and archbp William as 'legatus ecclesie sancte Romane', though only the long version adds 'et primas tocius Britannie'. If abbot Hugh I d. on 29 March 1126, as *Heads* i 36 reads John of Worcs. iii 168 (and cf *EEA* xiv p. 124 for the death of the bp of Chester/Coventry, the preceding entry, in 1126), then this should be abbot Hugh II, blessed on 12 June 1127, since William could barely have arrived in England as legate before Hugh I's death. However, John of Worcs. is here ambiguous, as the editor notes.

Wrotham: In another version of the sulung list in *Domesday monachorum* found in

---

[25] *Consuetudines Burienses* 119, 124. Dr Gransden interpreted 'Willelmus Turbius archiepiscopus Cantuar' as a bungled reference to William Turbe of Norwich, the bungling being perhaps the consequence of reluctance to admit that the local bishop could have conducted such an act of order. It is here taken as a more modest and less tendentious muddle over William 'de Corbeil'; for the archbp's devotion to St Michael see above pp. xlix–l.

[26] There are two medieval copies of the Custumal in the East Kent Archives Centre, Honeywood Road, Whitfield, Dover CT16 3EH: Sa/LC1 of *c.* 1375, and Boys' source, the s. xv Sa/LC2 (of which a transcript owned by Boys is Sa/ ZT2); there are numerous other later transcriptions of Sa/ LC2, including ibid. Sa/ LC 3–5 and Sa/ ZB 4/16, BL Cotton Julius B iv-v and Canterbury, Dean and Chapter Libr., ms Lit. B. 2, for which see *Arch. Cant.* cxv (1995) 395. I am grateful for much help from the staff of the East Kent Archives on these texts.

[27] For the *Reg. regum* reference to 'PRO Cartae antiquae [C 52], 18 [S] 274' read: Canterbury, Dean and Chapter, C. A. S 274 verso (s. xv); both versions are printed in van Caenegem, *Lawsuits* no. 254.

Lambeth ms 1212 p. 340 s. xiii[1] and Canterbury, Dean and Chapter Reg. P fos 28v-29 (damaged), s. xiii[2], discussed by R.S. Hoyt, 'A pre-Domesday Kentish assessment list' in *Medieval miscellany* 189ff, esp. 196–7, there are three consecutive entries referring to disputes over tenures on the archbishop's lands held before archbp William at Wrotham. Very tentatively (and rightly so) Hoyt suggested *c.*1136 as a possible date for what was presumably a single event.

St Osyth; A puzzling entry in the annals of St Benet at Holme in BL ms Egerton 3142, printed in an appendix to *Chronica Johannis de Oxenedes* ed. Henry Ellis (RS 1859) at 432 in later reprints, but not in the original edition, records archbp William with bps Richard of London, Everard of Norwich and John of Rochester at the translation of St Osyth on 3 June 1124. That the archbishop attended such an event is very probable (above, p. l). It may well have been the occasion on which the archbp and bp Richard secured the relics which they later gave to their cathedrals (*EEA* xv no. 22; Bethell, 'Richard' 307–8). However, if the St Benet annal were to be taken strictly, the event could scarcely have occured in 1124, when there is no reason to believe bp John had even been nominated. He was consecrated on 24 May, 1125 after election soon before 12 April (*Fasti* ii 76). Since bp Richard d. in January 1127 (*Fasti* i 1), the possible years would be 1125 or 1126. The same annals place the entry of the canons into St Osyth in 1120, where other related sources prefer 1121 (above 56 n). 1124 would be possible if John were only called bp by anticipation.

INDEX OF PERSONS AND PLACES

References are only given to notes where the name does not appear in the main text. Roman numerals refer to the introduction; arabic numerals refer to acts, followed by W if the person named is a witness; arabic numerals preceded by p. refer to the appendices. Places in England and Wales are assigned to both current and medieval counties.

INDEX OF SUBJECTS

HITLER'S
HEROINE